2-92

Baseball in '41

Also by Robert Creamer

Season of Glory (WITH RALPH HOUK)

Stengel: His Life and Times

The Yankees
(COAUTHOR)

Babe: The Legend Comes to Life

Rhubarb in the Catbird Seat
(WITH RED BARBER)

Jocko
(WITH JOCKO CONLAN)

The Quality of Courage (WITH MICKEY MANTLE)

VIKING

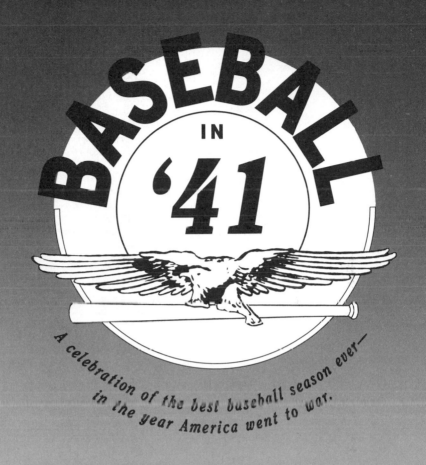

BASEBALL IN '41

A celebration of the best baseball season ever—
in the year America went to war.

ROBERT W. CREAMER

VIKING
Published by the Penguin Group
Viking Penguin, a division of Penguin Books USA Inc.,
375 Hudson Street, New York, New York 10014, U.S.A.
Penguin Books Ltd, 27 Wrights Lane,
London W8 5TZ, England
Penguin Books Australia Ltd, Ringwood,
Victoria, Australia
Penguin Books Canada Ltd, 2801 John Street,
Markham, Ontario, Canada L3R 1B4
Penguin Books (N.Z.) Ltd, 182–190 Wairau Road,
Auckland 10, New Zealand

Penguin Books Ltd, Registered Offices:
Harmondsworth, Middlesex, England

First published in 1991 by Viking Penguin,
a division of Penguin Books USA Inc.

1 3 5 7 9 10 8 6 4 2

LIBRARY OF CONGRESS CATALOGING IN PUBLICATION DATA
Creamer, Robert W.
Baseball in '41/Robert W. Creamer.
p.   cm.
Includes bibliographical references and index.
ISBN 0-670-83374-6
1. Baseball—United States—History—20th century. 2. Baseball
players—United States—Biography. I. Title. II. Title: Baseball
in 'forty-one. III. Title: Baseball in 1941.
GV863.A1C69   1991
796.357'0973—dc20   90-50747

Printed in the United States of America
Set in Cheltenham Book
Designed by Beth Tondreau Design

*This book
is for my children*

Jim Creamer of Boston

Tom Creamer of Chicago

John Creamer of New York

Ellen Sitron of Philadelphia

Bob Creamer of Tuckahoe

Preface

I f you read the dedication, you may recall that it said, "This book is for my children." As I write this, one of my children is in his twenties, two are in their thirties, two are in their forties. Although they are my children, they are not exactly children. They are verging toward middle age. One has a child who has graduated from college. In short, they are adult Americans with the usual interests that Americans have, including an affection for sports, with perhaps a special feeling for baseball.

Middle age begins, I think, when you first recognize that events in your generation's present are now in another generation's past. I became aware that I was edging into middle age when I was thirty-two, in 1954, the year I began working for *Sports Illustrated*. I had seen my first major league game in 1931, and the baseball of the thirties and forties had always been part of my present. But in 1954 the thirties were suddenly a long time ago. I met people on the staff—my contemporaries, I considered them, although they were ten years younger than I—who had few, if any, memories of the years before World War II. I had become part of an older generation, unable to share personal memories of twenty years before.

Now I am pushing seventy, and the 1954 contemporaries are pushing sixty, and I still can't share my prewar memories with them. What did a kid of eight know about the world an eighteen-year-old lived in during 1941? There are relatively few people out there with whom I *can* share memories of that vivid year.

Much of this book therefore is not turning the pages of an album but an effort to explain to my children and their contemporaries what 1941 felt like to me. I bridle when I see current movies about the thirties and forties that stress snap-brimmed fedoras and shiny old automobiles, as if those sum up the period. Sure, practically all men wore snap-brimmed fedoras in those days, but you didn't *notice* them then the way you notice them in the films. Hats were just part of the background and not an important part. I writhe, too, when I see old cars on the screen; every one is spanking clean, polished, gleaming with fourteen coats of deep-dish, crystal-clear enamel. But cars in those days were usually dirty, or at least dull, and a lot were dented. It took hours of hard work washing and "Simonizing" to get the family heap to look pretty, and then it would be only a day or so before the dirt and the dust returned.

I tell my children that. And in this book I'm trying to tell them and others who weren't around then what baseball and other matters were like in 1941. Or, at least, what they were like for me. It's not a comprehensive account. It's merely an attempt to tell them how I felt, to talk a little baseball, to explain some heroes, and to puncture a few myths, although myths are puncture-proof and never die.

Tuckahoe, New York
January 20, 1991

Contents

Cast of Characters

JOE DiMAGGIO	A streaker
TED WILLIAMS	A fireman
LARRY MacPHAIL	A roaring redhead
LEO DUROCHER	A lip
YANKEE STADIUM	The home of champions
THE YANKEES	The champions
BROOKLYN	A state of mind
EBBETS FIELD	A raucous place
THE DODGERS	A rowdy crew
RED BARBER	A revelation
THE POLO GROUNDS	A memorable stage
FRANKLIN D. ROOSEVELT	A speech maker
WINSTON CHURCHILL	A sailor
SPORTSMAN'S PARK	A battleground
THE CARDINALS	A year away
BRANCH RICKEY	A sly fox

PEE WEE REESE	A ballplayer
PETE REISER	A falling idol
MICKEY OWEN	A fall guy
HUGH CASEY	A disaster
BURTON K. WHEELER	A loser
CHARLES A. LINDBERGH	A loud loser
HUGH MULCAHY	A losing pitcher
JOE CRONIN	A loving scold
HANK GREENBERG	A most valuable soldier
THE TIGERS	A Hankless team
THE INDIANS	A year older—and sadder
BOB FELLER	A boy genius
DIXIE WALKER	The people's choice
DOLPH CAMILLI	A very strong man
PHIL RIZZUTO	A very small rookie
TOMMY HENRICH	A reliable fellow
CHARLIE KELLER	A bad man with a stick
JOE GORDON	A nonpareil
ED BARROW	A tyrant
JOE McCARTHY	A curmudgeon
AL BARLICK	An unpopular judge
LARRY GOETZ	A peacemaker
GEORGE MAGERKURTH	A meathead
JACOB RUPPERT	A retiring colonel
BEN LEAR	A general nuisance
RUDOLF HESS	An aviator
THE *BISMARCK*	A boat
JOHNNY MURPHY	A grandma
FRED FITZSIMMONS	An aging warrior
MARIUS RUSSO	A line-drive hitter
ADOLF HITLER	A lunatic
BENITO MUSSOLINI	An also ran
PRINCE KONOYE	A wishful thinker
GENERAL TOJO	A tough guy

BOB BOWMAN	A head hunter
JOE MEDWICK	A head case
WHITLOW WYATT	A hard case
KIRBY HIGBE	A flagbearer
BILLY HERMAN	The missing piece
BILLY SOUTHWORTH	A magician
CREEPY CRESPI	A name to remember
MARTY MARION	A shortstop to remember
MORT COOPER	A big brother
WALKER COOPER	A little brother, but big
JOHNNY MIZE	A big cat
ENOS SLAUGHTER	A country boy
TERRY MOORE	A center fielder
STAN MUSIAL	A walk-on
ESTEL CRABTREE and COAKER TRIPLETT	An odd couple
JOHNNY STURM	An odd single
LONNIE FREY	A villain
HARRY LAVAGETTO	A cookie
LUKE HAMLIN	A hot potato
BABE PHELPS	A grounded blimp
KEN KELTNER	A stopper
LEFTY GROVE	An old Moses
LOU GEHRIG	A death
PEARL HARBOR	An interruption
MYSELF WHEN YOUNG	A naif

PART 1

1

EXPLAINING THE OBVIOUS

My god, what a year 1941 was. I was eighteen when it began, and I turned nineteen that summer on the day Joe DiMaggio hit safely in his fifty-fourth straight game. He had kept the streak going to my birthday; it ended three days later.

1941 was the year Ted Williams batted .400—.406, to be precise. And the year the Dodgers, the rowdy Brooklyn Dodgers of Leo Durocher and Larry MacPhail, survived a tumultuous, season-long, nose-to-nose pennant race to win for the first time in twenty-one years—and then lost the World Series when what would have been a game-ending third strike got past their catcher, Mickey Owen.

Is this the heritage of the hapless baseball fan, that he remembers 1941 for Joe DiMaggio and Ted Williams and Mickey Owen instead of Pearl Harbor?

BEFORE you pass judgment, listen. I concede that if you were to ask the general run of Americans what they associate with 1941, most would say "Pearl Harbor" or "The year the war began." Especially those who are a decade or more younger than I am.

But when you were eighteen and nineteen and *living* in the year, 1941 wasn't Pearl Harbor—not most of it, anyway. The Japanese attack on America's big naval base in Hawaii didn't take place until December 7, which means that for eleven of the year's twelve months, or for all but twenty-five days of 1941, most Americans my age had never heard of Pearl Harbor. When the news came over the radio that December Sunday that Pearl Harbor had been bombed by Japanese planes, most of us looked around wonderingly and said, "What's Pearl Harbor? Where is it?" Charles Einstein, the writer and anthologist, was fifteen at the time, living in New York. That afternoon he left the family apartment to get something at a store, where the proprietor told him the news. Charlie went back to the apartment and solemnly told his mother and his stepfather, "We're at war. The Japanese have bombed Belle Harbor." Belle Harbor was a beach resort near Coney Island. His stepfather said, "They bombed *what?*"

Charlie and the rest of us found out soon enough what Pearl Harbor was, but at the moment most of us didn't know. For me and my generation 1941 was not a year of Pearl Harbor and war but of peace, the last year of peace, a shaky, fraying, disintegrating peace, but nonetheless peace.

It was also a year of utterly wonderful baseball. Roger Angell wrote, in commenting on the 1989 season (that sorry time when baseball was knocked sideways by the Pete Rose gambling scandal, the sudden death of baseball commissioner A. Bartlett Giamatti, and the earthquake-shattered World Series), "It was a miserable year, the worst in memory." It takes a certain confidence to make such a sweeping judgment, but Angell is probably right. In any case, he gives me the confidence to say, equally sweepingly, that 1941, with Pearl Harbor still hidden in the future, was a marvelous year, the best baseball season ever.

ROBERT W. CREAMER
‹‹‹‹‹‹‹‹‹‹‹‹‹‹‹‹‹‹‹‹‹‹‹‹‹‹

I won't argue the point. For me, it was by far the best, most rewarding season of my lifetime, but it certainly wasn't for fans of the Detroit Tigers and the Cleveland Indians. A year earlier, the Tigers and the Indians fought each other for the American League pennant until the last forty-eight hours of the season before the Tigers won it by a game. In 1941 both teams collapsed and fell below .500. For the Hall of Fame ballplayer Hank Greenberg, 1941 was a memorable year but hardly a delightful one. In 1940 Greenberg batted .340, was first in home runs and runs batted in, led his team to the pennant and was named the American League's Most Valuable Player. In 1941, at the age of thirty, the peak of his career, Greenberg was drafted into the army and was gone from baseball for all or most of five seasons. And while 1941 was a stimulating year for the St. Louis Cardinals, their elderly fans will tell you in one voice that 1942 was much, much better.

Mine is therefore a subjective judgment—but only to a degree. I was a Yankee fan in those days, and the Yankees, with DiMaggio leading the way, had a glorious time in 1941, which pleased me very much. But DiMaggio's fifty-six-game hitting streak tran-scended the Yankees and Yankee fans. It transcended New York; it transcended baseball. Everyone was caught up in it. No athlete before or since—not Babe Ruth or Jack Dempsey or Bobby Jones; not Jackie Robinson or Mary Lou Retton; not Muhammad Ali; not even Bo Jackson—has held the country's fascinated attention day after day, week after week, the way DiMaggio did in 1941. Andy Crichton told me that he and his brother Bob and two high school friends drove across the country that summer in an old jalopy. In Montana they stopped for coffee at a dusty cafe in a dusty town. Farm hands and ranch hands came into the cafe for breakfast. This was before television, remember, and radio news was sketchy before we got into the war, particularly in smaller towns. You found out what was happening from newspapers. Almost every man who came into the cafe, Crichton said, would glance toward a newspaper lying on the counter and ask the proprietor, "He get one yesterday?" He didn't have to explain who "he" was, even though this was two thousand miles from New York and a thousand miles west of the westernmost major league city, which in those days was St. Louis. Every day, all over the country, people asked, "Did he get one yesterday?"

As for Ted Williams, I wasn't from Boston and I wasn't a Red Sox rooter or a Williams fan, but Ted's pursuit of .400 and his success in attaining that lofty plateau grabbed me as it grabbed everyone who followed the game. His achievement has had no parallel in the half century since, and I haven't even mentioned the electrifying three-run homer Williams hit with two out in the last half of the ninth inning to win the 1941 All Star game for the American League.

I wasn't a Brooklyn fan either, but in 1941 the Dodgers, like DiMaggio, transcended the game. In fact, it was the Dodgers more than anyone else (*pace* DiMaggio, *pace* Williams) who made 1941 so continually exciting from the first day of spring training to the last day of the World Series. DiMaggio was an extended diversion in the middle, Williams a shorter one at the end; the Dodgers were a constant all year long. I know that that season, despite being a Yankee fan, I rooted for the Dodgers, too, and so did almost everybody else. They were like the New York Mets in 1969. After being perennial losers, year after year, the Dodgers captured the country's imagination with their climb to the heights.

This requires some explanation, which will be superfluous for some but necessary for others. As P. G. Wodehouse wrote in an early paragraph of one of his Bertie Wooster stories, "I don't know if you have had the same experience, but the snag I always come up against when I'm telling a story is this dashed difficult problem of where to begin it. It's a thing you don't want to go wrong over, because one false step and you're sunk. I mean to say, if you fool about too long at the start, trying to establish atmosphere, as they call it, and all that sort of rot, you fail to grip and the customers walk out on you. Get off the mark, on the other hand, like a scalded cat, and your public is at a loss. It simply raises its eyebrows, and can't make out what you're talking about."

I sense young eyebrows being raised all over the place. The Dodgers? Perennial losers? What are you talking about?

The remarkable success of the Los Angeles Dodgers, artistically and financially, over the past three decades, and the greatness of the old Boys of Summer Brooklyn Dodgers of 1947–56, tend to make people forget the old, old Brooklyn Dodgers. But you have to realize that before World War II, and especially during the 1920s and 1930s, the Dodgers—or Robins, as they were called through much of that period, after their rotund manager, Wilbert Robinson—were simply awful, an inept team that disappointed its devoted fans year after year. The old Dodgers/Robins were clowns— they were known as the Daffiness Boys—and Brooklyn fans hungry for victory and the self-respect that victory brings would leave Ebbets Field after each embarrassing defeat muttering, "Them bums. Them lousy bums." It was not an affectionate nickname, not at first. A bum was a bum, a no-good, and the Dodgers were a bum team, a club that in the Depression days of the 1930s was artistically and financially bankrupt.

Brooklyn lived on hope. "Wait till next year," fans would say in the fall, as another losing season ended. "You watch, we'll get 'em next year." But next year would see more of the same. Words and phrases like "Wait till next year" and "Bums" and Brooklyn locutions like "Thoid base" and "Leave us go out to the ballpark" worked their way into the sports pages. The borough of Brooklyn— Manhattan's Sancho Panza—was America's joke city, a larger Peoria, a bigger Podunk. The Brooklyn accent seemed hilarious. Danny Kaye took it to boffo extremes in one of his later routines when the character he was playing declared, "I'm fwrom Bwrooklyn. My whole family's fwrom Bwrooklyn. I was bawn and bwred in Bwrooklyn." Radio comedians always got a laugh when they mentioned Brooklyn. For all of Brooklyn's hope, the Dodgers were a joke team from a joke town.

Then in 1938 Larry MacPhail, a redheaded whirlwind, blew in from the West to run the Dodger front office. In 1939 Leo Durocher became manager, Red Barber began broadcasting Brooklyn games, and the lowly Dodgers squeezed into third place on the last day of the season. In 1940 they challenged for the pennant for half the year before falling back and finishing second, twelve games behind. In 1941 they challenged again and this time—a miracle, a miracle—they didn't fall back, they didn't disappoint. They held on, fighting off the Cardinals through one of the fiercest day-by-day pennant races in major league history, and they won.

The rags-to-riches story seduced America. Everyone was taken by them. It became an in thing to be a fan of the Dodgers. A prominent composer wrote a symphony for them. In time just about every war movie had "a kid from Brooklyn" in it, usually comic and dumb, though sometimes heroically comic and dumb. Russell Baker, writing about memorials to honor the war dead, said, "If you'd watched Hollywood's World War II movies you may have thought one of the main things they died for was to save baseball, or at least to save the Brooklyn Dodgers. The basic-war-movie formula of the period called for a kid from Brooklyn to chatter away about the Dodgers between bombardments and kamikaze attacks. Confronted with villainous Axis performers like Conrad Veidt and Richard Loo, Hollywood leading men were apt to declare that the Axis could never crush the spirit of a nation that rooted for the Dodgers."

YOU tend to magnify things when you recall the past, but I don't believe I am magnifying the 1941 season. I was talking about this book in its early stages with my brother-in-law, Joseph (Bud) Schelz. A few days later he phoned to tell me of a conversation

ROBERT W. CREAMER

he had had with a neighbor of his named Henry Demayo, who grew up in Brooklyn.

"Henry is about our age," Bud said, "and I knew he was a great baseball fan. I didn't mention your book to him. I just said, 'Henry, do you remember anything about the 1941 baseball season?'

"He looked at me as though I were crazy. 'Are you kidding?' he said. '1941? That was the *greatest* baseball season that ever was!' "

Some time later a dignified, intelligent man named E. M. (Bud) Livingston phoned me. (The presence of two Buds in successive anecdotes is not so much coincidence as it is a sign of the times. Many boys born after the First World War in the 1920s and 1930s were nicknamed "Buddy" by fathers influenced by the widespread use of the term among soldiers during that war. A teary song called "My Buddy" about guys from the old neighborhood who had gone off to fight and die in the trenches of France was extremely popular for a time, especially in barrooms.)

Bud Livingston had heard that I was writing about baseball in 1941, and he wanted to share his memories and clippings and souvenirs of that year. During our conversation I happened to tell him the story of my brother-in-law and his friend Henry Demayo. When I got to the part about the "greatest baseball season ever," Livingston all but shouted over the phone.

"Absolutely!" he cried. "Absolutely!"

So it isn't just me.

2

JOE AND TED

One of the problems in writing about the past is that the present keeps getting in the way. Knowledge of what has happened between then and now distorts our emotions and colors our reactions to people and events.

How do you tell what it was like then? It wasn't just Pearl Harbor that I had never heard of when the 1941 season began. I had never heard of Willie Mays. Willie didn't exist. Oh, sure, he was a ten-year-old kid in Alabama that spring, but in baseball he hadn't happened yet. There was no Jackie Robinson in 1941—never heard of him. No Roy Campanella, no Ernie Banks, no Frank Robinson, no Rod Carew, no Tony Gwynn, no Reggie Jackson, no Bo.

I had heard of Satchelfoot Paige (that's what he was called when I first heard of him) and Josh Gibson, and I knew they were great ballplayers, but the acute unfairness of their disbarment from the major leagues because they were black failed to register with me. I had a good friend named Elmer Morris when I was in high school, a big colored kid ("colored" was a polite word then) who was the best football player, the best basketball player, and the best baseball player in the school, and one of the finest lefthanded pitchers around. His brother Willie caught for him. Both were beautiful athletes but it never occurred to me that neither had a chance at making the big leagues. That might have been social density; it might also have been that it never occurred to me that *anyone* I knew had a chance at making the big leagues.

But it wasn't just black major leaguers that hadn't happened. Mention Mickey Mantle to me or any baseball fan in 1941 and you'd get a blank stare. Duke Snider? Harmon Killebrew? Never heard of them either. José Canseco? Don't make me laugh. Talk about third basemen if you want to, but don't mention Brooks Robinson, Mike Schmidt, Eddie Mathews, Ken Boyer, Graig Nettles. They hadn't happened. In 1941 a list of the ten best lefthanded pitchers of all time—or the fifty best, or the one hundred best— would not have had Sandy Koufax on it, or Warren Spahn, or Whitey Ford, or Steve Carlton. Talk about righthanders with strike-out speed, like Walter Johnson and Bobby Feller, but don't confuse me with names I never heard of, like Nolan Ryan, Bob Gibson, Tom Seaver, Roger Clemens, Doc Gooden. Who are these people?

It was a different world. Consider Joe DiMaggio. In the five decades since 1941 DiMaggio has taken on something of the aura of George Washington in Grant Wood's painting *Parson Weems' Fable*. The Reverend Mason Weems was a man who in the early 1800s wrote uplifting if not always accurate stories about great men. He made up the famous anecdote about Washington chopping down his father's favorite cherry tree. Weems said that when the angry parent demanded to know who had done it, young George said bravely, "Father, I cannot tell a lie. I did it with my little hatchet."

The story became part of Washington's legend, with its telling indication of our first president's honesty and integrity. Grant Wood's painting, done in the 1930s, shows Parson Weems drawing back a curtain to disclose the scene: a stylized cherry orchard, one tree chopped down lying on its side, an angry father, and a small boy with a hatchet looking up at him. Except that the head of the eight-year-old Washington is the white-wigged, stern-jawed Washington of the Gilbert Stuart portrait, the Washington of the one-dollar bill. Legend obscures fact; the present distorts the past.

DiMaggio today is like Washington in the painting. The dignity and grace of the man over the forty years since he quit baseball, combined with story after story about his accomplishments on the diamond, have created an indelible image of perfection. Mention DiMaggio as he was when 1941 began and there are instant images of DiMaggio later, of the man with the hitting streak behind him, the postwar DiMaggio gallantly overcoming injuries, the DiMaggio of 1949 coming back to the Yankees late in June after missing spring training and the first half of the season to destroy the Boston Red Sox single-handedly and propel the Yankees toward the first of Casey Stengel's ten pennants. There are simultaneous recollections of the Joe DiMaggio who retired tastefully after the 1951 season, the Joe who married Marilyn, the Joe who put a rose on her grave and declined to meet Bobby Kennedy, the Joe of the Mr. Coffee commercials, the Joe who was given an honorary degree by an Ivy League university, the Joe of "Where have you gone, Joe DiMaggio? A nation turns its lonely eyes to you."

It wasn't that way when 1941 began. DiMaggio had completed five big league seasons and he was undoubtedly a star of the first magnitude. He had led the league at times in home runs and runs batted in, and he was coming off two straight batting championships. But he was only twenty-six years old, a young, shy, not very good-looking fellow who had recently married a pretty blond actress no one had ever heard of. Her name was Dorothy Arnold, and the young couple were expecting their first child that fall. DiMaggio was the star of the Yankees, the successor to Babe Ruth and Lou Gehrig, but he was not yet fully accepted. Gehrig, whose

ROBERT W. CREAMER
≪≪≪≪≪≪≪≪≪≪≪≪≪≪≪≪≪≪≪≪≪

career had ended only two years earlier, was working as a parole commissioner in New York City. The sportswriters loved Gehrig, and so did the fans; Lou was still their hero. And Babe Ruth, then only in his mid-forties, was alive and vigorous, and he made news whenever and wherever he appeared in public, which was often.

In this Ruth-Gehrig environment DiMaggio was still the new kid on the block. He had stirred up resentment and bad publicity in 1938 when he held out for a big raise, which he felt he deserved but which owner Jacob Ruppert and general manager Ed Barrow adamantly refused to give him. The holdout hurt him with both fans and sportswriters, who often grew annoyed when players held out for big raises in those Depression years.

DiMaggio wasn't helped by an ethnically biased press that commented stupidly and demeaningly on his Italian background, his Italian "traits." Because of anti-Italian prejudice in the newspaper business the sportswriter Joseph Nichols, who wrote for *The New York Times* for many years, was obliged as a young man to change his name from Fappiano to avoid discrimination; Nichols gained a measure of satisfaction in later years when a racing stable named a crack sprinter "Fappiano" after him; Fappiano's son, Unbridled, won the 1990 Kentucky Derby.

DiMaggio surrendered in 1938 and signed for what the Yankees offered, but he missed the start of the season and when he made his first appearance in the Yankee lineup he was roundly booed. He was always late to sign, and the booing continued at times in 1939 and 1940. At the beginning of 1941, despite his great skill as a player, DiMaggio was still not overwhelmingly popular. During his first five years as a Yankee he missed more than eighty games— more than half a season—because of injuries or his penchant for holding out into spring training. He had been in the opening-day lineup only once in his five years with the club. In 1941 he was Joe DiMaggio, a very good ballplayer, but he was not yet DiMaggio the god, or even George Washington.

The image of Ted Williams in 1941 is even more distorted by

time. Today we see Williams as a big, handsome man who as he aged grew ruggedly better looking in the true-blue, 100-percent American, John Wayne manner, a man engagingly outspoken and opinionated, a charmer. We see him through four decades of baseball (he began in the major leagues in 1939 and finished in 1960), through six batting championships, through World War II and Korea (in both of which he fought bravely as a fighter pilot) through crippling baseball injuries and extraordinary comebacks. We see him through the melodramatic home run he hit in his last time at bat in his career, and we see him through the impeccable prose of John Updike describing that home run.

But in the spring of 1941 John Updike didn't exist any more than Willie Mays did. There still wasn't an American World War II for Williams to fight in, Korea was a little-known peninsula, sometimes called Chosen, that the conquering Japanese had occupied thirty years earlier, and Williams had not won even one batting title, let alone six.

He'd been in the major leagues for only two years. He was twenty-two, a tall, thin, gangly, awkward-looking boy with a rather goofy grin, so young looking and artless in his behavior that the other players called him "the kid," a nickname that stuck throughout his career (the headline on Updike's story in *The New Yorker* in 1960 was HUB FANS BID KID ADIEU.)

His height (he was six foot three when relatively few players were much over six feet) and his thinness earned him a sportswriter's manufactured nickname, "The Splendid Splinter." He was also at various times called the "Stringbean Slugger," the "Willowy Walloper" and "Toothpick Ted."

He was thin, but he could hit. There was no doubt about that from his very first game as a big leaguer when, playing for the Red Sox against the Yankees in New York on opening day in 1939, batting against the perennial twenty-game winner Red Ruffing, he sent a flat line drive over the second baseman's head that shot like an arrow to the right-centerfield fence in Yankee Stadium. He

ROBERT W. CREAMER

batted .327 that year after a relatively slow start and led the league in runs batted in, and a year later, in 1940, he batted .344. But in 1939 when he hit .327 he finished seventh in the batting race, more than fifty points behind the victorious DiMaggio; and though he finished third in 1940, only eight points behind Joe, he had never really been a factor in the close struggle for the batting title that year among DiMaggio, Luke Appling of the Chicago White Sox and Rip Radcliff of the St. Louis Browns.

He was considered a good ballplayer, in other words, but not yet a great one. He could hit, but he couldn't field worth a damn and on the bases he ran with a long-legged lope that seemed almost comical. Ile often appeared distracted in the outfield, where he occasionally practiced batting swings between pitches. And he was a behavior problem, or what baseball and the press and the public considered a behavior problem. He dressed oddly, which is to say he wouldn't wear a tie in an era when wearing a tie in public was almost as important as wearing shoes. He had temper tantrums. Sometimes, angry after popping up or hitting an easy ground ball to the infield, he wouldn't run hard down the line to first base but would peel off toward the dugout. He was scolded several times by the Red Sox manager, Joe Cronin, who liked him and treated him gently. Jimmie Foxx, the powerful Boston first baseman who also liked Williams and admired his ability, called him a spoiled kid. The crowd began to get on Ted, and Williams, who had rabbit ears, yelled unkind things at the crowd. He was criticized by the press, which called him "Terrible Ted." The Boston sportswriters, a frightening group of news hounds back then when the city seemed to have fifty newspapers, all barking for lively stories, climbed all over the youngster; they made mountains out of every molehill difficulty Williams got into and gave him scant credit when he did something well. When he hit the homer that won the All Star game in 1941, a headline in a Detroit paper said POPOFF MAKES GOOD. Bill Cunningham, a Boston sports columnist whom Ted didn't much like, wrote once that Williams took "as brutal and as cruel a cuffing from some elements of the sports press as a kid was ever called upon to suffer. Maybe from one way of looking at it he asked for it . . . [but] whether he asked for it or not he got it and there was never anything in modern times exactly like it." Williams' reaction was defiance, loud and clear.

He was impulsive, outspoken and rash. Buddy Hassett, playing with the Boston Braves, or Bees, as they were called then, said that early in 1940 he was riding in a car with Williams when Ted told him of an interview he'd just had with a Boston sportswriter. Ted had blasted what he called "this god-damned town," and the sportswriter was apprehensive, Ted said. "He said, 'You don't want me to print that,' " Williams told Hassett, "and I said, 'Yes! Print every damn word.' "

Hassett, knowing how such a story could hurt Williams in Boston, said, "Ted, let me out here and I'll phone the guy. He won't print it if we ask him not to." But Williams pounded the steering wheel and said, "Nope!" and wouldn't stop the car.

"I think that might have been the beginning of his troubles," Hassett said.

The culmination came in another story, written in the middle of the 1940 season, not by a Boston writer but by a nationally syndicated reporter named Harry Grayson, who was talking to Williams one day in Cleveland. Williams complained to Grayson about the pressure he was under in Boston. Ted mentioned that he had an uncle who was a fireman in Mount Vernon, New York, a suburb just a few miles north of Yankee Stadium. When the Red Sox were in New York Williams would sometimes stop by the firehouse to visit his uncle. He always got along better with what are called little people, particularly blue-collar types, than he did with the more glamorous people who flock like hungry pigeons around baseball stars, and he got along well with the men in his uncle's firehouse. He'd stay there for hours sometimes, talking and kidding around, relaxing. He told Grayson what a pleasant life his

ROBERT W. CREAMER
<<<<<<<<<<<<<<<<<<<<<<<<<

uncle had and how unpleasant his own had become and, impulsively, he said, "Nuts to this. I'd rather be a fireman."

Grayson leaped on that, and the story ran all over the country. Williams wants to quit baseball to become a fireman. Players on other teams leaped on it, too. Williams took an inordinate amount of riding from fans and bench jockeying from rival players, who put on toy fireman's hats, made fire-siren sounds and shouted in falsetto, "I want to be a fireman!"

Thus, despite his hitting, no one yet really took him seriously. He was still that quirky kid in Boston, the angular, awkward one who couldn't field and who didn't pay attention to his manager, the one who wanted to be a fireman. The term "flake" had not yet come into vogue, but Williams at the beginning of 1941 was considered a flake—a hell of a hitter, yes, but not yet a real ballplayer.

The all-time all-star outfield as 1941 began consisted of Ruth, Ty Cobb and Tris Speaker. Joe Jackson, the banned Chicago Black Sox star, was the only other outfielder who was considered to be in their class. A few observers were beginning to suggest that DiMaggio might some day challenge Speaker for the centerfield spot in that august outfield, but no one at the beginning of 1941 would have dreamed of including Ted Williams.

3

THE YANKEES

W hile some people and events are magnified by time, others are diminished. I think of what the Yankees were in 1941—and what they are now. Back then they were the most feared team in baseball; now they are an empty shell of the past. Fans bask in nostalgia, and Yankee publicity grinds out promotions glorifying the old days. There are the plaques to Ruth, Gehrig, Mantle and the others beyond the left-field fence in Yankee Stadium—the graveyard, we used to call it in the press box—and the oversize photographs of past heroes in the corridors under the grandstand.

It seems wistful, a little sad. The Yankees today are like Austria, an unimportant little country that has monuments to the days when it ruled half of Europe. Today Austria relies on Olympic skiers for its brief moments in the sun, and the Yankees on an occasional Mattingly.

But the Yankees fifty years ago—well, even imperial Austria had its rivals, but the Yankees stood alone. Baseball writers love to talk of "dynasties." Let a team sweep through a season and win the World Series and there we are reading headlines like "ARE THE METS A DYNASTY?" The astute Roger Angell wrote early in 1990 that if the Oakland Athletics could win a third straight American League pennant they would be the "first baseball dynasty" since the Cincinnati Reds of the 1970s. The Athletics did win, but the Reds altered that dynastic image in the 1990 World Series.

But just what is a dynasty? Egypt was filled with them, as I recall, and China had several that devoted much of their time to making vases. I assume that a dynasty is a long-term ascendancy, a ruling family or tribe or group that stays in control of things for a long, long time.

Applying that criterion to American sports yields very few dynasties. There have been powerful teams that were forces to be reckoned with over a length of time, such as Notre Dame in college football, or Vince Lombardi's Green Bay Packers in professional football, or—hi there, Roger—the Reds of the 1970s in baseball, but offhand I can think of only four teams that absolutely dominated their sports for a long period of years the way a proper dynasty ought to. These were UCLA and the Boston Celtics in basketball, the Montreal Canadiens in hockey and, beyond all others, the New York Yankees in baseball.

I don't mean to dismiss Angell's anticipation of Oakland's future or, more to the point, his recollection of Cincinnati's past. The Reds won the National League West six times in ten years in the 1970s and were second three other times; they won the National League pennant playoff four times in six tries and captured two of the four World Series they played in.

But they lost one of those World Series to Oakland, which won the American League West *five* years in succession (the most division titles the Reds won in succession was two) and the A's won the World Series three years in a row (the Reds lost two, won two). The three-year sweep of pennant playoffs and World Series by the Athletics in 1972–73–74 is the most impressive achievement by a major league team in the past quarter century. Of all the teams that have played major league baseball in all the years the big leagues have been in business, Oakland is the only club that ever won the World Series three years in a row—with one exception.

The exception, of course, is the Yankees—and now we get back to the word "dynasty." In the movie *Crocodile Dundee* the Australian actor Paul Hogan is accosted by a would-be mugger bearing a dangerous but normal-size knife. The woman with Hogan cries, "Look out! He's got a knife!" Hogan smiles and says, "You call that a nahf? That's not a nahf. Now *this* is a nahf," and he whips out an evil-looking blade that's about a foot long.

To Roger Angell, offering the Reds, I say, "You call that a dynasty? That's not a dynasty. Now *this* is a dynasty." From 1921 through 1964, a period of forty-four years, the New York Yankees won twenty-nine American League pennants, or just about twice as many as *all* the other teams in the league combined. They won twenty of the twenty-nine World Series they played in, with most of their losing Series either at the beginning or ending years of the dynasty. In the middle, from 1927 through 1953, they won fifteen of the sixteen World Series they were in.

The point of all this as far as 1941 is concerned is that the most domineering period of the lengthy New York dynasty was from 1936 through 1939, when the Yankees won four straight pennants and four straight World Series. Baseball purists will leap to point out that Casey Stengel's Yankees won *five* straight pennants and *five* straight World Series from 1949 through 1953. That was an astonishing, unparalleled accomplishment, but Casey's Yankee pennants came hard: In the first four of those five pennant races they fought off persistent rivals all season long and won by margins of one game in 1949, three in 1950, five in 1951, two in 1952. In their winning World Series they trailed the Giants two games to one in 1951 before going on to win, and in 1952 and 1953 they fought epic struggles with the Dodgers before coming out on top.

What about 1955–1964 when the Yankees, managed first by Stengel and then by Ralph Houk, won nine pennants in ten years? But those latter-day Yankees lost five of the nine World Series they engaged in.

What about the earlier Yankees, the Babe Ruth Yankees, the 1927 Yankees? The Babe Ruth Yankees won six pennants in eight years in the 1920s but lost three of the first four World Series they were in. Ruth's 1927 Yankees, who won 110 games and swept the Pittsburgh Pirates four straight in the Series, are often called the greatest baseball team of all time, and that may well be true, but the same club a year earlier lost the World Series and a year later had to scramble late in the season to win the flag by a bare two and a half games. The challenging Philadelphia Athletics then usurped the Yankee throne by winning three straight pennants themselves in 1929–30–31. In Ruth's fifteen seasons (his last year in New York was 1934) the Yankees won seven pennants. From 1929 through 1935, although they finished second five times and third once, the Yankees won only one pennant.

That diffidence ended in 1936. The aging Ruth was gone and the vibrant young DiMaggio had arrived. Gehrig was still at his peak, and the Yankees moved into high gear. The 1936 club won the pennant by nineteen and a half games (the 1927 Yanks won by nineteen) and set a new major league record of 182 home runs (the 1927 Yanks hit 158). In 1937 they won by thirteen games and hit 174 home runs, the second highest team total to that time. In 1938, Gehrig's last season, when the effects of his fatal condition began to show, they still won by nine and a half games and again hit 174 home runs. In 1939, with Gehrig gone, they regrouped, won by seventeen games and hit 166 home runs.

Never before or since has a baseball team been so overwhelmingly dominant. The pitching was deep and excellent—the staff had the lowest earned-run average in the league for four straight years—but it was the Yankees' powerful, unrelenting hitting that awed rival teams and earned them the nickname the Bronx Bombers. In 1941, in a list of the leading home-run hitting teams of all time, the 1936–37–38 Yankees were one-two-three, and only two other teams had ever hit more than the post–Lou Gehrig team of 1939. Everyone in the lineup could pop the ball. In 1938, when Hank Greenberg led the league with fifty-eight home runs and Jimmie Foxx was second with fifty, DiMaggio, the Yankee leader, was a distant fifth with thirty-two, yet the Yankees as a team had thirty-seven more home runs than Greenberg's Tigers and seventy-six more than Foxx's Red Sox. The 1936–39 Yankees led the league by wide margins each year in scoring runs, and they led by wide margins in keeping opponents from scoring. They were overwhelming.

They were just as impressive in World Series play. No team had ever won more than two straight World Series titles before, but the Yankees won the Series four straight times, and they won smashingly: by four games to two in 1936, 4–1 in 1937, 4–0 in 1938 and 4–0 in 1939. In the second game of the 1936 Series they humiliated the New York Giants 18–4, an unheard-of score in the World Series; half a century later it was still the record for most runs scored by one team in a Series game, and their fourteen-run superiority was still the biggest margin of victory. In the final game of that Series they stomped the Giants again, 13–5. In the 1937 Series they won the first three games by scores of 8–1, 8–1 and 5–1—a 21–3 superiority in runs scored. In 1938 they outscored the Cubs 22–9 in sweeping four games, and in 1939 outscored the Reds 20–8 in sweeping them in four games.

In the nineteen World Series games they played from 1936 through 1939 the Yankees won sixteen and lost three—against the best teams the other league had. A club winning sixteen of its first nineteen games in the regular season would be described as getting off to a runaway start. The Yankees played runaway baseball in the World Series.

Add that to the record of the Yankees' three previous pennant

ROBERT W. CREAMER
≪≪≪≪≪≪≪≪≪≪≪≪≪≪≪≪≪≪≪≪≪≪

winners in 1927, 1928 and 1932, each of which swept the World Series, and you find that in the thirty-one Series games the Yankees played from 1927 through 1939 they won twenty-eight and lost three.

No other team ever smothered the opposition the way this team did. They seemed invincible, and their aura of invincibility infused the American League, which as 1939 ended had won nine of the twelve previous World Series, including the last five in a row, and six of the seven All Star games since the inception of that annual affair in 1933. Only once in those seven All Star games had fewer than half a dozen Yankees been named to the American League roster, and in 1939 there were nine Yankees on the squad. Yankee pitchers—specifically, Lefty Gomez and Red Ruffing—started six of the first seven All Star games and received credit for four of the wins.

I go on at this length because of my memory of what it was like then: At the beginning of the 1940s the Yankees were an utterly dominating team, and there was no indication that their stifling superiority would not continue. Douglass Wallop's book *The Year the Yankees Lost the Pennant* (on which the musical comedy *Damn Yankees* was based) was still fifteen years into the future, but the cry "Break up the Yankees!" was already heard in the land.

Ruth was gone and Gehrig was going, but superb young players kept arriving: DiMaggio in 1936, Tommy Henrich in 1937, Joe Gordon in 1938, Charlie Keller in 1939. And the Yankees made a few astute trades, notably before the 1936 season when they acquired the veteran pitchers Monte Pearson and Bump Hadley. Pearson and Hadley won 102 games for the Yankees in 1936–37–38–39, or 25 percent of the club's victories in that glowing period. The Yankees also traded for Jake Powell, a tough, useful outfielder, and Roy Johnson and Billy Knickerbocker, good utility men. After the 1938 season they traded for another veteran pitcher, Oral Hildebrand, and Hildebrand went 10–4 for them in 1939.

Hildebrand's success made the rest of the American League go a little crazy. Walt Disney's *Snow White and the Seven Dwarfs* was a big hit in the late 1930s, and inevitably the eight-team American League came to be called Snow White and the Seven Dwarfs. Perhaps that was what moved the league to action after the 1939 season, or maybe it was Jimmy Dykes' loud and persistent criticism of the Yankee juggernaut. Dykes, the witty, acerbic manager of the White Sox, had chased the Yankees vainly through the 1936–39 quadrennium, and he reacted irritably one day when Joe McCarthy, the Yankee manager, was praised as a genius. The snappish Dykes, envying McCarthy's seemingly unlimited supply of good players, growled, "Genius, my ass. Whenever McCarthy needs a ballplayer, all he has to do is push a button, and there he is." Dykes' outburst angered McCarthy, particularly since it gave the Yankee manager the colorful if unfair label "Pushbutton Manager."

At any rate, after the 1939 season the seven dwarfs passed a new league rule that barred a pennant winner from trading for or buying players from the other teams. It seemed a petulant rule because, except for Hildebrand, the Yankees had done very little dealing since 1936. However, what the seven other teams were thinking of was first base. The once mighty Gehrig had ended his career after eight games of the 1939 season and his place had been taken by a light-hitting benchwarmer named Ellsworth (Babe) Dahlgren. Every other team in the league had a better first baseman than Dahlgren, and the powers-that-be were determined to keep the Yankees from using their money and their surplus of players to get one of them. If that was the rule's purpose, it succeeded, for Babe Dahlgren was the Yankee first baseman again in 1940 and, to my utter shock and chagrin, the immutable, invincible, unshakable Yankees lost.

ROBERT W. CREAMER

4

A LITTLE HISTORY

I don't want to leave the impression that in 1941 people of my age had little or no interest in the world beyond our immediate concerns, which in my case centered so much on baseball. I mean, sure, I was aware of Adolf Hitler. I had been aware of him since early in 1933 when I was ten and read on the front page of *The New York Times* that he had been made chancellor of Germany by President Paul von Hindenburg. The word "chancellor" was new to me and it impressed me, as so many things did that I found in the newspapers. Reading newspapers was a practice that I picked up from my brother, who was six years older than I. Jerry was an intense sports fan, and a sports fan had to read the papers. I loved the sports sections; they were fun to read, with much more copy than now and far fewer photographs and "graphics" and minitype statistics. The sports columnists wrote every day, or at least six days a week, and you looked forward to reading them each day the way you looked forward to seeing your friends in school or around the neighborhood.

I also read the funnies (even then they were technically called comic strips but everyone I knew called them the funnies), and I read the front page. I recall the banner headlines in November 1932 that proclaimed Franklin D. Roosevelt's "landslide" victory over Herbert Hoover in the Presidential election; "landslide" in that sense was a new word, too. I was surprised that Roosevelt won because my cousin Jack Kelly had voted against him. Jack was twenty-four and voting in his first presidential election; he had been only twenty in 1928 and thus too young to vote in that year's election. Jack had come to our house to visit my mother, who was sick (she died later that month), and he announced in his ringing voice that he wasn't going to vote for Roosevelt because Roosevelt was a cripple and how could a cripple run a country? That seemed logical to my ten-year-old mind, and I was surprised that the country had not agreed with Jack.

After Roosevelt was inaugurated on March 4, 1933, my brother saved the newspapers every day for a week during the famous "bank holiday" that Roosevelt imposed on taking office, when he closed every bank in the country for several days to prevent depositors from making a run on their money and plunging the country into a financial panic. There was no Federal Deposit Insurance Corporation then to protect banks and individual savings accounts; that came into being later as part of Roosevelt's New Deal, one of the many innovative bits of legislation that were introduced under Roosevelt.

"This is history," my sixteen-year-old brother explained when I asked why he was saving the newspapers. "These papers will be valuable some day."

I don't know what happened to the papers, but I remember him saving them and I remember the bank holiday, and I remember that despite everything some banks failed, including the Mount

ROBERT W. CREAMER
≪≪≪≪≪≪≪≪≪≪≪≪≪≪≪≪≪≪≪≪≪≪

Vernon Trust Company, where Jerry had a savings account. He lost all the money he had saved from odd jobs he had worked at—I think it was eighty-three dollars. Yet he went on to study business and finance in college and he became a banker himself.

So I was aware of Roosevelt and of Hitler, and I know I didn't like Hitler. He went quickly from being "chancellor" to being Der Führer, the leader, the dictator—like Benito Mussolini, the big-jawed, big-mouthed boss of Fascist Italy, who was Il Duce, also the leader. Hitler was weird looking, with his stupid haircut and his silly mustache, and he was German. Germans were the enemy in the stories and books we read about the World War—the first one, which in the 1930s did not yet have a number—when Spads and Nieuports fought Fokker triplanes over the trenches in France. Hindenburg, the man who brought Hitler to power, was an eighty-five-year-old relic of Germany's past, the chief German general at the end of the 1914–18 war and the man for whom Germany's supposedly impregnable "Hindenburg Line" was named. American heroes from the "Fighting Sixty-Ninth" and other storied regiments were always hurling themselves at the Hindenburg Line in the stories we read. The dirigible or zeppelin that burst into flames and fell to the ground in New Jersey in 1937 was named after Hindenburg. We liked the dirigible, but we didn't like Hindenburg or Hitler.

I particularly disliked the way Hitler behaved at the Berlin Olympics in 1936, the summer I was fourteen. I was an Olympics nut. In 1932 during the Olympic Games in Los Angeles I must have read every story and the detailed results of every heat in every event in every sport. One of my first sports heroes was Eddie Tolan, the little American sprinter who won the 100 and 200 meters in 1932, and in 1936 I loved Jesse Owens, of course, and John Woodruff, the tall young University of Pittsburgh freshman who won the 800 meters at Berlin. I watched Woodruff in big American track meets later on, and after all these years I still think he's the best runner I ever saw. Hitler insulted these men at Berlin, according to what I read and believed, calling them "America's black auxiliaries," and that cemented my dislike of him.

I became aware of Hitler's persecution of Jews, not the detailed horrors that were exposed after World War II but enough to know the terror that Jews lived under in Germany. In 1939 the *Reader's Digest* ran a short story called *"Addressant Unbekannt,"* or "Address Unknown," a rather melodramatic account of Nazi anti-Semitism told through an exchange of letters between a Jewish refugee in America and a non-Jewish friend in Germany that brought home vividly to my adolescent mind what cruel treatment Jews were undergoing.

Paul Fussell, in his 1989 book, *Wartime,* a blunt, tough report that endeavors to lay bare the stupidity and ugliness of war, implies that Americans in World War II looked upon Japan as a greater enemy than Germany. Not where I lived. I was an Irish Catholic, growing up in a largely Catholic community, and I knew very few Jews when I was young, but there was never any doubt in my mind: When I thought of enemy I thought of Germany and Hitler. He was a bully and so were the Germans. They started the first world war (I was unaware of the subtleties and ramifications of international economics and politics) and they started the second one. They enjoyed pushing people around (I'd read a lot about the German "rape" of little Belgium in World War I). So did Mussolini and his Fascist government in Italy. In 1935 when Italy invaded Ethiopia, or Abyssinia, as it was also called, we rooted for Ethiopia.

I was not as clear in my feelings about the civil war in Spain that started in 1936. I didn't understand the politics—I knew that the Russian Communists were backing the Loyalist government in Spain, and that Hitler and Mussolini were backing the rebels under General Franco, who eventually won. The Catholic Church openly favored Franco because he was a Catholic and the Communists were atheists, but I don't recall being pro-Franco. I remember a discussion in the late 1930s in my high school history class in which a very bright girl who knew a lot more about the world than I did queried our teacher on where she stood. The girl was for the Loyalists; the teacher for Franco. I didn't have to take a stand one way or the other, so I didn't. What I remember better about high school in the late 1930s was listening to a World Series game on the radio during our afternoon math class. It was a small class and we felt so damned grown up when Mr. Evans, the math teacher, told us it was okay to bring a radio in during the Series, as long as we kept the sound low and got our work done.

We had a student activity in high school called "Forum" which had replaced the old debating club, with its formal rigidities and its technical arguments in which you were sometimes obliged to defend something you didn't believe in or to attack something you did. The Forum was a precursor of the panel discussions you see on television. Instead of debating, teams of students from different high schools would sit on stage before an audience (other students usually; sometimes students and parents), with a teacher acting as moderator, and toss opinions back and forth about a specific topic. Whatever the topic was the forums always seemed to come down to a discussion of "The Democracies versus the Dictatorships." The democracies were essentially Britain, France and the United States; the dictators were Hitler, Mussolini and Joseph Stalin of the Soviet Union. The incongruity that for much of this time Stalin and Hitler were enemies (see Spain) was usually overlooked; it made sense after Stalin and Hitler joined hands in August 1939, just before I started my senior year in high school.

Hitler had been bullying his way around Europe. He pressured Austria and incorporated that compliant country into Germany in the spring of 1938. That was a major event; it greatly increased the size of Germany. I recall vividly a newspaper map showing the new, enlarged Germany looking like a huge mouth about to swallow a Czechoslovakia it now enclosed on three sides. Hitler nibbled at the Czech border in September 1938 when the infamous Munich

Pact engineered by British prime minister Neville Chamberlain to assure "peace in our time" let Hitler extend Germany's borders into the Sudeten Mountains, leaving Czechoslovakia's western extremity looking diseased and eaten away. Six months later, in the spring of 1939, Hitler gobbled up the rest of the country.

Yes, indeed, I was aware of Hitler and what he was doing. I was at the New York World's Fair in August 1939 with my aunt Florence and my aunt Gertrude—my father's sisters, lovely ladies who after my mother's death did many kind things for my brother, my two sisters and myself. That was the day when the stunning news came that the Russians and Germans had agreed to their nonaggression pact—neither would take up arms against the other—which gave Hitler free rein to move east into Poland. My aunt Florence, a freethinker who had given me Plutarch when I was fourteen and who gravely told me once that she no longer thought of herself as a Catholic or even a Christian, said calmly to my aunt Gertrude, "This means there'll be a war." She meant another world war. Eight days later I was riding into New York City on a train with my friend Arnold Benson when the banner headlines in the morning papers were screaming that before dawn that day Hitler had invaded Poland, and that the war had begun.

Poland was destroyed in less than a month. I was working as a bus boy at a big outdoor clambake put on by a Westchester County political club in a picnic grove on a nice old place called Schmidt's Farm, which is now a housing development, when word came that the Russians had moved into Poland from the east and had agreed to divide the country with Hitler. Later that fall the Russians invaded Finland. We knew nothing about "protecting one's flanks" or that the Soviet Union, despite the Nazi-Soviet pact, still considered Hitler the enemy and was moving ruthlessly to strengthen its defenses. We rooted for little Finland, fighting the Russian bear in the snow and ice of the wintry north. Robert Sherwood wrote a prize-winning play called *There Shall Be No Night* about the Russian invasion of Finland, and the Finns attacked the Russian

ROBERT W. CREAMER
≪≪≪≪≪≪≪≪≪≪≪≪≪≪≪≪≪≪≪≪≪≪≪

armor with homemade fire bombs—gasoline in bottles with a flaming wick attached to the outside and which exploded in flames when a thrown bottle shattered against a tank. These deadly little bombs, in mocking tribute to the Soviet foreign minister who helped engineer the Nazi-Soviet agreement, were called Molotov Cocktails.

We knew all this, we read all this. Sports section, yes, and the funnies, yes, but the front page, too. In the spring of 1940, as my beloved, unbeatable Yankees stumbled and slumped early in the pennant race, Hitler moved again. First, he raced rapidly northward into Denmark and Norway, which shocked me; Denmark and Norway, like Sweden and Switzerland, seemed beyond politics; they were career neutrals, not part of the unseemly vortex of European power politics. But Hitler violated them anyway. He put them in his pocket and a month later turned westward and rolled into Belgium, Holland and France. The Germans had crushed little Belgium in the First World War; now they were doing it again. Worse, this time they also crushed Holland, another traditional neutral, and little Luxembourg, which we'd hardly heard of. It was shocking. It was like shooting a gun in church. Hitler was despicable; he had no respect for tradition, for convention, for decency.

Hitler's conquests were often dramatized in the newsreels and movies that we saw by superimposing the crooked-cross swastika of the Nazis on maps or characteristic scenes of the conquered countries—Holland's windmills, France's Eiffel Tower. The defacing swastika became so repellent that even today when I see an occasional swastika scribbled on a wall by an ignorant child or a pinhead adult, I am more viscerally shocked than I am by the sight of a scrawled obscenity. I explained this once to one of my sons, when he was little. "For me," I said, "it's worse than seeing shit or fuck." He was shocked by my language, as I intended him to be.

Hitler's slashing invasions brought the word "*Blitzkrieg*" into common usage. The English came to use "the blitz" to describe the sustained German air attacks on Great Britain later in 1940, but the term, literally "lightning war," really meant something sudden, surprising. Bud Schelz, my brother-in-law to be, was in his freshman year at Fordham when the war began, and he took a course taught by an old German Jesuit who, when he tossed a surprise quiz at his class, called it a "blitz."

In May and June 1940, as the Yankees floundered, we followed the advance of Hitler's lightning war through the Low Countries and into France in the newspaper maps that appeared every day. Great huge arrows plunged across borders and curved deep into France. The British army, which had crossed the English Channel the previous autumn to join the French along the German border, retreated to Dunkirk and back across the Channel. In June, the week I graduated from high school, France fell. The ground war came to a halt. Hitler and his allies now had all of Continental Europe except for Portugal, Switzerland, Sweden and the Balkans.

I was aware of what was going on, but I was still politically naive. I know that in the summer of 1940 I paid more attention to the pennant races than to the presidential campaign. That was the year Roosevelt was nominated by the Democrats to run for an unprecedented third term as president, but I don't remember anything about the Democratic convention that nominated him. I do remember that the Republican convention was held in Philadelphia and that I listened to it on the radio and rooted hard for the underdog Wendell Willkie to get the nomination, which he did. I was too young to vote—you had to be twenty-one, although at eighteen I was old enough to drink legally—but as a member of a Republican family I wore a "No Third Term" button and that fall as a college freshman wrote a paper for my political science class on James Knox Polk, a strong American president who had declined to run for a *second* term. I thought it was a telling argument. My poly sci professor wasn't impressed, and Roosevelt won anyway, which didn't bother me. I was more upset by the Yankees' inexplicable season; they remained in their early season slump

ROBERT W. CREAMER

until August, and when they finally began to play well it was too late, and they finished third, which seemed as shocking to me as Hitler invading Denmark and Holland. That seems unpardonably facetious, but I'm pretty sure it's the way I felt that summer when I was eighteen, and sports meant more to me than the world did.

5

ENTER LARRY MacPHAIL

The Dodgers' heady climb out of baseball's depths really began a decade earlier in Columbus, Ohio, where Larry MacPhail was running an automobile agency and dabbling in real estate. MacPhail, then forty, had never played professional baseball, had never managed and had never worked in any capacity for a professional team, major or minor. Yet when a group of Columbus businessmen bought an option on the moribund Columbus Senators of the American Association in order to keep the sickly franchise from being moved away from Columbus, they picked MacPhail to run the club.

MacPhail was intelligent and imaginative, but his principal assets were a loud personality and an untamed coil of runaway enthusiasm. He could be gracious and courtly, or he could be as abrasive as a sheet of sandpaper, but he got things done. He came from a well-to-do Midwestern family, attended Beloit College and the University of Michigan, and at the age of twenty earned a law degree from George Washington University. Before he was twenty-one he was married, was working for a prominent Chicago law firm and had been admitted to practice before the Illinois State Supreme Court.

When he was twenty-five he moved to Nashville, Tennessee, to run a department store he had done legal work for. Three years later, during the First World War, MacPhail went overseas as a captain of artillery and saw combat. After the war ended he was in France as part of the Allied occupation force when his commanding officer decided to kidnap the Kaiser. Kaiser Wilhelm of Germany had been the Hitler of World War I, the principal enemy of Britain, France and the United States. Allied war propaganda called him the "Beast of Berlin." Slogans like "Hang the Kaiser" were popular. When the armistice that ended the war was signed in November 1918, the Kaiser fled from Germany into Holland, which had been neutral during the war. The commanding officer of MacPhail's regiment, Colonel Luke Lea, who was something of a wild man, conceived the idea of driving into Holland, without official permission, and nabbing him.

Lea enlisted a few trusted associates: MacPhail, another captain named Henderson, a lieutenant, three sergeants and a corporal. He got five-day passes for his party, commandeered a couple of automobiles and after losing most of the five days to various unanticipated delays arrived at the castle where the Kaiser was staying.

Lea entered the castle with MacPhail and Henderson while the others waited outside. He asked politely to speak with the Kaiser. He was politely received and asked to wait. As the three Americans waited people kept moving in and out of the room. Lea suspected that Dutch authorities were being sent for. Kidnapping the Kaiser now seemed out of the question, and he knew that he and his little band would be interned in Holland if they were caught, so he decided to retreat. On their way out of the castle MacPhail swiped an elaborate metal ashtray as a souvenir of the expedition.

They got back to France safely, but the Dutch complained to the Allies about the intrusion and there was a hell of a fuss. Among other things, what about the ashtray? Lea said he didn't know anything about an ashtray and was reprimanded with a slap on the wrist. MacPhail brought the ashtray back home to America, kept it proudly on his desk and entertained newsmen for decades with his story about kidnapping the Kaiser. (His son Lee MacPhail, who was president of the American League from 1974 to 1983, has the ashtray now. Another of Larry's sons, Bill MacPhail, was sports director of CBS-TV and ESPN. A daughter, Marian, for many years headed the research department at *Life*. Lee's son Andy became general manager of the Minnesota Twins. All in all, a remarkable family.)

After the war MacPhail moved to Columbus and ran a glass-making business before getting into automobiles and real estate. Everybody knew him in Columbus. He was an operator, a wheeler-dealer, a man who leaped at opportunities. In 1929 he poured a lot of money into a project for a new medical center. The idea was good, the timing bad; the stock market crash occurred that October, and in 1930 MacPhail found himself starting over again.

The stock market crash also affected the fortunes of the Columbus Senators. Most minor league teams were independently owned then, and minor league baseball was much more important than it is now. A man running a top minor league franchise could make a lot of money at it and be a person of prominence in the community. The American Association, for example, was a remarkably stable organization. With the International League and the Pacific Coast League it was one of the three Class AA, or highest level, minor leagues in the country (the term "Triple A" was not introduced until 1946). For more than fifty years it had eight teams in the same eight cities—Minneapolis, St. Paul, Milwaukee, Kansas City, Indianapolis, Louisville, Columbus and Toledo—except during World War I, when Toledo played home games in Cleveland.

ROBERT W. CREAMER

Four of those eight cities are now represented in the major leagues. The American Association was big-time stuff.

But in 1930 Columbus was a weak franchise. It hadn't won an American Association pennant since 1907, while every other team in the league had won at least once since then, and most of them two or more times. Worse, Columbus had finished in the second division for fifteen straight years.

Let me pause to explain "second division" to those for whom the term has little or no significance. For the first half of the twentieth century the classic, constant number of baseball teams in a league was eight. Not six, not ten, not twelve, not fourteen. Eight. The American League had eight teams, the National League had eight. The three top minor leagues each had eight, and so did the Texas League and the Southern Association, the next highest minor circuits. Most lesser leagues also had eight teams.

Even if a club failed to win the pennant, it was important to finish second, third or fourth—that is, in the upper half or first division of the league. It was a matter of pride and money. First-division teams drew better crowds and earned bigger salaries. Major league teams that finished second, third or fourth shared in World Series receipts. A player's share might be only a few hundred dollars, but a few hundred dollars was a hefty bonus in those days when a big-league salary might average less than a hundred a week for the entire year. Most major leaguers took jobs in the off season to augment their incomes.

But players on teams in the second division did not earn bonus money. Such teams were looked down upon as failures. A team "fell" into the second division; it "rose" into the first division. "First division" came to mean something admirable; "second division" was denigrating, as in "He's a second-division ballplayer."

The Columbus Senators were a chronic second-division team when MacPhail took charge. The first thing he did was to look for help from a major league club. Only a few big league clubs owned minor league teams. Most simply bought players directly from independent minor league operators, or drafted players from the minors at a set fee. Players owned by the big league clubs were "loaned" to minor league teams for seasoning until they were deemed ready for the bigs. Some big league clubs had arrangements with minor league teams in which they provided most or all of the players and paid most or all of their salaries; in exchange, they had a storage bank of reserve players. This was called a working agreement.

MacPhail wanted such an agreement for 1931, his first season, but he had no luck interesting a big league team in Columbus until he met Branch Rickey, who was running the St. Louis Cardinals for owner Sam Breadon. Rickey went a step further; he said the Cardinals would like to buy the club outright. This pleased the Columbus investors, and it pleased MacPhail, who received a two-year contract to continue as president of the club, which was renamed the Columbus Red Birds.

The arrangement worked beautifully, for a while. Rickey supplied Columbus with good ballplayers and MacPhail supplied the promotional spark. He had the old ballpark painted a bright red, gave ushers and ticket takers red hats and red ties to wear, painted red birds on the outfield fence, even painted the flagpole a brilliant red. Rickey and MacPhail established a "knothole gang," which let kids in free on weekdays. Special season passes were sold to women. Attendance jumped, the team improved, and the Red Birds finished fourth. They were in the first division!

The Cardinals decided to replace the rickety old Columbus ballpark with a brand-new stadium. MacPhail supervised the construction, argued with the workers and got one of them so angry that he threw a wrench at MacPhail's head. But the stadium was built and at MacPhail's urging lights for night games were installed. Night baseball had been played experimentally here and there for half a century, but the first night game in Organized Baseball did not take place until 1930, at Des Moines in the Western League.

ROBERT W. CREAMER
《《《《《《《《《《《《《《《《《《《《《《《《《

In 1931, MacPhail's first season, Indianapolis introduced night ball to the American Association. Now in 1932 under his direction it began in Columbus and attracted big crowds. It was a great year for MacPhail. The Red Birds finished second and drew 310,000 people, which in that dark Depression year was better than six big league clubs did, including Rickey's Cardinals, who drew only 279,000 in St. Louis.

You'd think all would be sweetness and light between them, but MacPhail and Rickey were on a collision course. MacPhail's energy had been vital in getting the Red Birds up and flying, but his freewheeling way of operating didn't fit with Rickey's way of doing things. Rickey had been in baseball for more than twenty years, to MacPhail's two. He knew the game thoroughly and he wanted people who worked for him, including MacPhail, to do things his way. The new Red Birds did not exist for MacPhail and Columbus; they existed for the St. Louis Cardinals. They were an essential part of the "farm system" Rickey was developing for the Cardinals.

Before Rickey, when the standard procedure was for major league clubs to replenish their rosters by buying players from the minors, teams like the Cardinals were handicapped because richer clubs like the Chicago Cubs and John McGraw's New York Giants could outbid them. To circumvent this Rickey assembled a network of minor league teams that were owned or controlled by the Cardinals. On these "farms" they could grow, so to speak, their own players. That's the way it's done today, but it was a novel idea when Rickey introduced it. He bought Columbus from MacPhail because the Cardinals' system needed another team at the Double-A level. He was constantly adding teams. By 1940 the Cardinals owned or controlled thirty-three minor league teams, and the flow of fine ballplayers from the minors to the Cardinals was astonishing. The Yankees began their own farm system after Rickey paved the way, and they, too, kept bringing up outstanding rookies.

The farm system concept infuriated Judge Kenesaw Mountain

Landis, the baseball commissioner, who was of the old guard that wanted minor league clubs to remain pretty much free of big league control. Landis particularly objected to the practice of keeping promising players "hidden" by switching them back and forth from roster to roster and up and down from one minor league classification to another to avoid exposing them to the annual baseball draft. The draft had been designed to prevent independent minor league clubs from keeping good players on their rosters year after year instead of letting them rise to the majors. After the majors took control of minor league clubs it was supposed to prevent them from stockpiling quality players on their farms for use at some future time when the parent club needed them.

Landis hated the farm system. Rickey's counterargument was that the minor leagues could not survive without farm-system subsidization by the majors. In the long term he was proved right, but in the 1930s Landis watched Rickey and other operators like a hawk and he swooped down and "freed" minor leaguers—made them free agents—whenever he decided there had been a "cover-up." The Yankees acquired the admirable Tommy Henrich as a free agent in 1937 after Landis freed Tommy from the Cleveland Indians' system.

In any event, Rickey in developing his farm system knew exactly how he wanted his minor league teams to function. He wanted the men who operated those teams, men like the shrewd Warren Giles, who later became president of the Cincinnati Reds and whose son Bill ran the Philadelphia Phils, to be cogs in a smoothly running machine. But MacPhail could not be a cog in a machine— by nature he was more of a sabot. Inevitably, he and Rickey clashed. MacPhail was annoyed by the cavalier way Rickey moved players in and out of Columbus; Rickey was irritated by MacPhail's attitude, particularly his tendency to ignore the complicated paperwork involved in farm-system transactions.

He was also offended by MacPhail's carefree way of life. Rickey, brought up in a strict Methodist home, was a teetotaler. When he went into baseball he promised his mother he would never go to a ballpark on Sunday. Despite the obvious difficulties that caused, Rickey stuck to his promise. MacPhail on the other hand was a high roller. He wore panama hats and two-toned shoes. He was something of a woman chaser. He liked to drink. He liked to drink a lot. Drinking got him into trouble because his temper became even more explosive when he had a few under his belt.

One night when he was on the road traveling with the Columbus club, MacPhail got into a heated argument with the night manager of a hotel where the team was staying. He said something threatening about pulling his club out of that hotel. The manager said something unsoothing in reply and MacPhail roared that by God he was going to take his club out of the hotel right now, God damn it. And he did, going around in the middle of the night banging on room doors, rousing the players and moving them down the street to another hotel. That did not sit well with Rickey.

Branch, who was notoriously close with a dollar (Enos Slaughter said, "He'd go to the safe to get you a nickel change"), was also bothered by MacPhail's extravagant way of running the ball club. When he found out after the new stadium was completed that Larry had a paneled office bigger and more luxurious than his and Breadon's in St. Louis, he blew the whistle. MacPhail was called to St. Louis, where the usually genial Breadon scolded him, saying, "Do you see any wood paneling on the walls of this office or Oriental rugs on the floor?"

"It was easy to guess who had been carrying tales," MacPhail said. He resented Rickey's interference. He claimed that the stadium job had come in under budget, thus earning the contractor a substantial bonus. "He said he'd like to do something for me," MacPhail argued, "to show his appreciation for the way I had been of help to him."

That was not Rickey's version. "The job went far over budget," Arthur Mann wrote in a biography of Rickey. "The workmen didn't like MacPhail because of his interference. Rickey interceded and sat far into the night with union representatives to placate workers on the job." Mann, it should be noted, was Rickey's employee and friend as well as his biographer.

Whatever the truth, the differences between the two men came to a head early in 1933. The Columbus club was accused of violating the minor league rule against paying players more than the four-hundred-dollar-a-month salary limit. Rickey said MacPhail had broken the rules. MacPhail said the violations had been the Cardinals', not his. Rickey asked MacPhail to resign. MacPhail refused. Rickey then fired him.

ROBERT W. CREAMER

6

THE CINCINNATI KID

Six months later MacPhail was back in baseball, this time in the major leagues as vice president and general manager of the Cincinnati Reds. The Reds were a terrible team in those days. They had finished last three years in a row and their season attendance had fallen to 218,000. The club went into receivership, and the Central Trust Company of Cincinnati invited MacPhail to come in and run things.

Later, there was a conflict of opinion between MacPhail and Rickey as to how he got the job. The Rickey version was that Branch had been asked to run the Reds. He said he was committed to St. Louis and recommended MacPhail for the job. MacPhail in rebuttal said, "The only thing Rickey ever did for me was fire me from Columbus." MacPhail said he had known the people at Central Trust long before he was called in to take over the Reds and that Rickey had nothing to do with it.

Despite their differences the two remained friends, at least on the surface. They sat together at ballgames, got together on trades, gave jobs to each other's sons. Lee MacPhail and Branch Rickey, Jr., were lifelong friends. Branch Rickey III and Andy MacPhail are friends. Beneath the surface, however, antagonisms festered and after World War II they stopped speaking to one another.

In Cincinnati MacPhail was quick to attract attention to himself and the ball club. He began to trade players. He spruced up the ballpark. He devised a season-ticket plan, said to be the first such ticket plan ever offered by a big league club. Until then tickets were usually sold on a game-to-game basis; relatively few box or reserved seats were sold much ahead of time.

A young radio announcer just up from Florida named Red Barber was given the job of doing the Reds' games on radio, although MacPhail's part in Barber's hiring was coincidental. Red had come to Cincinnati as a staff announcer, and the station assigned him to do the games. The first Cincinnati game Barber broadcast was the first major league game he ever saw. But MacPhail liked baseball on radio. His games in Columbus had been broadcast. He felt it was great publicity. He had Barber do live interviews with players and managers three hours before game time, in the hope that Barber's interviews would stimulate fans to come out to the ballpark for the games.

Despite everything the Reds finished last again in 1934 and attracted even fewer fans than in 1933: a season total of 207,000. Two major league teams did worse. The Phillies drew 170,000, the St. Louis Browns 115,000. Attendance in those Depression years was—well, depressing. The 115,000 the Browns drew in 1934 was actually pretty good for them. They drew only 88,000 a year earlier and only 81,000 and 93,000 the following two years. For the eight seasons from 1932 through 1939 the Browns attracted a *total* of 853,000 spectators.

Even Rickey's colorful Gas House Gang Cardinals of 1934, one of the most famous of all baseball teams, winners of the National League pennant after an exciting race, drew only 325,000. The

ROBERT W. CREAMER

highest attendance in 1934 in the National League was 731,000 by the Giants. In the American League the Tigers, winning the pennant for the first time since 1909, drew 900,000, but that was almost triple what they had drawn a year earlier.

Now and then there were big crowds at ballparks, usually at doubleheaders (a bargain relished by the cash-poor fans of the 1930s) and especially for doubleheaders on the three big holidays—Memorial Day, the Fourth of July and Labor Day. There'd be doubleheaders almost every Sunday in most ballparks. On most weekday afternoons (there was no night ball in the majors when MacPhail arrived in Cincinnati) there'd be only a few thousand spectators scattered through the stands. A crowd of 10,000 at any time was gratifying; one of 20,000 was exceptional. A season attendance of 500,000 meant a team was doing fairly well at the gate. A season attendance of a million was extremely rare.

Even so, the 207,000 the Reds drew in MacPhail's first year was pretty bad, and after the season he appeared at the winter baseball meetings with a forty-page paper pushing the idea of night baseball. He spoke for three hours, and when he was finished he was given permission to try night ball in Cincinnati in 1935. He could schedule one night game at home against each of the seven other teams in the league, with the proviso that each team reserved the right to refuse to play at night.

MacPhail scheduled the first night game against the Phillies, an attendance-poor team that would not object to efforts to hype the gate. MacPhail promoted the game for all it was worth and even arranged to have President Roosevelt touch a telegraph key in Washington that would turn on the lights at the Cincinnati ballpark. At dusk, just as the sun was going down, Roosevelt, who understood publicity as well as MacPhail did, pressed the key, the lights came on and there was a great "Ahhh!" from the crowd.

For their seven night games, all of which were played on weekday evenings, the Reds drew about ten times as many people as they would have if the games had been played on weekday afternoons. There was opposition, especially in the American League. The Yankees' general manager, Ed Barrow, said, "It's just a fad. It'll never last after the novelty wears off." But Cincinnati's season attendance more than doubled. The team climbed out of the cellar, finished sixth and continued to improve.

However, Larry's truculent personality did not please the conservative Powell Crosley, who had become owner of the club. Crosley wanted MacPhail to fire James (Scotty) Reston, the Reds' traveling secretary, after Reston criticized the club owner for renaming the ballpark Crosley Field and for installing a big replica of a Crosley-manufactured refrigerator on the outfield fence. MacPhail refused, saying, "If he goes, I go." The immediate problem was resolved a short time later when Reston left to join the Associated Press. (He later became chief Washington correspondent of *The New York Times.*)

Despite the Reds' improvement on the field and at the gate, MacPhail and Crosley couldn't get on together. The ultimate break came in 1936 when MacPhail got into a fistfight with a Cincinnati police sergeant in a hotel elevator. Newspaper stories played up the incident. Sporting a black eye, Larry read the headlines and said gleefully, "Man, how do you like *that* for publicity?" Crosley didn't like it at all. When the season was over MacPhail resigned and went back home to Michigan to work with his father in the banking business.

This time fifteen months passed. Then in January 1938 he was hired by the Dodgers, and Brooklyn was never the same again.

ROBERT W. CREAMER

7

LARRY AND LEO
AND RED

I f the Reds were terrible when MacPhail arrived in Cincinnati, the Dodgers were a mess when he reached Brooklyn. It wasn't just the Depression and the general sense of economic malaise. In a down time for the country, the Dodgers were an exceptional mess.

MacPhail was an odd choice for the job. He had held only two positions in baseball and had been bounced from both of them. He had only three years of major league experience. He was a well-educated Midwesterner moving into the dese-dose-dem environment of Ebbets Field.

And he fit it like a glove.

Maybe he just liked messes, problems, complications. He certainly found them in Brooklyn. Charlie Ebbets, who was president of the Dodgers from 1898 to 1925, gave the club a certain sense of direction through the first quarter of the century, but he had died more than a dozen years before MacPhail's arrival and the interregnum was chaotic. Ebbets had sold a half interest in the Dodgers to Ed and Steve McKeever, who were influential in Brooklyn business and politics. After Ebbets and Ed McKeever both died in 1925, Steve McKeever was left alone to work with Ebbets' heirs, and they didn't get along. The front office had little direction and the club kept doing haphazard things. Occasionally someone in the front office would make a show of leadership, but when a firm decision was made it was usually a dumb one. The club was heavily in debt, yet twice in the money-scarce thirties the Dodgers rewarded managers with multi-year contracts and then fired them a year before their contracts were up, which meant that twice the club paid a man a full year's salary for not managing. At a time when half the big league teams were hiring player-managers in order to save money on salaries, it seemed an extraordinary extravagance.

The Dodgers fell into the second division and stayed there. The financial and organizational status of the club was so shaky that the Brooklyn Trust Company, in a move similar to that which had occurred in Cincinnati, moved in and took control. The bank wanted an independent baseball man to run the club. Ford Frick, then president of the National League, suggested MacPhail. (At least, that's one story. In later years Rickey said he had recommended MacPhail. His grandson, Branch Rickey III, suggests quite reasonably that with baseball's penchant for networking it's more than likely that his grandfather was asked his opinion of MacPhail and gave an approving one.)

Despite his meager experience MacPhail was so sure of his ability to run a baseball club that he held off until he got the terms he wanted. It wasn't money, although his salary at Brooklyn was much higher than that of any of his players (which is the way it was in baseball in those days). What he wanted was to be in charge. At Columbus and Cincinnati he had chafed under the higher authority of Rickey and Crosley. This time he wanted control. He

ROBERT W. CREAMER
<<<<<<<<<<<<<<<<<<<<<<<<<<<

wanted to run everything, subject only to financial approval by the bank.

He and George McLaughlin of the Brooklyn Trust Company hit it off. When he joined the club he was called the executive vice president, and a year later his title was officially upped to president. He was the boss.

Of what? Except for a couple of years around 1930 the Dodgers had been relentlessly mediocre since Ebbets' death. They finished in sixth place five straight times after Charlie died and were sixth again in 1933 and 1934, leading to a newspaper comment one season that "overconfidence may yet cost the Dodgers sixth place." Then, in a variation on the theme, they were fifth and seventh before finishing good old sixth again in 1937.

And they were seventh in MacPhail's first year, although it didn't seem to matter much. At least they were trying. MacPhail borrowed money from the bank and, as was his custom, spruced up the old ballpark. He bought a hard-hitting, smooth-fielding first baseman from the Phillies named Dolph Camilli, one of those fine players who don't meet the standards that Hall of Fame selectors look for but who in their time are among the very best in the game. Tommy Henrich and Charlie Keller and Joe Gordon of the Yankees were like that. Ken Keltner of the Indians. Terry Moore and Marty Marion of the Cardinals.

MacPhail found some legitimate major leaguers on the roster he inherited. One was Harry (Cookie) Lavagetto, a good third baseman who had been miscast as a second baseman in previous seasons. Another was Luke (Hot Potato) Hamlin, who won twenty games a year or so later. A third was shortstop Leo Durocher, who was soon to become the team's manager.

Burleigh Grimes was still the manager when MacPhail arrived and he had a year to go on his contract. Grimes, known as Old Stubblebeard, was a hard-nosed manager, professionally tough. In MacPhail's first year, long decades before women became a regular part of the baseball beat, the Dodgers heard that one of the New York papers was sending a "girl reporter" to Ebbets Field to do a color story on Grimes. The "girl reporter" turned out to be a sophisticated, smartly dressed woman who was one of the paper's top feature writers. "Wait'll she tries to talk to old Burleigh," someone said. Grimes, who had been informed of her arrival, was sitting grumpily at one end of the dugout. The woman approached him and said, "Hello, I'm supposed to interview you."

"I have nothing to say."

"I know," the woman said sweetly, "but shall we get on with the interview anyway?"

MacPhail had no intention of following the Brooklyn tradition of paying a man not to manage, so he held on to Grimes for the time being. But in spring training the quick-thinking, garrulous Durocher, known as "the Lip," was loudly in evidence; he became *de facto* and eventually *de jure* team captain and heir to the managerial post. MacPhail added players and subtracted some and although his first Brooklyn club did finish seventh it improved from twenty-nine games below .500 to only eleven below.

Attendance rose nearly 40 percent, largely because MacPhail got people to pay attention to Brooklyn. He introduced night baseball. It had been three years since President Roosevelt turned the lights on in Cincinnati, and no other big league team had yet followed McPhail's lead. Ed Barrow of the Yankees and other hardliners seemed justified in thinking night ball was a fad. Attendance in Cincinnati had leveled off after the initial impetus of night games and had even dropped a little in 1937, when the MacPhail-less Reds dropped into last place. (They revived in 1938 and won pennants in 1939 and 1940, and attendance rose dramatically in those years.)

The Yankees and the Giants didn't want MacPhail to install lights, but he put them in anyway, and the first night game in New York City was played in Brooklyn on June 15, 1938. As everyone who follows baseball knows, it was an astonishing success. There was a capacity crowd, and Cincinnati's Johnny Vander Meer, who had tossed a no-hit, no-run game four days earlier, pitched his second successive no-hitter, one of the signal events in baseball history. More than anything else, the outrageous melodrama of that night established MacPhail in Brooklyn.

A week later MacPhail irritated the Yankees again by signing Babe Ruth to a contract as a Dodger coach, and the Babe spent the rest of the season waving runners past first base and entertaining the fans during batting practice by belting out long taters. The only Dodger who resented Ruth's presence was Durocher. Leo wanted to succeed Grimes as manager and he felt the publicity-conscious MacPhail might appoint Ruth to the job. One day Leo executed a perfect hit-and-run play and when a newspaper gave Ruth the credit for signaling for the hit and run from the coach's box, Durocher exploded.

"For Christ's sake," Leo protested in his rasping voice. "How the fuck could he call the play? He doesn't even know the fucking signs."

Ruth got mad, there was a vocal exchange, and Leo shoved Ruth against a locker. Grimes got between them before Ruth could retaliate. "I was hoping they'd both punch Grimes," said Buddy Hassett, at that time a Dodger outfielder, who had reason to dislike the Brooklyn manager.

The season ended and Grimes was let go. Ruth's contract was not renewed. In Chicago during the 1938 World Series MacPhail named the volatile, imaginative, irritating, combative Durocher the new manager and the Dodgers were off and racing. With Leo at the wheel the new era in Brooklyn moved into high gear. Where the Dodgers used to be clumsy but amusing, unskilled but endearing, now they became tough and pugnacious, cocky and over-achieving, the bad boys of the league.

MacPhail brought Red Barber to New York in 1939 to be the Dodgers' play-by-play announcer. He grabbed new players right and left, claiming discards from the waiver lists, signing free agents, beefing up Brooklyn's farm system. Most of the players he picked up did not work out—the Dodgers used nineteen different outfielders from 1938 to 1940—but as MacPhail picked through other team's junk heaps he found a few prizes. One in 1939 was a thirty-one-year-old righthanded pitcher named Whitlow Wyatt, who had won only twenty-six games in nine big league seasons. He won seventy-eight for the Dodgers over the next five years, most of them big ones. A second find was a brittle twenty-nine-year-old outfielder named Fred (Dixie) Walker, who had ruined his shoulder and damaged his knee and seemed near the end of a disappointing career. Walker had nine fruitful seasons in Ebbets Field and was one of the most popular players in Brooklyn's history—known as "the People's Cherce." A third was a burly right-hander named Hugh Casey, who won fifteen games in 1939, most of them as a starting pitcher, and who then became one of the best relief pitchers in the game.

There were others who made shorter or longer appearances on the Ebbets Field stage—the outrageous Cletus (Boots) Poffenberger, one of the oddest of odd balls; the fading but still dangerous fastballer Van Lingle Mungo; the likable but not very productive second baseman Pete Coscarart; the hard-hitting, poor-fielding catcher Gordon (Babe) Phelps, who had a nickname on his nickname—Babe was called Blimp. There was a small lefthanded pitcher named Vitautis Casimirus Tamulis, a Lithuanian who was called the Italian "Vito" for short; a thirty-three-year-old pitcher named "Tot" Pressnell; and a small utility infielder named Johnny Hudson, called Mr. Chips by the fans after the popular 1930s movie *Goodbye Mr. Chips* because Hudson was considered a good man in the clutch, when the chips were down.

Durocher took this patchwork team and in August of 1939 had it playing .500 ball, the best a Dodger team had done that late in the season since 1932. Then Durocher got it to play even better. The Reds and the Cardinals were fighting for the pennant and were out of reach, but just ahead of the Dodgers were the Cubs and the

ROBERT W. CREAMER

Giants. In 1939 the Cubs and the Giants were still thought of as the quality teams in the league, the big winners over the years, the old guard, the defenders of the faith. Chicago and New York, Frank Chance and John McGraw, Gabby Hartnett and Mel Ott, winners of twenty-two pennants in thirty-eight years. They were the Establishment. They were the target.

The Dodgers won thirty-one of their last forty-six games. They passed the Giants to move into the first division and they challenged the Cubs. They fell back again—that old Brooklyn habit of lifting the fans' hopes and then dashing them—but Durocher wouldn't let them quit. On the last day of the season the Cubs lost and in rainy Ebbets Field the Dodgers won and finished the season in third place, half a game ahead of Chicago. Third place! My god, it was unbelievable.

The Dodgers drew a million people that year, according to MacPhail's count, and everyone in New York was captivated by them, especially during that last stretch drive. I wasn't one of the million who went to Ebbets Field. Brooklyn was a long way from where I lived, and when I saw the Dodgers play it was in the Polo Grounds against the Giants. Not that I saw that many games in those days. Going to a big league ballgame was an occasion. I got most of my baseball from the newspapers and from Stan Lomax's nightly roundup of ball scores on radio. And, of course, from Red Barber. Late in the 1939 season my father was away and I borrowed his car and drove with a friend named Eddie Miller to the top of a hill where there was good radio reception. We must have sat there for two hours listening to Barber broadcast another late-season Dodger victory. I was still a loyal Yankee fan but the Dodgers were fascinating, and listening to Barber was fun. MacPhail and Durocher were always doing something, always raising hell about one thing or another. Durocher would rage at umpires and arouse the crowd, which loved to watch Leo argue, his mouth flapping, his face shoved into an umpire's face.

MacPhail would explode at anyone around him. He fired the

Ebbets Field press-room bartender. He got mad at Harold Parrott, a *Brooklyn Eagle* sportswriter (later a club official with the Dodgers), for something Parrott wrote and barred him from Ebbets Field; he made up with Harold and his editor at an amiable lunch a few days later. He took swings at John McDonald, his wisecracking righthand man. He fired Durocher, or told him he was fired, several times and always hired him back the next day. He fired his secretary the same way and later married her. Buzzie Bavasi, two or three years out of college, had begun working for the Dodgers, and he and his wife were sitting with MacPhail when an opposition player slid home past Phelps. The umpire called him safe and MacPhail bellowed his disagreement, shouting at the umpire from his box. When he sat back he said to Bavasi, "What did you think of that?" Bavasi said, "I thought Babe missed the tag." MacPhail glared at him. "You're fired!" he said, and Bavasi's wife started to cry. She thought MacPhail meant it.

He kept buying and selling and trading ballplayers, improving the club, creating interest, casting about for new ideas. He experimented with protective helmets. He experimented with a yellow baseball (the dye came off on the players' fingers). He got NBC to do the first experimental telecast of a major league game from Ebbets Field in August 1939, with Barber doing the commentary.

But who had a television set? I never saw television until after Margaret and I were married in 1947. Radio was the medium, and it was a treat to listen to Barber broadcast this great Brooklyn soap opera. Baseball on radio was a novelty. There were no major league baseball broadcasts in New York when I was growing up, except for the World Series and the All Star game. From 1933 to 1938 the Giants, Yankees and Dodgers had a written agreement not to broadcast, the theory being that fans would stay at home to listen rather than go to the ballpark. When the agreement expired at the end of 1938 MacPhail declined to renew it, despite

ROBERT W. CREAMER
≪≪≪≪≪≪≪≪≪≪≪≪≪≪≪≪≪≪≪

outraged bleats from the Yankees' Barrow and the Giants' Horace Stoneham. Barrow said if MacPhail went ahead with the broadcasts, the Yankees would go on a bigger station and blow the Dodgers "out of the water."

MacPhail went ahead anyway and the Yankees and Giants, forced into action, entered into an odd agreement in which the two teams used the same play-by-play announcer and the same station and broadcast only their home games. Under the major league schedule then in use the Yankees and Giants never played home games on the same day. When one was at home the other was on the road. However, when the Dodgers were at home they were almost always confronted by either a Yankee or a Giant game across town, and now they also had to confront a broadcast of that game. No wonder Barrow was confident that their broadcasts would blow the Dodgers out of the water.

But the rival broadcasts didn't hurt the Dodgers at all. General Mills, makers of Wheaties, the principal sponsor of the Yankee-Giant broadcasts, drafted a folksy old baseball announcer named Arch McDonald from Washington, D.C., to do the games. McDonald had been very popular doing play-by-play for the Senators in Washington, but he was a bust in New York. His very slow, rambling style irritated New Yorkers, who much preferred Barber. For all Barber's Southern accent and country idiom (tearin' up the pea patch, walkin' in tall cotton, sittin' in the catbird seat) he fit New York. He was sharp and intelligent, a thoroughly modern, refreshing broadcaster whose straightforward way of reporting the action attracted not only Dodger fans but baseball fans in general.

After a while even non–baseball fans became hooked on Barber and baseball and, usually, the Dodgers. Barber blew McDonald out of the water. Mel Allen, a young staff announcer at that time, assisted on the Yankee/Giant broadcasts, which meant he got to spell McDonald for a couple of innings in each game. "Arch was a country boy," Allen said, "and he didn't feel easy in New York.

.

After the season he went back home to Tennessee." Allen succeeded McDonald as the principal broadcaster and after military
service in World War II went on to fame as the Yankees' longtime
play-by-play announcer. But in 1939 and for a long time after,
Barber and the Dodgers dominated baseball broadcasting in New
York.

ROBERT W. CREAMER

8

DREADFUL YEAR

The Yankees began their disastrous 1940 season at the same time Hitler was beginning to rip western Europe apart. The big world was turning upside down and so was my little world of baseball, although I didn't realize it at first.

Early in 1940 the Associated Press asked sixty-seven sports-writers which team would win the American League pennant and sixty-six of them picked the Yankees. The sixty-seventh was, I assume, a wise guy. When the Yankees began the season sluggishly I dismissed it as an early season slump, one they would soon break out of.

But they didn't break out of it. They continued to play poorly, losing more often than they won, and nearly two months into the season they were still under .500. DiMaggio, batting .296, was more than eighty points below his league-leading .381 of the year before. The other Yankees were worse. In a hard-hitting baseball era when anything under .300 was considered undesirable and anything under .280 pretty damned bad, Charlie Keller was hitting .241, Joe Gordon .238, Tommy Henrich .234, Bill Dickey .208, Red Rolfe .200, Frank Crosetti .161.

The greatest team in baseball was last in the league in hitting—and not just last, but a woeful, distant last. At the end of May the Yankees as a team were batting only .234, which in that high-average day was almost literally unbelievable. The next worst team was batting thirty-four points higher, and the two leading teams were more than fifty points ahead of the Yankees.

They were better in June, but not much. They didn't improve in July, and in August they lost seven of nine games to fall below .500 again. Two thirds of the season was gone, and the Yankees were still under .500! I couldn't believe it. As late as August 16 they were in fifth place, the lowest they had been that far along in the season since 1925, the terrible year when Babe Ruth was sick, rebellious and suspended, and the team finished seventh. I was only three in 1925 and hadn't noticed. In 1940 all I knew was that nothing like this had happened to the Yankees in my years of rooting for them.

I could not understand it. The powerful Yankee hitters seemed strangely paralyzed. Why weren't they hitting? Inevitably, some people took "paralysis" literally, thinking of Lou Gehrig and the sclerosis that had struck him down a year earlier. After Lou's consecutive-game streak ended early in the 1939 season, he went to the Mayo Clinic in Rochester, Minnesota, for a complete physical checkup, and there the nature of his disease was disclosed. He had "amyotrophic lateral sclerosis," which was described as a form of "infantile paralysis," the term commonly used then for poliomyelitis. Parents lived in chilling fear of infantile paralysis in those days before Jonas Salk's discovery of the polio vaccine, and as children we learned the dreaded term early, before we could read or write. For a long time I thought it was "infintallaparalysis," all one word.

The seriousness of Gehrig's condition was dramatized for us by

ROBERT W. CREAMER

the use of the term and now, a year later, whispers went around that perhaps Gehrig had infected the other players on the club. Jimmy Powers, a gossipy sports columnist for the *New York Daily News,* changed the whisper to a shout when he discussed the likelihood of such infection in print. He received a torrent of shocked criticism in return, plus lawsuits filed by Gehrig's attorneys and Yankee players. It was terrible to be suspected of having infantile paralysis; people shunned you the way they shun AIDS patients today. Powers and the *Daily News* quickly published a retraction and an apology, but the issue wasn't defused until the Yankees finally began to play the way they were supposed to.

A twenty-seven-year-old rookie righthander named Ernie Bonham was the catalyst. The Yankees brought him up from the minors on August 12 to help fill a gap in the pitching staff created by Lefty Gomez's season-long inability to pitch. Gomez and Red Ruffing had given the Yankees a powerful one-two pitching punch for nine years, but in 1940 Gomez had a chronic sore arm and was able to start only five games. Bonham, arriving on the scene just as the team began to hit, started twelve games, completed ten of them, won nine, pitched three shutouts (best in the league that year was four) and had an earned-run average of 1.90 (well below Bobby Feller's season-long league best of 2.61). Bonham was a sensation.

DiMaggio had run off a twenty-three-game hitting streak in July, the longest in the league that season, and had lifted his average into the .320s. In August he took off on another sustained batting binge that lifted his average to .352 by the end of the year, good enough for his second straight batting championship. The other players also began hitting, and the team suddenly looked like the old Yankees again.

Baseball legend has it that once they began to play well the Yankees dominated the league the rest of the way and missed winning the pennant in 1940 only because they started their sprint too late and ran out of time. It wasn't quite that way. When they came out of their slump in mid-August they won twenty of their next twenty-three games, and by the morning of September 11 had moved to within one game of the lead. That afternoon, Bonham beat Feller 3–1 in the first game of a doubleheader with Cleveland, and the Yankees moved into first place for a couple of hours. They lost the second game to fall behind again, lost five of their next six and were never a real factor during the last two weeks of the pennant race. When the Tigers clinched the pennant by beating the Indians two days before the season ended, the Yankees were a relatively distant third, three and a half games back. They picked up a meaningless game and a half on the final Saturday and Sunday of the season, so that their place in the final standings looks mighty close:

Detroit	90–64	—
Cleveland	89–65	–1
New York	88–66	–2

But it wasn't as close as it looks. The Yankees were beaten, well beaten, and I—in a slow-motion, long-term sense of the word—was shocked.

To this day I can't figure out what happened to the Yankees that season. Why did everyone stop hitting? Marvin Breuer, a good second-line pitcher with the Yankees at the time, said, "Everybody has a slump now and then. They all just happened to have one at the same time." But an entire team, for four months?

Some point to the absence of Gehrig and the presence of the light-hitting Babe Dahlgren at first base. But the Yankees won with Dahlgren at first base in 1939, and without Gehrig they went on to win three more pennants in 1941–42–43 by an average of more than thirteen games a year. They couldn't have missed Lou all that much. What happened in 1940?

You could point out that Casey Stengel's Yankees of 1949–58 would have won ten straight pennants except for a second-place

ROBERT W. CREAMER

finish in 1954. These things happen. But the 1954 Yankees played excellent baseball; they won 103 games, more than any of Casey's pennant-winning teams, and were beaten only by a very strong Cleveland club that won 111 games.

You could also mention the 1959 Yankees, the only other Yankee team not to win a pennant from 1949 through 1964. They finished third, too, and their 79–75 record was worse that that of the 1940 Yankees. But the 1958 pennant-winning club played poorly the last six weeks of the season and, unlike the powerful 1939 team, barely won the World Series. The 1959 slump was not all that surprising. And to start winning again in 1960 the Yankees needed the injection of Roger Maris, acquired in a blockbuster trade with Kansas City; Maris won the first of his two Most Valuable Player awards in 1960. In contrast, the winning Yankees of 1939 and the winning Yankees of 1941 were substantially the same team as the losing Yankees of 1940.

Why did they slump in 1940? In a way it *might* have been Gehrig's illness that affected the club—not physically, but mentally. Sometimes it takes a while for something so shocking to sink in, and the Yankees might not have felt Gehrig's absence fully until they reported for spring training in 1940. That was the first spring without Gehrig's imposing presence for *everyone* on the club, from manager Joe McCarthy on down (Gehrig was in his sixth season as a regular when McCarthy became manager in 1931). Bill Dickey, the Yankees' Hall of Fame catcher, was a particularly close friend of Gehrig, and Dickey's 1940 season was much the worst of his impressive career.

Perhaps Lou's departure contributed to a general sense of things falling apart, a loss of stability. There was Gehrig, still only thirty-six years old as 1940 began, slowly dying. There was the war, with the old order changing rapidly, established countries collapsing one after the other like dominoes. And there was the absence of Colonel Jacob Ruppert, the wealthy New York brewer who had owned the Yankees for nearly a quarter of a century and who had died in 1939. Maybe the Yankees missed the comforting presence of Jake.

Ruppert, urbane, sophisticated, impeccably dressed, had come to personify the superior quality of the Yankees. He was the quintessential owner, a quiet, mannered rich man with an aristocratic reserve. He was always in evidence as the owner of the Yankees on the appropriate occasions, such as opening day, the World Series, signing Babe Ruth to the highest salary ever paid in baseball, issuing a statement disciplining Babe when the big fellow got off the reservation. Yet he never publicly interfered with the day-to-day operation of the club, which was handled for him by Barrow.

In the funny papers rich men like Daddy Warbucks in "Little Orphan Annie" were almost always portrayed wearing morning clothes or tuxedos, wing collars with ascots, *something* that showed they were rich. Ruppert's clothes were more tasteful than Daddy Warbucks', but whenever you saw a photograph of him on the sports pages he *looked* rich, he looked elegant, he looked terrific. In short, he looked like the patrician owner he was.

None of the other owners could quite convey that quality. Walter O. Briggs, who owned the Tigers, was very wealthy and very powerful, but he conveyed the image of a tough, self-made man who had come up from the ranks. Ruppert gave the impression that he had always been up there. Philip K. Wrigley of the Cubs probably came closest to the patrician idea, but Wrigley was a young man—he'd succeeded his dead father as owner only a few years earlier—and he seemed more genial and friendly, a nice young fellow who happened to have money. Wrigley probably had a lot more money than Ruppert, for that matter, and so did Briggs, but they didn't *look* rich. Ruppert did.

Tom Yawkey of the Red Sox was another young owner at that time, the heir to millions whose family had purchased a ball team for him. Yawkey in time proved an exemplary owner, but as far as I was concerned half a century ago he was a parvenu, a new

ROBERT W. CREAMER
≪≪≪≪≪≪≪≪≪≪≪≪≪≪≪≪≪≪≪≪≪≪≪

guy who threw a lot of money around buying great players from other clubs (Joe Cronin, Lefty Grove, Jimmie Foxx) in order to build up his own artificially. (Ruppert had done the same thing two decades earlier, buying Ruth and other top players one after the other like a drunk at a yard sale, but that had happened long before my memory, and time has a way of sanctifying yesterday's sinners.)

Powell Crosley of Cincinnati had wealth and position, but he used the Reds to promote himself and his business interests, much the same way Gussie Busch did later with the St. Louis Cardinals: Crosley Field, Busch Stadium. When Ruppert built his great stadium in 1923 he called it after his ball team.

Horace Stoneham, the youthful, chubby-cheeked owner of the Giants, had inherited his team from his father, Charles, a few years earlier. Charlie Stoneham was sometimes described in the newspapers as a former "bucket-shop operator." I didn't know what a bucket shop was, and I'm not sure I know now, but I gather it was a somewhat sleazy form of investment trading. In any case, neither old Charlie nor young Horace had the stature, the unflappable dignity, that Ruppert had.

A couple of clubs, the Boston Braves and the Dodgers, had silent, or hands-off, or confused ownership that stayed in the background. Connie Mack, the ancient manager of the Philadelphia Athletics, had become the principal owner of his club, but Connie didn't seem like an owner. The crosstown Phillies were a poverty-level team, and owner Gerry Nugent was known to us sports-page readers as a desperate dealer, one who repeatedly sold off his best players for the cash he needed to keep the club going. When Nugent sold pitching star Kirby Higbe to Brooklyn, Higbe asked Nugent for a percentage of the cash the Phils received in the deal. "Kirby," Nugent said, "it's already gone." Clark Griffith, a former player and manager, owned the Washington Senators, supposedly a financially shaky club that Griffith held together with shoestrings and safety pins. I don't know about that. Clark and his heir and successor, Calvin Griffith, lived pretty well down there in the Virginia countryside, so the Washington club was making *some* money. But the image was that of Nugent, constant scrambling.

The Cleveland Indians were run by Alva Bradley and the Pittsburgh Pirates by William Benswanger, and I assumed both owned the teams they operated. I'm not sure of that, but it doesn't matter. They were the ones we thought of as owners, and Ruppert outshone them, too. The White Sox belonged to the Comiskeys, but the old Comiskeys, father Charles and son Louis, were both dead, and Lou's widow, Grace, the nominal head of the club, stayed pretty much in the background. The St. Louis Browns were owned by a hustling businessman named Don Barnes, and the Cardinals were owned—or at least I thought they were owned—by Breadon and Rickey. The two names were linked together in print so frequently that I assumed they were partners. It was years before I realized that Breadon was the owner and Rickey a hired hand, although a very powerful and talented hired hand. In any event, they were hands-on workers, not the aloof king that old Colonel Ruppert was.

Ruppert stood alone. When he died something classy went out of baseball, and out of the Yankees. In 1940 his heirs, none of whom were known to or meant anything to the players, were trying to sell the club, and repeated rumors of new ownership coming on in the Colonel's place could have been upsetting—although it took five years before the sale of the club was finally accomplished.

Who knows what happened to the Yankees in 1940? All I do know is that for one young Yankee fan at the beginning of 1941 the old confidence was shaken, and the future, echoing the world itself, was strangely uncertain. A lot of things had happened to me in 1940. I reached my eighteenth birthday, and that changed things a lot. In New York State, where I lived, being eighteen meant that my junior driver's license, with its restrictions against driving a car at night or in New York City, was upgraded to a senior license, with no limits on time and space. Being eighteen meant that in

ROBERT W. CREAMER
〈〈〈〈〈〈〈〈〈〈〈〈〈〈〈〈〈〈〈〈〈〈〈〈〈〈〈

New York I was now old enough to drink legally in bars and restaurants. Drinking and driving, however offensive that combination sounds now, were important elements in such matters as dating girls and feeling grown up—particularly when you were legally entitled to such privileges.

I graduated from high school in 1940. I went off to college, the first time I had been away from home and family by myself. I was scholastically shaky and socially inept, even with my senior driver's license and my new legality in bars. I had grown five inches in a year and was now over six feet tall, but I weighed only 138 pounds, and that fragile stature (I was nicknamed "the Dead Man" by college friends who were amused by my pale, thin appearance) reflected the fragility of my maturity.

I was very young for my years and for my height. I lacked sophistication and confidence, and now I wasn't even sure about my baseball team anymore. Going into 1941 I was uneasy about the Yankees and I was vaguely pessimistic about life.

9

A VERY FAST START

B rooklyn fans, on the other hand, were wildly optimistic. Led by MacPhail and Durocher, broadcast by Barber, the Dodgers had taken over New York. It was a revolution. You have to remember how dominant the Giants and Yankees had been and how downtrodden Brooklyn was, even beyond the matter of all those sixth-place finishes. Brooklyn had been a separate city, but it lost its independent status when it was absorbed into Greater New York in 1898. In that era it won back-to-back National League pennants and was the dominant team in New York. But just as it lost its political independence it lost its baseball eminence. After McGraw became manager of the Giants in 1903 Brooklyn ceased to be a baseball power. The Giants won thirteen pennants and were first or second twenty-four times in the next thirty-five years; during that same period, 1903 to 1938 (the year MacPhail arrived), the Dodgers won only twice and finished in the second division twenty-nine times. Even the Yankees, who didn't exist until 1903, overshadowed the Dodgers, and after Babe Ruth hit town they were out of sight.

The Dodgers were nothing compared to the Giants and the Yankees. The Polo Grounds held 55,000 people, Yankee Stadium 65,000. Ebbets Field, squeezing people in, might have seated 34,000. The Borough of Brooklyn had more people than Manhattan, where the Giants played, and the Bronx, where the Yankees were, but from 1903 through 1938 the Dodgers outdrew the Giants only twice and the Yankees only three times, the last in 1916. Brooklyn was second-rate.

About the only time the Dodgers seemed important was when they were playing the Giants. In the old eight-team league, teams played each other twenty-two times a year, and the Dodgers and Giants played each other twenty-two times in the same city. That internecine warfare was epic; I can think of no more accurate word to describe it. The Giants were the better team and usually dominated, but any Dodger victory at any time was a sweet moment of vindication, a spasm of triumph, for Brooklynites.

Now and then it got better than that. The best was at the end of 1934 when the Dodgers knocked the Giants out of a pennant. Bill Terry succeeded McGraw as manager of the Giants in mid-1932, and in 1933 he led the Giants to the National League flag and victory in the World Series. Terry was a decent man, intelligent, a gentleman, but he projected a bad public image—he seemed surly, arrogant, contemptuous. In the spring of 1934 when he was discussing prospects for the coming season with reporters, he was asked, "What about Brooklyn, Bill?" Jokingly, presumably responding the way a man involved in the annual Dodger-Giant rivalry ought to respond, he said airily, "Brooklyn? Is Brooklyn still in the league?"

That off-the-cuff comment in an unimportant press conference was blown into headlines, and Terry became the most hated name in Dodger history. On the last weekend of that same season, his Giants were tied for first place with the Cardinals. Each team had two games to play. The Giants' last two were at the Polo Grounds against the Dodgers. Thousands of Brooklyn fans surged across the East River and had a deliriously happy time as the Dodgers beat the Giants twice while the Cardinals were winning in St. Louis. The Giants finished second and the gleeful cry went up: "Hey, Terry! Is Brooklyn still in the league?"

In 1939, what with night ball and Durocher and finishing third, and not only finishing ahead of Terry but beating his Giants sixteen games to six during the season, the Dodgers drew a million fans to little Ebbets Field. That was a quarter of a million more than the Giants drew to the Polo Grounds, and nearly 100,000 more than the Yankees drew to Yankee Stadium. Hey, Terry! Hey, Barrow! Who owns New York?

Nineteen-forty was even more satisfying. The Dodgers had had bursts of glory before but followed them with pratfalls. After winning the pennant in 1916 they dropped to seventh the next year. After winning in 1920 they were fifth in 1921. After finishing only one and a half games behind in 1924 they fell to sixth in 1925. In 1930 after winning eleven straight in September to move into first place they lost seven straight and finished fourth. Why should 1940 be different?

But it was. Durocher got his team off to a very fast start. (I recall an interview years later in 1955, when Durocher was managing the Giants. It was just before opening day and an earnest New York baseball writer asked, "Leo, do you intend to get your team off to a fast start this year?" Durocher looked at him contemptuously and rasped, "No, you stupid son of a bitch, I'm gonna lose the first ten games.") In 1940 his Dodgers won the opening game, won again, and again, and again. They won eight straight and then took a train west to meet the league-champion Reds in Cincinnati. At that time the major league record for an undefeated streak at the start of a season was nine, held by the Giants. Could the Dodgers match it? Durocher started Tex Carleton, another of MacPhail's retreads, a worn-out pitcher who had spent 1939 in the

ROBERT W. CREAMER
‹‹‹‹‹‹‹‹‹‹‹‹‹‹‹‹‹‹‹‹‹‹‹‹‹‹

minor leagues after seven seasons in the bigs. Carleton pitched beautifully and not only had a 3–0 lead going into the last half of the ninth inning; he also had a no-hitter going.

I remember that game well. I was home from school in bed with a bad cold, and I listened to Barber's broadcast. I wasn't alone in that. During that last inning I don't believe there was a baseball fan in or near New York with access to a radio who wasn't listening as Carleton tried for his no-hitter.

Carleton got the first out and then the second out. Barber was doing the game via the Western Union wire, which was the way out-of-town games were handled then. Radio technology was considered too expensive to have play-by-play announcers go on the road to do live broadcasts of out-of-town games, although they did for All Star games and the World Series. Instead, the broadcaster went to the radio studio and worked from a telegraphed report, a pitch-by-pitch account of the game. The wire would report things laconically: "Lavagetto up. Ball. Strike. Ball two. Lavagetto out, fly to first. Camilli up. Ball. Single to right. Two runs in. Camilli to second on throw."

Like other broadcasters Barber would wait for the wire description of a play to be completed before padding it out and passing it on to his listeners, and we'd hear the telegraph wire chattering. Some announcers gussied up their broadcasts with sound effects of bat hitting ball and fake crowd noise in an effort to con listeners into feeling they were hearing a live broadcast. Ronald Reagan, who as a baseball broadcaster in the 1930s did ticker games for KRNT in Des Moines and WHO in Chicago, got a lot of mileage out of a story he liked to tell about the time the wire went out when he was broadcasting. "I had the batter foul off twenty-seven pitches before the wire came back in," Reagan would say, chuckling.

Barber told me that story in 1966, fourteen years before Reagan was elected president, when I was working with him on his autobiography, *Rhubarb in the Catbird Seat*. Red had heard Reagan tell it three decades earlier at a meeting of baseball broadcasters in Chicago, and he said he wondered then why Reagan hadn't simply told his listeners the wire was out instead of continuing to fake it. We didn't use the story in the book—Barber felt it would be unkind—but later on it became apparent that Reagan loved it. Maybe he liked faking people out.

Barber used none of the showboat devices that some announcers dragged in to give their broadcasts a simulated reality. He simply reported the game, depending on his knowledge of the players and the situation to give life and excitement to the bare bones of the wire report. Of course, between pitches we always listened intently to the tickety-tick of the wire in the background, wondering what it was saying. Rumors persisted that professional telegraphers could "read" the sound and win bets on upcoming plays from innocent strangers. We would try to guess from the tone of Red's voice what he was about to report (a home run? a strikeout?). But we never could. Red's voice would be calm and objective as he waited for the completion of the wire description before amplifying it for his listeners.

However, this day in his broadcast of the game in Cincinnati he did something utterly different. There were two outs in the ninth, the world-champion Reds were still hitless against Carleton and the Dodgers were on the verge of winning a record-equaling ninth straight game. I was lying in bed, listening. I forget what the count was, or even if there was a count. I don't remember the batter. What I do remember is listening to the chatter of the ticker, wondering what it was reporting, when suddenly Barber cried, "It's a no-hitter! I don't know what happened yet, but it's a no-hitter!"

The wire had reported something like "Frey up. Strike one. Frey out . . ." and Barber didn't wait for the rest of it. What was on the wire was what Brooklyn wanted to know. A lesser man might have milked the moment, creating a show out of it, but Barber didn't hesitate. His listeners in Brooklyn and all around New York were waiting to find out what happened, and Barber reported the big news the instant he had it and added the details afterward. Red was head and shoulders above other baseball broadcasters back then, and in the years since only a few have attained his level of intelligent skill. He was truly professional, and so, too, it was becoming increasingly evident, were the Dodgers.

10

DUCKY WUCKY MEDWICK

The Dodgers lost the next day to Bucky Walters, Cincinnati's ace, but the opening streak lifted them into a struggle for first place with the defending-champion Reds that lasted into mid-summer. MacPhail was so delighted with the way his ball club was playing that at the end of that first western trip he chartered two airliners (in those days one plane wasn't big enough to carry all of the thirty-five or forty players, newspapermen and front-office people in the Dodger party) and flew them back to New York. As far as I can determine that was the first time a major league club had flown.

The Reds caught the Dodgers and passed them in May, the Dodgers took the lead back in June, the Reds grabbed it again, the Dodgers grabbed it back. Not until after the All Star game in July did Brooklyn slip back to second to stay. Too many things had happened. On June 1 Pee Wee Reese, the admirable rookie shortstop MacPhail had bought from the Red Sox a year or so earlier, was hit on the head with a pitched ball in Wrigley Field. This was when players wore soft cloth caps when they batted, not helmets. Reese suffered a concussion and spent several days in a Chicago hospital. Later he returned to the lineup, but in August he was hurt again, this time breaking a bone in his heel sliding into second, and he was gone for the rest of the season.

In June, ten days after Reese was beaned, MacPhail, gunning for the pennant, engineered a trade that changed the Dodgers forever. It was the first of four MacPhail deals that in eleven months transformed Brooklyn from one of those have-not teams that occasionally produce good seasons into the perennial baseball power the Dodgers have been ever since.

MacPhail wanted a power-hitting outfielder, and Branch Rickey had one. Rickey was shaking up the Cardinals, who after challenging the Reds for the pennant in 1939 were floundering in 1940. He fired manager Ray Blades early in June and gave the job to a recovering alcoholic named Billy Southworth, a manager in the Cardinal farm system whose experience as a major league manager consisted of one boozy half season with St. Louis more than a decade earlier. Southworth, an astute baseball man, had straightened out his life and showed confidence and command when he took the managerial reins again. Under him the 1940 Cardinals, who were 15–29 before he became manager, played .633 ball the rest of the season and finished a strong third.

The influx of young players coming up from the vast Cardinal farm system let Rickey exercise his talent for trading away headline players before they passed their peak and lost value in the market. Rickey always said he'd rather trade a star a year too soon than a year too late. When MacPhail came looking for a power hitter, Rickey decided it was time to peddle Joe Medwick, who was only twenty-eight and who for several years had been the best all-around hitter in the National League.

Medwick was a slashing line-drive hitter whose lifetime average at that point was .338. In his seven full seasons in the National

League he had averaged 120 runs batted in a year and more than eighty extra-base hits. In 1937 he led the league in homers, runs batted in and batting average to win the Triple Crown. That year he also led the league in hits, doubles, runs scored, total bases and slugging average and won the Most Valuable Player award, even though the Cardinals finished fourth.

Medwick was called Ducky Wucky because of the way he walked, but he was tough. He was in the lineup nearly every day; in his seven seasons he had missed only twenty games. He liked to swing the bat. He was a bad-ball hitter, dangerous on anything thrown near the plate.

In the spring of 1940 he was considered one of the great hitting stars of the game, on a par with DiMaggio, Greenberg, Jimmie Foxx and Mel Ott. Ted Williams? Not yet. In June of 1940 a baseball fan would have laughed if anyone said that young Ted Williams was a much better hitter than the great Joe Medwick.

But Medwick was also a selfish ballplayer, an arrogant, abrasive, bad-tempered man who got in squabbles with teammates, angered managers, irritated sportswriters and in Rickey's opinion had outlived his usefulness to the Cardinals. So Rickey gave MacPhail both Medwick and Curt Davis, a fine starting pitcher who won twenty-two games for St. Louis in 1939 but who was almost thirty-seven and too old for the Cardinals' youth movement. In return, St. Louis received $125,000 and four lesser players from the Dodgers.

It was an absolutely stunning trade. Getting a star like Medwick legitimized the Dodgers, established the team as a serious contender and eliminated once and for all the image of the Brooklyn club as a collection of clowns and misfits. Never mind that Medwick was a misfit himself with the Cardinals. When Durocher played shortstop for St. Louis he and Medwick had been great friends— the abrasive Joe would play for the abrasive Leo. What mattered most was that Medwick was a great ballplayer, and now the Dodgers had him.

And a week later they lost him. He had played five games for the Dodgers when the Cardinals came to town. In the first game he played against his old teammates Medwick went hitless. The next morning he and Durocher were riding down in the elevator at the Hotel New Yorker, where both were living and where the Cardinals stayed when they were in New York. On the elevator they met Bob Bowman of the Cardinals, a hard-throwing right-hander from the mines of West Virginia who was starting for the Cardinals that afternoon. Words were exchanged, rough challenging words. How much was heavy-handed banter and how much was genuine threat is impossible to determine, but Medwick said something to the effect that he'd knock Bowman out of the box that afternoon and Bowman said something to the effect that Medwick had better duck first. Whatever was said, Bowman's first pitch to Medwick that afternoon hit him on the head and knocked him unconscious.

"He hit Joe on the head just about as hard as I've ever seen anybody get hit," said Enos Slaughter, the Cardinal right fielder.

Medwick fell as though he'd been shot and lay flat on his back in the batter's box, his arms spread wide. Bowman ran to the plate and bent over, obviously concerned. Durocher sprinted from the dugout. The first-base coach ran in. Charlie Dressen, Durocher's righthand man, came in from the third-base coaching box. Players spilled onto the field from both dugouts. Dodger players accused Bowman of deliberately throwing at Medwick. There were angry words and some pushing and shoving, but no real fight. It was a beaning, that's all, and beanings were appallingly commonplace then. Reese had been hit the week before. Billy Jurges, the Giants' elegant fielding shortstop, was badly beaned a couple of weeks later and was out for the rest of the season.

What made Medwick's beaning so shocking was the star quality of the man hit, and the timing. The Dodgers had just got him, for God's sake. Brooklyn's agony was personified by MacPhail, who had been watching the game from the press box level. He roared in anguish and rushed downstairs to the Dodger dugout. Furious and shouting angrily, he tried to go out onto the field but was held back by a couple of Dodgers. After Medwick was carried off on a stretcher MacPhail did go on the field. He stormed over to the Cardinal dugout and raged at them. Medwick was taken to a hospital. MacPhail was persuaded off the field. Southworth took Bowman out of the game, and baseball went on.

MacPhail demanded an investigation, and in time Ford Frick, the president of the league, interrogated Medwick, Bowman, Durocher and others. Nothing conclusive came from his investigation. MacPhail charged that it was a deliberate act and William O'Dwyer, later mayor of New York but then the Brooklyn district attorney, made political points by declaring that his office was going to look into the matter. Nothing came of that either.

Bowman was traded to the Giants after the season, a provocative move on the Giants' part. Early in 1941, exposed now to the Dodger-Giant rivalry, Bowman said, "I expect Dressen and Durocher will keep on me all year because I beaned Medwick. That wasn't my fault. Dressen was stealing the signs and tipping off the batters. He'd whistle when he thought a curve was coming. Don Padgett [the Cardinals' catcher the day Medwick was hit] and I decided to cross him up, with Padgett signing for a curve and me coming in with a straight high one. Poor Medwick was looking for a curve and he couldn't get out of the way."

Years later Slaughter told Don Honig, "Some people thought it was done intentionally, but I never thought that. Dressen was great at stealing the signals and letting the batter know what was coming. Every time Bowman threw the curve Dressen picked it off and whistled up to the batter. So Padgett went out and told Bowman to hold the ball like he was going to throw the curve and then throw the fast ball. That's one way to put a dent in somebody's head. But that's the batter's lookout. Bowman faked a curve, Dressen whistled and Medwick stepped into a fast ball and got hit, hit hard."

Medwick missed only a handful of games and was back in the

ROBERT W. CREAMER

Dodger lineup surprisingly soon, and he batted .300 for the Dodgers that season and .318 a year later. But he was not the same ballplayer. He was plate-shy, which was understandable, and while he was still a useful player he just wasn't the same Medwick.

Before the beaning he was a major force. He had finished first or second in various batting categories twenty-eight times. After the beaning he never led the league in anything and was second only once. In St. Louis he batted below .319 only once; after the beaning he hit higher than that only once. Before the beaning he averaged 208 hits a year. The most he ever had after it was 175.

Here's a comparison of the two sides of Medwick's baseball life:

Seasons Played	Years	Age	Games Played	AB	H	R	RBI	HR	XBH	TB	PCT	SA
8	1932–39	20–27	1084	4420	1492	771	873	145	579	2442	.338	.552
9	1940–48	28–36	900	3215	979	427	510	60	279	1410	.304	.439

He was a diminished figure. No wonder MacPhail, sensing this, went berserk.

11

TALL COTTON

I t was a frustrating time for MacPhail, an impatient man who wanted the pennant now. The most frustrating moment of the 1940 season came in a tense game with the Reds in Ebbets Field, when the Dodgers still had hopes of catching Cincinnati. Lonnie Frey, an ex-Dodger who was unpopular in Ebbets Field because he slid hard into Pete Coscarart and then fought with him, beat the Dodgers with a home run against the right-field screen. Ordinarily, a ball against the screen was just a hit, not a home run. A ball *over* the screen into Bedford Avenue was a home run. A ball off the screen or the concrete wall below the screen was still in play. But Frey's fly ball hit the screen, dropped straight down and stopped on a narrow ledge atop the concrete wall. It stayed there, defying gravity, while the Dodgers waited for it to come down. As they waited, Frey circled the bases with a home run and the Reds went on to win the game. After the game a still angry MacPhail ordered workmen onto the wall, where they installed a beveled cover on the ledge to prevent a batted ball from ever acting that way again.

Frey's homer summed up the Dodgers' 1940 season. They struggled and came close, but they couldn't win. They finished second, which was gratifying, but they faded in the stretch and ended the season twelve games behind the Reds and just ahead of the rapidly rising Cardinals.

After the season MacPhail went hunting for more ballplayers. Everyone was after one of the Phillies' two good starting pitchers, Kirby Higbe and Hugh Mulcahy. Mulcahy pitched a great many games for the terrible Phils and lost a great many: eighteen in 1937, twenty in 1938, sixteen in 1939, twenty-two in 1940. From the frequency with which the notation "Losing pitcher—Mulcahy" appeared in the box scores, he came to be called Hugh (Losing Pitcher) Mulcahy and is so listed in *The Baseball Encyclopedia.* Higbe, a year or so younger, led the league in strikeouts in 1940. Both were solid pitchers, but MacPhail had his heart set on Higbe. In November he beat the Giants and other interested clubs to the prize by giving the Phils $100,000 and three players for the righthander.

A month later he swung his third big deal. He and Durocher were dissatisfied with the Dodger catching, which had mostly been in the hands of Babe Phelps, the Blimp, whose powerful bat could not make up for his ineptitude and his indifferent attitude behind the plate. Casey Stengel, when he was managing Brooklyn in 1935, admonished the Blimp for not calling for more knuckle balls from a pitcher whose best pitch was a knuckler. Phelps said, "That knuckler is hard to catch."

Durocher wanted a better catcher. The Cardinals had one in Mickey Owen, not much of a hitter but one of the best fielding catchers in the game. Rickey had an exceptional rookie catcher named Walker Cooper coming up from the minors; he let it be known that Owen was available, and MacPhail got him for $65,000 and two players. MacPhail sometimes boasted that he conned

Rickey into letting him have Owen by keeping the Higbe deal secret until the Owen transaction was completed—the idea being that if Rickey knew MacPhail had acquired a pitcher as good as Higbe he would not have let him strengthen the Dodgers further by letting him have Owen, too. But Rickey never worried about dealing a star to a contending club as long as he got his price.

The $65,000 St. Louis received for Owen plus the $125,000 for Medwick accounted for almost all of the $200,000 dividend the Cardinals paid their stockholders that season. MacPhail spent a lot of money—more than a quarter of a million dollars for Medwick, Higbe and Owen—but Larry, and presumably the Brooklyn Trust Company, felt it was worth it. Attendance was flourishing, and much of Brooklyn's substantial debt was rapidly being retired.

The Dodgers were markedly better going into 1941 than they were when they opened the 1940 season. Medwick, even diminished, was a class player, and so were Higbe and Owen. Curt Davis was a valuable addition to the pitching staff. Reese was healthy again, and a promising rookie named Pete Reiser, who had been brought up from the minors in July 1940, looked like the real thing.

Brooklyn was walking in tall cotton. There'd be no more "Wait till next year" now. *This* was the year. Going into 1941, Dodger fans could see nowhere to go but up.

ROBERT W. CREAMER

12

A LITTLE MORE
HISTORY

During the latter part of 1940—late summer, autumn, the early weeks of winter—the war was mentioned only in passing among us young. No serious fighting took place after the fall of France, except for the German air raids on Great Britain. These attacks—the blitz—and the English struggle to fend them off later came to be known as the Battle of Britain, and God knows those were terrible months for the English. In retrospect it became clear that the bravery of the Royal Air Force rising day after day to fight the strength of the Luftwaffe, the German air force, deserved the overworked term "gallant."

But we had no TV in those days, and while black-and-white photographs in newspapers and magazines and film clips in the newsreels showed the devastation and horror, for us the air war over Britain simply did not have the impact of traditional, old-fashioned war news. We were used to communiques in the newspapers, reports from the front, maps showing battle lines shifting back and forth, breakthroughs, territory lost, cities captured, countries conquered. I remember the spring of 1940 mostly for the Nazi blitzkrieg, the evacuation from Dunkirk, the fall of France. I remember the fall of 1940 mostly for the third-place finish of the Yankees, the World Series between the Reds and the Tigers, football games.

That may have been dumb of me, but realize that in the ten months from September 1939 to June 1940 the Germans had taken Poland, Denmark, Norway, Holland, Belgium, Luxembourg and France, while the Russians had taken Finland, Estonia, Latvia, Lithuania and the eastern part of Poland that the Nazis hadn't gotten to. But from July 1940 into the early months of 1941 the Russians didn't move and the fearsome Nazi war machine did nothing—except bomb England. While we recognized that the bombing was awful, innocents like me saw no territorial gains by the Nazis, no maps showing specific defeats. The Germans were standing still. The Russians were sitting back.

The Japanese did move into what was then called French Indochina, known now as Viet Nam, but they did it bloodlessly, pressuring the Vichy French to let them in. In Europe a great swath of northern and western France along the English Channel and the Bay of Biscay was occupied by the Nazis; what was left in the interior in the south and east was governed by French "collaborationists" (collaboration was a bad word; it meant you helped the Nazis) under the leadership of Marshal Henri Pétain, an eighty-five-year-old French war hero from World War I, a rival of von Hindenburg, who sucked up to the Nazis. Because Paris was occupied by the Germans, the puppet government established a secondary French capital in the resort town of Vichy. The Vichy regime changed France's motto from the glorious *Liberté, Egalité, Fraternité* (Liberty, Equality, Fraternity) to the utilitarian *Famille, Travail, Patrie* (Family, Work, Country). They did what the Germans told them to do and let the Japanese into Indochina.

I was hardly aware of this. I can't recall anyone talking about

ROBERT W. CREAMER

Indochina. Europe was where the war was, and as 1940 waned there wasn't much war there. Italy, Germany's ineffective ally, had occupied little Albania on the far shore of the Adriatic Sea in April 1939, when the world was busy watching Hitler gobble up the rest of Czechoslovakia, and late in October 1940 Mussolini launched an invasion from Albania into Greece. We were all delighted when the pugnacious Greeks resisted fiercely and shoved the Italians back into Albania.

But that was a little war, and so was the fighting in North Africa where Italian forces from Libya, then an Italian colony, moved several miles inside British-held Egypt and sat down for a couple of months before the British pushed them back into Libya. Later in the war the desert fighting in North Africa became very big news indeed, but it wasn't that way in the waning months of 1940.

Really, the summer and fall of 1940 seemed quiet in the aftershock of the violence of the spring. The only news outside of sports that interested me was the presidential election, and even that did not focus heavily on the war or the international situation.

Willkie, the Republican candidate, represented the more liberal, progressive wing of the party, and his main argument seemed to be that he could run the government more efficiently than Roosevelt could. The big issue, the one people argued about, was whether Roosevelt or any president deserved a third term in office. It was a phony issue at the time, but phony issues are often the key to success or failure in American politics. The Republicans (adolescent me among them) cried, "No third term!" The Democrats, alluding marginally to the perils of the international situation, cried, "Don't change horses in midstream!" The people, voting with their pocketbooks, stuck with Roosevelt, who had done more for them than the old-line Republicans ever had.

Those old-line Republicans, who reluctantly supported the liberal Willkie, were still outraged at what they felt was Roosevelt's betrayal of "his class," meaning the wealthy, ruling aristocracy that had pretty well dominated America for much of its history.

Joseph Alsop wrote that the WASP ascendancy in this country did not begin to fall apart until the Depression/New Deal 1930s. He meant the old, established, white, Anglo-Saxon, Protestant families who for well over a century had pretty much controlled banking and finance, business in general, public morals and standards of dress and behavior in the United States. Alsop wrote, for example, that when he was a young man in college he would not have dreamed of going out of doors without putting on a hat; you can see evidence of that dutiful practice in old movies and in old photographs of crowds at baseball games.

Roosevelt was of that same ruling class, yet his New Deal was more than just a device for economic recovery. It stimulated great social change, too, so that in time the powerful Daddy Warbuckses of the country—the J. P. Morgans, the Vanderbilts, the Whitneys, the Cabots, the Lowells, the Gods—were no longer in command. People began behaving the way they wanted to. When I was a little kid members of the common herd—my people—read "Emily Post on Etiquette" seriously in order to learn what to wear and how to behave at, for instance, weddings or dinner parties. But all that deference to class was slowly going out the window. It was a revolution, and the old guard couldn't stop it, and it drove them crazy, and they blamed Roosevelt, who was, they said, a traitor to his class. "That man in the White House," they called him. *The New Yorker* ran a Peter Arno cartoon showing a wealthy, richly dressed dowager calling to some friends, "Come along! We're going to the Trans-Lux to hiss Roosevelt!" (The Trans-Lux was a newsreel theater, and FDR was always in the newsreels.)

The old-line Republicans waited impatiently for the Roosevelt administration to end, for the day when FDR would no longer be in the White House. This explains the point of another *New Yorker* cartoon that I remember well and which still makes me laugh. The time is early 1940, before Roosevelt had committed himself to running for a third term. The scene is an exclusive club where half a dozen men in evening dress are gathered around a large

ROBERT W. CREAMER

console radio listening to a political speech. One is lifting his head in anguish, another is clutching his brow in despair, the others are studies in gloom. The voice on the radio is saying ". . . hope that the great pilot who has steered us so surely through the perilous currents of the past eight years may be prevailed upon . . ."

Roosevelt ran for a third term, of course, and won handily, and as the year was coming to a close he made a speech over the radio a couple of days before New Year's Eve. I was home on Christmas vacation from my freshman year of college, and I didn't listen to it. It was a Sunday night, and an eighteen-year-old freshman home from college didn't sit around on Sunday nights listening to presidents make speeches. That was the weekend between Christmas and New Year's, party weekend, and I was at a party.

But my parents listened, and so did most grown-ups around the country. It was one of Roosevelt's "Fireside Chats," the fifteenth that he had delivered to the nation during his two terms in office. "Fireside Chat" was the folksy name that the president or some bright person in his administration had dreamed up to describe the informal talks he made directly to the nation from time to time—talks that were not State of the Union addresses, or formal speeches to this group or that one, or reactions to crises, or carefully worded responses to questions at press conferences. The radio talks were the route Roosevelt took to reach the people directly. Remember that in those days there was no television, with its daily photo opportunities and carefully orchestrated sound bites. What the president wanted to say to the people had to filter its way through mostly Republican newspapers, and if an editor or publisher was antagonistic—and most of them were—their slanted stories and opinionated headlines could mute or distort much of what the president wanted to get across.

But Roosevelt, like Larry MacPhail, was quick to recognize the power of radio. It was a relatively new medium, barely a decade old in the big broadcasting sense when Roosevelt took office, and it was extraordinarily popular. In the 1930s and early 1940s people listened to the radio (we always said "the" radio) the way we hang on television today. In 1941 it was estimated that 35 million people listened every Sunday night to Jack Benny's comedy show, at a time when the country's population was 135 million, or 115 million fewer than today. That's quite a "share."

Roosevelt was a skillful radio performer, a speechmaker of rare ability. His somewhat nasal tone and his upper-class–Groton–Harvard–squash-court accent fascinated the public. People turned on the radio to listen to Roosevelt as much for entertainment as enlightenment, in much the same way that farm people in the nineteenth century traveled long miles in hard-riding wagons over rough roads to spend all day Sunday at church, where they often listened to a long sermon in the morning and another long sermon in the afternoon. In an era when people worked six-day weeks and ten- and twelve-hour days, church was a change. It was different. It was stimulating. Damn it, it was exciting. Roosevelt had much the same hold on the people as those oldtime country preachers had.

His Fireside Chat on December 29, 1940, was something special. It was an extraordinary speech, probably the most important one Roosevelt ever made, except for his "the only thing we have to fear is fear itself" address almost eight years earlier. If I didn't listen to it that Sunday night, I knew all about it Monday morning because the papers were filled with it: big banner headlines, comments, reactions from around the world.

What Roosevelt did that night was drag the war onto the center of the American stage, which was hard to do. We loved the idea of neutrality, of staying out of Europe's fights, of not getting involved with England. Today, now that Great Britain is just another average-size country well below the level of a superpower, it is hard to realize that up until World War II Britain was considered *the* major power in the world. The maps on the walls of our

ROBERT W. CREAMER
‹‹‹‹‹‹‹‹‹‹‹‹‹‹‹‹‹‹‹‹‹‹‹‹‹

classrooms and in our geography books showed England and its possessions in pink, and pink was everywhere: Canada was pink, Australia and New Zealand were pink, India and Pakistan and Ceylon were pink, the West Indies were pink, much of Africa, from Egypt on top to the Union of South Africa on the bottom, was pink. Spots of pink showed in the Near East, in the Mediterranean at Malta and Gibraltar, in Central America and the north coast of South America, on island after island in the Atlantic, the Pacific, the Indian Ocean. This was the British Empire.

The British were hot stuff, and a lot of Americans, remembering our colonial past, still resented them. Joseph Alsop tells of the crusty Senator Peter Gerry of Rhode Island, a direct descendant of the Elbridge Gerry who lived in Boston when the British Redcoats fought the Americans on Bunker Hill and who later signed the Declaration of Independence. Asked how he could be anti-British when Great Britain was in such danger, Peter Gerry replied, "You perhaps won't understand, but in families like mine we still remember the lobsterbacks."

Those ardently fostering the anti-British, antiwar attitude came to be known as isolationists. Those in favor of giving Britain more and more help in fighting Hitler were interventionists. I clearly remember the oft-repeated argument of the isolationists that we should follow the advice of George Washington, who warned us in the 1790s to stay out of "entangling foreign alliances." In 1940, even with Hitler riding high after the fall of France, there were Americans who said they didn't care who won the war just as long as we stayed out of it. Some American businessmen expressed annoyance at the naval blockade the British had imposed on continental Europe to cut off Hitler's supply of raw materials, because, they said, it was hurting trade.

Norman Thomas, who gathered a decent number of votes when he ran for president every four years on the Socialist ticket, dismissed the war between Germany and Britain as a struggle between two rival imperialisms. American Communists, a fairly strong voice in the country in the 1930s, rallied behind Stalin and his Nazi-Soviet pact and were loudly anti-British and antiwar. So were Anglophobe conservatives, like Colonel Robert R. Mc-Cormick, publisher of the virulently right-wing *Chicago Tribune,* who in their anti-British, antiwar fulminations did not seem at all abashed to find themselves in bed with the Communists. Not that they hated Communism the less but Britain the more.

There was a strong anti-British attitude among Irish Catholics in America, the majority of whom were the children or grand-children of immigrants who had fled British oppression in Ireland, and there was a general anti-European feeling among Italians, Poles, Germans, Scandinavians and other ethnic groups who had left Europe because they hadn't liked it there. There was little search for roots, little interest in our European forebears. We were American now and fiercely proud of it. Sometimes too proud. You wouldn't have dared to burn the flag then. You may recall e. e. cummings' poem about Olaf—"I sing of Olaf glad and big"—who defied superpatriots during the First World War by saying, "I will not kiss your f.ing flag." They "threw the yellowsonofabitch/into a dungeon, where he died."

This hyper-intense "Americanism" strengthened the cause of those who wanted to isolate America from the quarrels of the old world, those who invoked Washington's advice. Some thought the anti-British attitude stemmed from a latent pro-German feeling, but I don't think that was a major factor at all. Where I lived—and I lived in a community that was largely Catholic—Hitler was the en-emy, and he was utterly despised. There was a loony-tune fringe group in America called the German-American Bund, a collection of mostly recent German immigrants led by an imitation Hitler named Fritz Kuhn, but the vast majority of German-Americans disliked the Bund as much as they disliked Hitler. I remember my German-American father-in-law—at that time only the father of a girl I liked a lot—happily singing and spritzing his way through a popular novelty tune of the day called "Der Führer's Face," which

ROBERT W. CREAMER
≪≪≪≪≪≪≪≪≪≪≪≪≪≪≪≪≪≪≪≪

mocked Hitler and his concept of a race of German supermen. "Ja, ve is der supermen," the song went, "super-duper supermen." Each chorus ended with the phrase "Right in der Führer's face," followed by a ripe razzberry, which George Schelz rendered with vigor. His father had left Germany late in the nineteenth century to avoid compulsory military service, but George was a sergeant in the U.S. Army in World War I. His brother was in the navy. His two sons were in the army in World War II. He was the typical German-American in 1941, not Fritz Kuhn and his Nazi pinheads.

But that did not mean that anti-Nazi Americans were eager for the United States to go to war to help England fight Hitler. In the odd euphoria of the Nazi stasis after the fall of France the problem—how dangerous Hitler's aggression was to America—had been swept under the rug and forgotten by most of us. Roosevelt, in the speech he made on December 29, lifted the rug and shook it, and the war fell out.

He warned us that despite the apparent status quo Britain was in desperate trouble. He knew the Nazi bombings had hurt badly, that Nazi submarines—the glamorous U-boats—were constantly sinking ships bringing arms and supplies to England, that Great Britain could not last much longer without our vigorous help, and that this could not be a matter of indifference to our country. He reminded us that Hitler and his allies wanted to dominate not just Europe but the world (the Nazis had even mapped out four postwar "zones of influence" for the world, which his New Order would control with the help of Italy and Japan). Roosevelt said bluntly that the war was our war, that the enemy was Germany, Italy and Japan, and that our best hope was to help Great Britain. He warned that if Britain went down, "All of us in the United States will be living at the point of a gun." He said, "Never before since Jamestown and Plymouth Rock has our American civilization been in such danger." He scared hell out of us.

What we had to do, he said, was to shake up our industrial might and make planes, ships, tanks and guns in great quantities as quickly as possible and see to it that they were safely delivered to Great Britain and to Greece and China, the only other countries then actively resisting the Axis onslaught. He proposed a "lend-lease" arrangement that let us pool resources with England. He had already circumvented U.S. neutrality laws the previous September by "lending" Britain fifty overage American destroyers in exchange for "leases" on land in British territories in the Caribbean, Bermuda and Newfoundland for American naval and air bases. Now he wanted Congress to allow full-scale "lend-lease" help to Great Britain. In one of his most memorable phrases Roosevelt said, "We must be the arsenal of democracy."

His speech and the lend-lease proposal, which Congress finally passed the following March, fired up the internal battle between the isolationists and the interventionists. By this time the isolationists were a distinct minority (Gallup Polls showed Roosevelt with a 70-percent approval rating), but they were loud, they had money, and they were backed by two of the most widely read newspapers in the country: McCormick's *Chicago Tribune,* and the *New York Daily News,* owned by McCormick's cousin, Joseph Medill Patterson. Many Republicans, including Willkie, Roosevelt's defeated rival, came out in support of the President's lend-lease idea, but others reacted bitterly. Alfred M. Landon of Kansas, who had lost the 1936 election to Roosevelt, said, "If Willkie had taken this stand last summer, he would not have been nominated. If Roosevelt had taken it, he would not have been elected."

The most effective leader of the isolationists was a feisty, sharp-tongued senator from Montana named Burton K. Wheeler, who attacked Roosevelt at every opportunity. Leonard Wood, a former army general, led a very active group of isolationists who called themselves the America First Committee. The most glamorous personality on the isolationist side was Charles A. Lindbergh, the famous flier who became a national hero in 1927 when he made the first solo airplane flight across the Atlantic Ocean. After that flight he was probably the best known person in America. My sister

ROBERT W. CREAMER
‹‹‹‹‹‹‹‹‹‹‹‹‹‹‹‹‹‹‹‹‹‹‹‹‹‹

Martha reminded me that when we were little children in the late 1920s we would wave vigorously whenever an airplane flew over, which wasn't very often in those days, and shout, "Hi, Lindy! Hi, Lindy!" We knew a lot about "Lindy." We knew that he was called "Lucky Lindy," that his full name was Charles Augustus Lindbergh, Jr., that his real nickname was Slim, that his airplane was called *The Spirit of St. Louis* and that he usually referred to the plane and himself as "We." He was a national hero. Everyone was shocked in 1932 when his baby son was kidnapped and killed; we also felt a bit of resentment when he and his wife later pulled up stakes and moved to England to be away from the danger of another kidnapping in the United States.

Lindbergh was a prominent figure at rallies and meetings of the America First Committee and isolationist groups. Although he was a plodding speaker, he was vitally important to the isolationist cause for the simple reason that he was instant ink. Wheeler and Wood and other isolationists got their names and speeches in the papers, but Lindbergh, the celebrity, got headlines and photographs on the front page. He was the son of a onetime populist congressman from Minnesota who was an old-fashioned country-style radical with a deep-seated distrust of big business and big government, as represented by the wealth and aristocracy of the East. His national-hero son married into Eastern money and played footsie with big government—he was bedazzled on several visits to Nazi Germany by the strength and efficiency of Germany's military-industrial machine. He accepted an honorary award given to him by the Nazis, he made at least one anti-Semitic speech, and he was convinced to the point of fanaticism that there was no way Britain, even with American help, could stop Hitler. He urged a "negotiated peace," which meant surrender to people remembering Hitler's earlier "negotiations" with Poland and Czechoslovakia and Denmark.

Wheeler, Lindbergh and the others continued their rear-guard action against Roosevelt and the interventionists all through 1941, right up to Pearl Harbor, but not that many people paid them serious attention. Big crowds—20,000 or so—jammed places like Madison Square Garden to see and hear Lindbergh and the others, but there was little broad support. Hardly anyone disagreed with the isolationist desire to keep America out of war—nobody wanted war—but at the other end of the spectrum few wanted peace at any price. Something had to be done, and we hoped it could be done without our taking an active part in the fighting. Most Americans agreed with Roosevelt that Hitler (along with Mussolini and the Japanese) was wrong, a bad guy, and we wanted to see him defeated. Roosevelt's "arsenal of democracy" idea appealed to us.

Besides, beefing up industry for war production or "defense" meant jobs and money. The New Deal had lifted us out of the worst of the Depression, but even so the American economy was still thin and meager. "Defense jobs" ended that. The country suddenly was thriving. Defense spending started an economic boom that lasted for fifty years.

PART

II

13

HEADING SOUTH

The Yankees went south for spring training in 1941 outwardly unperturbed by their failure in 1940. Although they were no longer restricted by the no-trading rule that bound American League pennant winners—that was the Tigers' problem in the 1940–41 off season—the Yankees made no effort to swing a deal, not even for a first baseman to supplant Dahlgren.

This inaction was caused in part by concern for what the newly instituted peacetime military draft might do to baseball. The draft had passed Congress and been signed into law by the President in September 1940, and it called for all eligible males to register on October 16. Simply put, the call said, "If you are a man who has reached his twenty-first birthday but has not yet reached his thirty-sixth birthday you must register today for selective military service. If you have no valid reason for failing to do so you are liable to arrest and if convicted you may be sentenced to as much as five years in prison or fined $10,000." That $10,000 was an eye-opening figure in an era when few men made much more than fifty dollars a week.

At eighteen I was too young to register, but my brother Jerry, who was twenty-four, unmarried, with no dependents, was ripe. So were major league baseball players, almost all of whom were between twenty-one and thirty-five. Very few big-leaguers then were older than thirty-five and even fewer were younger than twenty-one. Charlie Gehringer of the Tigers, at thirty-seven, was the only member of the pennant-winning Detroit club who was too old to register, and pitcher Hal Newhouser, at nineteen, was the only one too young. Lefty Grove, the "Old Mose" of the Red Sox, was forty, well over registration age, but everyone else on the Sox, including player-manager Joe Cronin, had to sign up. The New York Giants of the National Football League—we called them the "pro Giants" or the "football Giants" because in those days "the New York Giants" meant the baseball team—had thirty-two players on their squad in the fall of 1940, and thirty-one of them had to register (the exception was a twenty-year-old tackle from Baylor named Monk Edwards). Joe Louis, the twenty-six-year-old heavyweight boxing champion, registered in Chicago and deflated reporters pressing him to declare which branch of service he'd prefer by saying, "I ain't choosey."

More than 16 million men registered, and the first draftees, or selectees, or inductees—the terms were used interchangeably—entered the army in November 1940. A second batch went in January 1941, and a third, larger group later on in the spring. A minor leaguer belonging to the Chicago White Sox, a twenty-two-year-old pitcher named Gene Stack from Saginaw, Michigan, was the first man on a major league roster to be called into service. Stack had an impressive 19–11 record in 1940 with Lubbock in the Class D West Texas–New Mexico League and had struck out 238 batters in 268 innings, an eye-catching strikeout ratio in that low-strikeout era. The White Sox had put him on their forty-man-reserve roster (which had to be reduced to twenty-five during the

ROBERT W. CREAMER
‹‹‹‹‹‹‹‹‹‹‹‹‹‹‹‹‹‹‹‹‹‹‹‹‹‹‹

season) and although Stack never appeared in a big league game, when he was drafted in January the White Sox proudly claimed him as the first major leaguer to be called into service. Stack, whose real name was Eugene Stackowiach, never did make the majors. He died in the service of a heart attack in June 1942, after pitching for an army team in Indiana.

Poor Stack. The odds of being called up were long in that first year of the draft. The armed forces wanted about 400,000 men from the pool of 16 million registered, or about one man in every forty. Relatively few went into uniform in the first and second draft calls; a somewhat larger number went in the later call-up in the spring. My draft-bait brother was still at home then.

Since there were about four hundred players on the twenty-five-man rosters of the sixteen big league clubs, the odds were that only about ten of them would be drafted in 1941, or less than one man per club. Because professional athletes were in better shape than the average man in the street and more likely to pass the draft physical, their odds of being picked should have been greater than one in forty, but it quickly became evident that men volunteering for the draft were helping to fill the quotas that each local draft board was required to provide. Connie Mack, the seventy-eight-year-old manager/owner of the Philadelphia Athletics, said enlistments in Pennsylvania made it likely that no major league players at all would be drafted from his state for the time being. Jeremiah Tax, who was my brother's age and who in later years was assistant managing editor of *Sports Illustrated*, told me that the same situation existed where he was living in Virginia, not far from Washington, D.C. Volunteers coming into the Virginia draft boards from poverty-stricken rural areas provided most of the quotas.

"The army was opportunity," Tax explained. "You have no idea of the poverty some of those people were living in then. The army meant food, and plenty of it. A little money, which they could send home to their families. *New* clothes! Real toilets instead of outhouses. Showers. A clean bed. Fresh blankets. Most of all, that food."

I remember when I was in basic training in the army a couple of years later we city boys had little trouble getting weekend passes from camp to go into town. The country boys, especially those from the South, wouldn't ask for passes; they preferred to stay in camp and eat the good Sunday dinners in the mess hall. And it wasn't just the country boys who were volunteering: In New York City 99 of the first 106 New Yorkers to enter the armed forces under Selective Service were volunteers.

Most baseball executives were not too concerned about the immediate effect that the draft would have on their teams. However, Barrow, the Yankees' general manager, when asked in January why his team had been so inactive in the trading mart replied that the Yankees had to be cautious because of the threat of the draft. He mentioned his prize rookie shortstop, Phil Rizzuto, then twenty-two, who was coming up to the Yankees for the first time after four years of brilliant apprenticeship in the minor leagues. Rizzuto, known even then as Scooter, had been named not only the Most Valuable Player in the American Association in 1940 but also the Minor League Player of the Year. He was expected to take the fading Frank Crosetti's place at shortstop but, Barrow explained, "How can we run the risk of trading someone like Crosetti and having a kid we're counting on to fill his shoes taken by the draft?"

But the Yankees had already jettisoned several veteran players who had been valuable in the 1936–39 pennant-winning era. Oral Hildebrand, who had been such a help in 1939, had been dropped in August 1940 when Bonham was brought up from the Yankees' farm in Kansas City. Asked to go down to Kansas City in Bonham's place, the taciturn Hildebrand, who was called "the silent man with the audible name," said nothing. Instead, he just packed his bags and went home, quitting the Yankees for good and terminating his major league career at the age of thirty-three.

From their failing 1940 team the Yankees also disposed of Monte Pearson, Bump Hadley, Billy Knickerbocker, Steve Sundra and Jake Powell (who during spring training in 1940 banged his head against a concrete outfield wall while making a catch and knocked himself unconscious). The first-string lineup remained unchanged.

"Even if we had the chance to weed out more of our older players," said Barrow, in his sensitive way, "we'd have to be cautious. The draft is the most serious problem we have to deal with. It means holding onto our veterans and going slow on our deals."

It didn't mean giving them raises, or even the same salaries they had in 1940. "Even Jolting Joe DiMaggio is unlikely to be in line for a raise," wrote one reporter after chatting with Barrow in the Yankee offices in New York. Word came that Red Rolfe, who had been a mainstay at third base for half a dozen seasons but who had been bothered by eye trouble and a bad back, was thinking of retiring to his home in Penacook, New Hampshire, where he owned a profitable gasoline station. A cynic noted that the gas station netted Rolfe about $2,500 a year, compared to the $15,000 he earned with the Yankees, but the possibility that Rolfe *might* quit added to the confusion about the once superb Yankee infield.

Everyone assumed that Rizzuto would take Crosetti's place, and many felt that the Scooter's minor league sidekick, second baseman Gerry Priddy, would replace Joe Gordon at second. Unobservant reporters, reaching for reasons why the Yankees had done so poorly in 1940, decided that Gordon had had "his worst year" at second base, which didn't make sense. Gordon had gone through the same early batting slump that the other Yankees had, but he finished strongly, ending the year with thirty homers, 112 runs scored, 103 runs batted in. Except for DiMaggio he was the most productive hitter on the team. In the field his exceptional speed, range and acrobatic flexibility had enabled him to lead all American League second basemen in assists for the second year in a row, while turning in a fielding average that missed by two points of being the best in the league. He was a great second baseman, but the antiquarian thinking that dominated baseball at the time noted only that Gordon had never hit .300 for a season and was therefore a mediocre hitter. Never mind your homers and your runs batted in. If you didn't bat .300 in those days, you were not considered a good hitter.

With Rizzuto penciled in at shortstop, the thinking was that Priddy should play second. The two youngsters had been together through most of their minor league careers, and it seemed logical that they should be the Yankees' keystone combination in 1941. Gordon was hardly mentioned during the winter. Then one day a reporter asked manager Joe McCarthy about Gordon. With Priddy at second, what about Gordon? Could he play third if Rolfe retired?

"Gordon can play anything, including the violin," McCarthy said. "He'd be as good at third as he is at second."

No one seemed to question the basic dumbness of moving the best second baseman in the league to make room for an unproven and really unneeded rookie. Rizzuto was *needed* at shortstop; Crosetti had indeed had the worst year of his career. But Priddy was not *needed* at second. Gordon was only twenty-six, was going into his fourth year as a major leaguer, and was at the top of his game.

ROBERT W. CREAMER

14

FAREWELL TO A
LESSER BABE

Nonetheless, the Yankees kept talking about Rizzuto at short and Priddy at second and about recasting the infield, meaning moving Gordon to third base. McCarthy said that Dahlgren, the fine-fielding, poor-hitting first baseman, was the only 1940 Yankee infielder who was sure of his post in 1941.

When the Yankees assembled in St. Petersburg for spring training late in February, seven of their regular players were absent, still holdouts. Rolfe had abandoned any idea of being a gas jockey that summer and had signed, but DiMaggio, Ruffing, Gordon, Henrich, relief pitcher Johnny Murphy and veteran outfielder George Selkirk, who had played 111 games in 1940, had not, and neither had Dahlgren. Three days later, with the seven still unsigned, the Yankees made a startling announcement. Babe Dahlgren had been sold to the Boston Bees, the once and future Braves. No players came to the Yankees in the deal.

Ordinarily, the sale of an undistinguished player like Dahlgren would not have provoked much comment, but the Yankees had five months during the off season to peddle him and hadn't, and during those five months they repeatedly said Dahlgren would be their regular first baseman in 1941. They had only one other first baseman in camp, an unheralded minor leaguer named Johnny Sturm, who was in the same good-fielding, weak-hitting category as Dahlgren. In Sturm's last three minor league seasons he batted just over .300 each time, but he had hit only eleven home runs in three years. Dahlgren hit harder than that.

So why did the Yankees suddenly decide to get rid of Dahlgren? George Weiss, later a Barrow-like general manager of the Yankees but at that time the club's farm director, praised Babe's fielding but said he couldn't hit, at least not the way a first baseman should hit. "First base is a position anyone can play adequately," Weiss told sports columnist Richards Vidmer, whom he had run into at the Hialeah racetrack a day or so after the Dahlgren deal, "but it's a position where hitting power must be produced. No matter how skillful a first baseman is on defense, if he can't hit he doesn't belong in the major leagues." Weiss also told Vidmer that some of the Yankee players who had been around for a while had begun to feel that they were indispensable and that Dahlgren was one of them. The club knew he would have to be replaced anyway, Weiss explained, so they let him go when they had the chance.

But, Vidmer argued, when a club trades a regular, they usually have a pretty good idea of who will take his place. The Yankees didn't seem to have any idea of who that would be.

"Well," Weiss said, "they have an idea it will be one of three men." He mentioned Henrich, who had played several games at first base during the previous three seasons, and Sturm, who had played with Rizzuto and Priddy at Kansas City. "It may be sacrilegious to say so," Weiss said, "but I think Sturm may be just as sweet a fielder as Dahlgren." Despite that praise, Vidmer said you could tell by the farm director's voice that he wasn't sure Sturm was ready for the big leagues.

ROBERT W. CREAMER
‹‹‹‹‹‹‹‹‹‹‹‹‹‹‹‹‹‹‹‹‹‹‹‹‹‹‹

Weiss raised a third possibility: Put the smooth-fielding Gordon there. "Imagine how he'd play first base!" he beamed.

Vidmer pointed out that Gordon was not a .300 hitter. "You have to have punch at first base," he said. Punch, in his lexicon, meant hitting .300. Weiss, who understood batting power better than Vidmer did, smiled and said, "Gordon hits lots of home runs every year and he has lots of runs batted in."

When McCarthy was asked about the sale of Dahlgren, the Yankee manager had a surprising opinion of the departed first baseman's fielding skill. McCarthy always took a patronizing attitude toward the baseball writers who covered the club. "Why don't you let me worry about that?" was his stock answer when a reporter asked him a tough question about the pitching staff or a possible change in the batting order. Now he told them that Dahlgren was not as good a fielder as he appeared to be. He said many of Dahlgren's spectacular fielding plays were really routine chances that looked difficult because of the way Dahlgren handled them.

The sportswriters, who had written that you had to go back to the days of Stuffy McInnis and Hal Chase to find a first baseman who fielded as well as Dahlgren, were surprised, but most of them dutifully swallowed McCarthy's disparaging remarks. Dahlgren had very short arms, McCarthy explained, and he couldn't reach balls that other first basemen could unless he leaped and stretched. And of course, he added, Dahlgren was not much of a hitter.

"He's a nice boy," McCarthy said, "but where would you get with nine Dahlgrens on your club?"

When questioned further about the logic of a deal that left the club at this late date without a bona fide major league first baseman, the manager stiffened. "I never made a deal I didn't figure would help my club," he said. "The Yankees can win without Dahlgren."

But the deal was actually made by Barrow, not McCarthy. No manager ever likes to give up a contributing ballplayer unless he gets one of at least equal ability in return. Why did Barrow make the deal? Judging from Weiss's remarks, it seems likely that Barrow, who was used to contract wrestling with star players, was outraged that Dahlgren, a marginal player at best, had the nerve to hold out into spring training as though he were a star, too. And I think that Barrow was losing his patience with the other holdouts and wanted to do something to shake them up. Selling Dahlgren so abruptly was one way to shock and scare the others into coming to terms. It seemed to work. Ruffing, Henrich, Murphy and Selkirk quickly signed, and Gordon followed suit a day or so later, leaving only the stubborn DiMaggio for Barrow to worry about while McCarthy worried about finding a new first baseman.

He used Sturm in early practice sessions, but when Henrich came into camp McCarthy told him to work out around first base. Henrich laughed. "This will be the third year in a row," he said when he went out to the bag. He didn't even have a first-baseman's mitt. "I carried one around with me for two years. I had it with me last year. But when I left the club"—Henrich had torn a ligament in his knee during a road trip and had been sent back to New York—"I left it behind and I don't know where it is now."

"Looks like you'll have to buy another one," someone suggested.

Henrich laughed again.

"Getting the glove is the easy part about playing first base," he said.

The very next day McCarthy switched again and announced that Gordon would play first base. "He'll play it," McCarthy said, "until he shows he can't." The rookie Sturm, who was elated when the Dahlgren sale made it appear that the job might be his, was downcast by the experiments with Henrich and Gordon, but he dutifully showed Gordon the basics of playing the position. The other Yankees kidded the out-of-position second baseman. When Gordon went high in the air to spear an errant throw, the carefree catcher Buddy Rosar cracked, "Ahh! Better than Dahlgren!"

Gordon was uncomfortable at first base. For a few days he was handicapped by a cheap first-baseman's mitt he bought in a local store, but even after he obtained a better one he still looked awkward and uncertain.

It was discouraging for a Yankee fan. Here were the Yankees beginning their comeback, and they had a rookie shortstop, a rookie second baseman and an untried first baseman whose back-ups at the position were a right fielder and a minor leaguer no one seemed to have much confidence in. As one reporter commented, "The Yankees have three men who can play a little first base but no one who can play a lot of first base."

Another one wrote, "Why did the Yankees ever sell Dahlgren?"

DiMAGGIO held out several days longer after the others signed, which didn't do much for his popularity. The belief was that he wanted $37,000, or $5,000 more than the $32,000 he was said to have earned in 1940. When he finally signed on March 7, it was assumed he had settled for $35,000, which made him the third highest paid player in the game, after Greenberg and Feller. To show relative values at that time, Joe McCarthy was already making $35,000 as manager, Barrow was making a lot more than that, and Commissioner Landis was making more than $60,000. The players were the low men on the baseball totem pole.

Joe did not arrive from California until March 11, more than two weeks after the first Yankees arrived in St. Petersburg. No one seemed too concerned. DiMaggio had never been much of an early factor with the Yankees. In 1936, his rookie season, he burned his foot in a diathermy machine and missed opening day. In 1937 he had a tonsillectomy and again missed opening day. In 1938 he held out until after the season started. In 1939 he was in the Yankee lineup on opening day for the first time but was hurt during the second week of play and missed more than thirty games that season. In 1940 he injured his leg in an exhibition game in Brooklyn just before opening day and sat out the start of the season for the fourth time in five years.

In St. Petersburg he was routinely asked about his physical

condition. "Give me about a week," he said, "and I'll be ready." Then a cliche-oriented reporter asked, and DiMaggio answered, a question that meant little at the time but in the reverse telescope of time rings with portent.

"Joe, do you have your heart set on any records this year?"

"No," DiMaggio replied, no thoughts of a hitting streak dancing through his head. "I'll just be in there swinging every day and we'll see what happens."

Meanwhile, a tremor from the draft shook the Yankee camp. Rizzuto received a letter from his draft board back home in Queens, on Long Island. The board told him to notify the local draft board in St. Petersburg of his presence there so that the Long Island board could send the St. Petersburg board "an order of transfer of physical examination." The confused rookie showed the letter to McCarthy, who phoned the St. Petersburg draft board. The board told McCarthy to tell Rizzuto to come in the next day to sign in so that the board would know where he could be reached when they wanted to find him.

Speculation ran wild. What was the rookie's classification? Would he be drafted? What would the Yankees do now that they faced the possibility of losing their brilliant rookie shortstop? The supposedly decrepit Crosetti was suddenly back in the picture. Earlier, McCarthy had been asked if he would give Crosetti a trial at shortstop during spring training, and the testy manager snapped, "I didn't know I had to after he's played shortstop for nine years." But, he was reminded, Crosetti batted only .194 in 1940. McCarthy said, "None of the boys except DiMaggio hit up to par last season. It was just one of those things."

Now, less testy, more apprehensive, facing the loss of Rizzuto, McCarthy said, "I can play Crosetti at short. Or I can play Gordon. Gordon came up as a shortstop. I can play him at short." It seems incredible to me now, although I confess I don't remember feeling upset about it at the time, that the Yankees would continue mucking about with their great second baseman. They were breezily

ROBERT W. CREAMER
〈〈〈〈〈〈〈〈〈〈〈〈〈〈〈〈〈〈〈〈〈〈〈〈〈〈〈〈

shifting him to first base in Dahlgren's place; to third base in Rolfe's place; and now to shortstop in Rizzuto's place. McCarthy was an admirable manager—any man who won nine pennants, as Mc-Carthy did, obviously knew his stuff—but I cannot fathom why he ever considered moving a fielder as good as Gordon out of a position as vitally important as second base. McCarthy's great forte as a manager was handling pitchers—he was exceptionally deft at building a staff, at using the right man at the right time against the right team, at nursing a shaky starter into a mode of confidence, at spot-starting second-rate hurlers to get maximum results from them. In the current era of emphasis on relief pitching, it is easy to forget that McCarthy was a pioneer in the way he used Johnny Murphy as a relief specialist year after year for a decade, during which the Yankees won seven pennants.

But I think he was just plain dumb to move Gordon off second base. Of course, it may well have been in deference to Barrow's wishes, since the Yankees had their prize rookie double-play combination in camp. Rizzuto was clearly the class of the two-man act, but the Yankee brass had boosted Priddy to the same level, which led to all the talk of switching Gordon around. After all, he could play anything, including the violin. Yes, and Bix Beiderbecke could play the piano, but if you were putting a jazz band together would you rather have Bix on piano or cornet?

Rizzuto went for his physical and passed it. He was the shortest of the group of fifteen men being examined, and he had a red pad strapped to his left thigh that he'd been wearing to protect a charley horse. He was five feet five inches tall and weighed 155 pounds. His vision was a perfect twenty-twenty. The St. Petersburg officials said the results of the physical examination would be sent to Rizzuto's draft board.

Ten days later he was classified 3A, physically okay but deferred from military service—at least for the time being—because of dependents. Rizzuto was not married but he contributed significantly to the support of his family.

Whew. We Yankee fans breathed a sigh of relief. Now we had Phil set at shortstop, and the recast infield was in place. Priddy showed that he could field well enough, although he had trouble at bat and everyone agreed that Rizzuto was a much better ballplayer. Rolfe was his smooth old self at third. The only worry was at the other side of the infield where, as one reporter wrote, "McCarthy has never had to teach anyone as much as he has had to teach Joe Gordon at first base."

DiMaggio did not play until March 23, but when he did he looked great. One day he had a home run, three doubles and a walk and reached base safely a sixth time when a long fly ball he hit to the outfield fence was dropped for an error. He had a hit in every spring training game he played in, and Henrich, Keller and Selkirk gave him a strong supporting cast in the outfield.

Rizzuto batted safely in eleven straight games, but he aggravated his charley horse and had to sit out several days. Crosetti filled in for him and batted over .400, although it was noted that he "didn't come close to a grounder that Rizzuto would have handled." When Rizzuto came back to the lineup he picked up where he had left off, hitting safely every day. DiMaggio was still hitting, and as the Yankees finished training in Florida and joined the Dodgers for a barnstorming trip north to New York, they didn't look bad at all.

Yet they were passed over in the annual poll of sportswriters, which a year earlier had produced that lopsided sixty-six-to-one vote in favor of the Yankees to win the pennant. This time the writers picked Cleveland to win. For the first time in years the Yankees were underdogs going into the season.

ROBERT W. CREAMER

15

THE ADVENTURES OF VAN LINGLE MUNGO

The Dodgers trained in Havana that spring. This was twenty years before Fidel Castro's revolution, and Cuba in those days was a favorite vacation place for Americans. Babe Ruth and John McGraw had wintered there, gambling in the casinos and making bets on the horses running at Oriental Park.

MacPhail had the Dodgers down in Havana early, a party of thirty-five players and club officials leaving New York on Valentine's Day, February 14. Not just pitchers and catchers for early camp; MacPhail had the entire Dodger squad in training by the middle of February. Well, almost the entire squad. Babe Phelps, the catcher, a reluctant traveler, chose not to go to Havana. He got as far as Miami, didn't like the idea of sailing over the ocean to Cuba on a boat, turned around and went back home to Maryland.

Some questioned the value of such a long spring training—it was more than two months until opening day. Did healthy young athletes like Reese and Reiser really need eight weeks to get into shape? And wouldn't such a long training session sap the team's strength in the long run, leaving it tired and worn out late in the season? MacPhail dismissed the criticism. He said he liked a team to be in top shape on opening day so that it could get a jump on its rivals. "Don't worry about August and September until they come along," he said. "Maybe the team will be tired by then, but that's too far off to worry about."

But the main reason for the early arrival in Cuba was simply that MacPhail had arranged with Horace Stoneham for the Dodgers and the Giants to play three exhibition games in Havana on February 28, March 1 and March 2, and he was giving his team a couple of weeks to get ready for them. The Giants, who trained in Miami, were beginning their training at a record early date, too. Then there would be three games with the Cleveland Indians and five games with a team called the Cuban All Stars before the Dodgers left Havana and went back to Florida to complete spring training at their regular base in Clearwater. MacPhail scheduled a record number of games that spring—everybody wanted to see the Brooklyn Dodgers—and in order to play them all the club was to be split into two squads, one under Leo, the other under coach Charlie Dressen.

It was an odd approach to spring training, but MacPhail was always up to something. During the winter he not only completed the trades for Higbe and Owen, which greatly strengthened the club, but he also presented Dodger fans with a variation of his Cincinnati season-ticket plan. The ticket plan was a novelty in New York. Ordinarily, only important people—politicians, actors, other celebrities—were assured of getting the same good seats on big game days. Others took potluck. But now MacPhail said any fan could buy the same good seats for every big game. He offered two packages, one for twenty-two dates, the other for ten. The twenty-two-date package included Opening Day, July Fourth, Labor Day, all seven night games and all twelve Sundays when the Dodgers were home. The package cost $36.30 for a reserved seat, $48.40

for a box. The ten-date package ($16.50 for a reserve seat, $22 for a box) didn't have the Sunday games.

MacPhail also pioneered in "upgrading" seats in name, if not in quality. Certain general-admission seats became reserved seats; certain reserved-seat areas became box-seat areas. He changed the name of the seats in far left field from "bleachers" to "pavilion" and doubled the price from 55¢ to $1.10.

He resodded Ebbets Field with turf from a polo field on Long Island where polo players from Great Britain, Argentina and the United States used to play international matches. He worked on his protective helmet idea. He had planned to have the Dodgers wear protective headgear as an experiment in the last game of the 1939 season, but the second game of the doubleheader scheduled for the last day was rained out and the experiment was abandoned. But the helmet idea nagged at MacPhail again when Reese and Medwick were beaned in 1940, particularly after Medwick went down.

"Medwick was really badly hurt," MacPhail said, "worse than we ever knew at the time. We rushed him back into action too quickly, partly because Ducky insisted on playing. A doctor told me later that Leo and I should have been arrested for sending him back that soon."

Protective helmets had been tried previously in baseball but had proved too heavy and bulky. This was before high-strength plastics, but MacPhail conceived the idea of using lightweight metal and he got Dr. George Bennett of Johns Hopkins Hospital in Baltimore interested in the idea. Bennett was an orthopedist who often treated baseball players for sore arms and similar injuries. He and others at Hopkins developed a helmet that was really just an ordinary-looking baseball cap with pockets into which curved metal plates could be inserted when a player batted. Bennett gave MacPhail credit for the genesis of the idea.

In 1941 Dodger players wore the protective caps in spring training and some players on other teams tried them. Resistant as always to new ideas, the major leaguers soon went back to wearing the soft flannel caps they had always worn. The war pretty much ended the experiment and protective helmets went on the back burner until the 1950s when Branch Rickey, then running the Pittsburgh Pirates, had plastic helmets made for his team and ordered players to use them. The Pirates took a lot of ribbing at first from the machos on other clubs, but it wasn't too long before all major leaguers and all baseball players everywhere wore the helmets.

MacPhail was very much in evidence in Havana in his sunglasses and flashy slacks. After practice he and Durocher would go off with Cuban friends to the horse racing. Judge Landis was supposed to grow apoplectic whenever baseball and horse racing were mixed, because of the gambling overtones, but if he heard about the Dodger afternoons at Oriental Park he didn't do anything about it.

The Giants came over from Miami and the Dodgers beat them three straight times, a sweep that exhilarated Brooklyn fans already wallowing in the 16–6 advantage the Dodgers had over the Giants in 1940. Higbe, who had beaten the Giants five times in 1940 for the Phillies, got credit for one of the victories, which seemed to be rubbing it in. Dixie Walker, who hit .450 against the Giants in 1940, had a key hit. It was a glorious weekend.

Medwick was happy and working hard. With the Cardinals he had held out into spring training, but with Brooklyn he signed his 1941 contract the day after the 1940 season ended. Owen, another refugee from the low-paying Cardinals, was not as quick to sign. MacPhail offered him a slight raise over his St. Louis salary, but Owen wanted more. He did go to Havana with the club and—because the Dodgers were shorthanded in the catching department with Phelps still home in Maryland—MacPhail soon came to terms with Owen.

Larry was not as genial with Phelps, who was still unsigned, or with Van Lingle Mungo, the onetime ace of the Dodger staff who had fallen on bad times. Mungo drank too much and raised too much hell when he did. He came to Havana on sufferance after solemnly promising to behave himself, and for the first three weeks in Cuba he was fine. He even made a cogent analysis of Cincinnati's chances of winning the pennant for the third straight time. The Reds were favored by the sportswriters and the oddsmakers, but winning three National League pennants in a row had been accomplished only twice in thirty-five years, both times by McGraw's Giants, and Mungo didn't think the Reds could do it.

"Paul and Bucky have been twenty-game winners two straight years," Mungo said. (Derringer and Walters, the Cincinnati pitching stars, had won fifty-two games together in 1939 and another forty-two in 1940.) "Each has to come back with another big season, and the odds are against it. Two pitchers on one team can't go on winning twenty games forever. One or the other is bound to start losing."

Mungo was right. Walters won nineteen in 1941 and Derringer only twelve, and the Reds finished third.

However, Mungo, the baseball analyst and well-behaved pitcher, didn't make it past the third week in Cuba. The temptations of the flesh and the grape, or sugarcane, were too abundant in wide-open Havana. The crisis came the weekend the Indians arrived in Cuba for their three games with Brooklyn. The Dodgers walloped them 15–0 in the first game on a Friday. Mungo celebrated a little that night. The Saturday game was rained out, and that gave Mungo a head start on Saturday night, which is when things got out of hand. He came back to the hotel in the early evening feeling mighty fine, talking loudly and offering to buy drinks for everyone in the hotel bar. Then he ran into Durocher.

In Durocher's autobiography, *Nice Guys Finish Last,* which his skilled coauthor Ed Linn turned into one of the most entertaining of all baseball books, Leo says he sent his errant pitcher "staggering" toward his room. A half hour later Mungo left the hotel again, accompanied by two women, one of them "Lady Vine," a singer at the hotel, and the other the female half of a Latin dance team. This time Mungo returned to the hotel in the early hours of the morning "in a mood to break things," as we gossip-loving fans read in the papers the next day.

Durocher told MacPhail, who, having accepted Mungo's promise to reform, felt betrayed by the pitcher's fall from grace. MacPhail wrote an angry formal letter to the pitcher, which was typed and delivered by his factotum, John McDonald. The letter informed Mungo that he was fined and suspended, that he was to leave Havana and report at once to the minor league Montreal Royals in Macon, Georgia, and that "You are being furnished transportation from Havana to Macon. You are to leave tonight, Sunday."

McDonald delivered the note to Mungo at the ballpark on Sunday before the game. The big pitcher was still not meticulously sober, and when he read its message he rose in anger and threatened to punch Durocher, who threatened to punch him back. A fight was averted, but Mungo left the ballpark. The rained-out Saturday game had been rescheduled as part of a Sunday doubleheader, the first and possibly the only time a doubleheader has ever been played in spring training. Havana had been promised three games between the Indians and the Dodgers, and three games were what they insisted on seeing. Bobby Feller, the most renowned pitcher in baseball, was starting for the Indians and a very large crowd was at La Tropical Stadium to see him. Feller won his game and the Dodgers won the second one, which was cut short to let the Indians catch their boat back to Miami.

That was the boat Mungo was supposed to be on, but he didn't make it. According to Durocher, who never was one to let a strict adherence to facts get in the way of a good story, Mungo continued to drink on Sunday after stomping out of the ballpark and ended up in bed with both Lady Vine and the female half of the dance team. The dancer's husband found out what was happening and came after Mungo with a carving knife. Somehow the Dodgers got

ROBERT W. CREAMER

Mungo out of the hotel and onto a plane, which flew him to safety and the Montreal Royals.

Mungo behaved in Macon and rejoined the team briefly early in the season, but he was no longer an effective pitcher. He lasted just long enough to pitch two uneventful innings, before leaving the Dodgers and Brooklyn forever.

16

HEADING NORTH

The Dodgers followed Mungo to the mainland a week or so later after winding up their stay in Havana playing the Cuban All Stars. One of the Cuban pitchers was a veteran lefthander named Luis Tiant, who had a little righthanded-throwing son named Luis who was not yet four months old.

In Florida Durocher settled on a starting lineup that had Pee Wee Reese at shortstop; Paul Waner, the once great star of the Pittsburgh Pirates who had been released by the Pirates and signed by MacPhail that winter, in right field; Pete Reiser in center; Joe Medwick in left; Cookie Lavagetto at third base; Dolph Camilli at first base; Pete Coscarart at second base; and Mickey Owen catching.

After Cuba spring training for the Dodgers became routine and matter of fact. They beat the Cardinals, lost three straight to the Giants, which didn't seem to matter much, and eventually went off on their split-team barnstorming tour. Phelps was still in Maryland, reportedly ailing now from a sinus attack. Arthur (Red) Patterson, a sportswriter for the *New York Herald Tribune,* said, "This is the screwiest of all baseball camps. There are enough ballplayers for three or four clubs. One battery, Mungo and Phelps, is strewn along the Atlantic seaboard. Funny thing is, they might win the National League pennant."

Maybe, but MacPhail and Durocher were not satisfied with the club. They felt there was a glaring weakness in the infield, where Coscarart, the regular second baseman for the previous two seasons, simply did not measure up to pennant-winning standards. Pete had never been much of a hitter and in spring training was worse than usual. Durocher, fretting about the weakness at the bottom of his batting order, said, "Pete's a grand second baseman, but I guess the hawks have got him. And Owen is a great catcher, a *great* catcher, but can I stand him at bat? What's he gonna hit?"

The Dodgers could carry Owen's weak bat if they could get some hitting at second base. MacPhail coveted Billy Herman of the Cubs, whom he'd been trying to get since the end of the 1940 season. Herman had been the Cubs' second baseman for nine years; he was a perennial .300 hitter, a genius at the hit-and-run, a superb fielder who was particularly adept at the double play, and was generally acclaimed as one of the smartest players in the game.

Herman had been unhappy in Chicago for a couple of years; he'd been discontented when the Cubs chose Gabby Hartnett as playing manager instead of him in 1938, and again, more obviously, when Hartnett was fired after the 1940 season and Jimmy Wilson was picked to succeed him. The Cubs had a new general manager named Jimmy Gallagher, who had been a Chicago sportswriter highly critical of Cubs management. Phil Wrigley reacted to the criticism by saying, in effect, "If you know so much *you* run the club," and hired Gallagher.

MacPhail had offered Gallagher the unhappy Phelps for the unhappy Herman. Gallagher said no. Not long after the Dodgers left

Cuba, MacPhail flew to California, where the Cubs were training, to talk to Gallagher again. Jimmy wanted more than Phelps for Herman, and MacPhail wired Terry of the Giants in an attempt to work out a three-club deal. In Florida Terry told the press that MacPhail had a proposal that went something like this: the Cubs would get the Giants' catcher, Harry Danning; the Dodgers would get Herman; the Giants would get Phelps and Coscarart from the Dodgers and outfielder Hank Lieber from the Cubs; the Cubs would also get outfielder Charley Gilbert from the Dodgers (Gilbert had been Brooklyn's center fielder during the season-opening winning streak in 1940 but got hurt and lost his job to Dixie Walker; he was still considered a Dodger regular, although it was clear that Walker was ahead of him and that Reiser was ahead of Walker).

Terry informed the press of all this and said he told MacPhail he wasn't interested. That was a pretty big story and it got a lot of play in the papers. The next day the Dodgers got a long rambling telegram from MacPhail—he loved to send telegrams—that said:

TERRY HAS ISSUED A STATEMENT THAT HE TURNED DOWN A THREE CORNERED DEAL WITH CHICAGO AND BROOKLYN SUGGESTED BY ME. TERRY'S CLUB MUST BE GIVING HIM NERVOUS INDIGESTION OR ELSE HE IS EATING LATE AT NIGHT AND DREAMING THESE DEALS IN HIS NIGHTMARES. TERRY HAS BEEN TRYING TO TRADE DANNING TO EVERY CLUB IN BASEBALL. HE ASKED US FOR PHELPS AND A PITCHER AND WE REPLIED BY TELLING HIM WE WOULD GIVE HIM COSCARART. TERRY HAS MY PERMISSION AND I CHALLENGE HIM TO SHOW MY TELEGRAM TO THE PRESS. WE HAVE NOT DISCUSSED ANY SUCH DEAL AS TERRY IS APPARENTLY TRYING TO PROMOTE WITH CHICAGO AT ANY TIME. PLEASE GIVE THIS INFORMATION TO OUR PRESS. L. S. MACPHAIL.

He added a P.S., perhaps the first P.S. in telegraphic history. It gave MacPhail's sarcastic reaction to that day's exhibition games, when the Dodger's A squad, managed by Durocher, lost to minor league Dallas while the Dressen-led B team defeated the American League champion Tigers. MacPhail's P.S. read: PLEASE TELL PRESS

ROBERT W. CREAMER

AND ADVISE ME BY WIRE WHETHER WE SHOULD OPEN SEASON WITH DRESSEN'S
TIGER TAMERS OR DUROCHER'S POWDER PUFFS.

THERE was no more trade talk for a while. Phelps, still unsigned, reported to Montreal at Macon. Medwick, tearing up the Grapefruit League with his batting, was being called "Jolting Joe" by the press. DiMaggio did not yet have a patent on the name or on hitting streaks. The baseball writers kept daily watch on Medwick as he hit safely in eighteen, nineteen, twenty straight exhibition games.

After the demeaning defeat in Dallas the Dodgers' A squad began to play sharply. The club won seven straight games, joined the Yankees in Atlanta and beat the New Yorkers there, beat them again the next day in Durham, North Carolina, beat them the day after that in Baltimore and beat them the day after that in Wilmington, Delaware. Their winning streak was up to eleven straight, they had beaten the Yankees four in a row, and they were sitting on top of the world. As the Dodgers returned in triumph to Ebbets Field for three last exhibition games with the Yanks before opening the National League season, Brooklyn was in a state of euphoria. There was no question at all about the future. The Dodgers were going to win the pennant.

17

HANK GREENBERG AND
THE DRAFT

Throughout the winter and spring the Selective Service procedure preoccupied baseball, particularly that part of it dealing with Hank Greenberg. Greenberg was the best ballplayer in the major leagues at that time—he had been voted Most Valuable Player in the American League in 1940 ahead of DiMaggio, even though DiMaggio had just won his second straight batting title—and he was ripe for the draft. That was big news because Greenberg was such a big name. I've been surprised to discover that few baseball fans of my children's generation know how good Greenberg was. I think the current preoccupation with career totals—3,000 hits, 500 home runs, 300 victories—has diminished the appreciation of superb players who had shorter careers. But you ought to know about Greenberg.

He broke into the majors with the Detroit Tigers in 1933 and retired in 1947, and in those fifteen years had only nine complete seasons. He broke his wrist in 1936 and missed all but twelve games, and he lost four years and half of a fifth to military service in World War II. Yet in that brief period he established himself as one of the best of all power hitters, possibly the best after Babe Ruth and Lou Gehrig. He wasn't much of a fielder, although he made a successful switch from first base to left field in 1940 at the request of the Tigers, who knew that first base was the only position another Tiger slugger named Rudy York could play. Greenberg made some oh-shit catches—those in which an outfielder charges in for a ball, realizes he's misjudged it, says, "Oh, shit!" and makes a fortuitous grab high over his head—but he was competent enough out there to be picked as the best all around left-fielder in baseball that year.

He was a hard worker, a good team man and, oh my, could he hit. He belted fifty-eight home runs in 1938 (the Babe's best was sixty, Lou's forty-nine). He drove in 170 runs in 1935 and 183 in 1937 (Babe's best was 170, Lou's 184). He hit sixty-three doubles in 1934 (the major league record is sixty-seven). In 1937–38–39–40, his last four seasons before going into the army, he averaged forty-three home runs and 148 runs batted in a year. He had ninety-six extra-base hits in 1934, ninety-eight in 1935, 103 in 1937, ninety-nine in 1940. Ruth is the only other player to have had as many as ninety-six extra-base hits in four different seasons. Gehrig had that many twice, DiMaggio once, Jimmie Foxx once, Rogers Hornsby once. Williams never had as many as ninety extra-base hits in one year. Mickey Mantle never had as many as eighty. Mike Schmidt's best was eighty-one. Willie Mays had ninety one year, Henry Aaron ninety-two.

The Tigers won three pennants in the seven seasons from 1934 through 1940 when Greenberg was their star; they were the only team other than the Yankees in that period to win an American League flag. He won the Most Valuable Player award twice. He was some ballplayer, a hell of a hitter and a great man to have on your club.

But in 1940 came the draft. Registration day was just one week after the last game of the World Series between Detroit and Cincinnati. Greenberg was driving from Detroit to New York with his brother Joe and they stopped to register in the upstate town of Geneva, New York. A man was not obliged to go to his local draft board to register; he could sign in at any board he happened to be near. The registrant's name, address and other salient data were forwarded to his home draft board for processing. The local board would issue his draft card and would rule on his status vis-à-vis military service.

When the Greenberg brothers registered, Joe listed his home address as the Greenberg family residence in the Bronx. Hank gave the name of the hotel in Detroit where he lived during the season. "I don't know what prevailed upon me to list my residence as Detroit," Greenberg said in his posthumous autobiography, edited by Ira Berkow. "Maybe I thought it would keep me from being drafted so soon. What a mistake that turned out to be."

Each draft registrant was given a local number. The numbers, which were substantially the same for each board, were put into a big bowl in Washington, D.C., and at a well-publicized ceremony shortly after registration day they were pulled out at random. Number 158 was the first number drawn and was therefore given "order number" one. Each subsequent number selected was given its order number. Greenberg's number was the 621st selected, a relatively low order number, although not as low as those of some other baseball people. Durocher (who was only nine months short of his thirty-sixth birthday when he registered) had order number 560. Bobby Feller, on the other hand, had number 2,857, which meant that he was almost certain not to be called for military training in 1941. Feller completed the season, but after Pearl Harbor he did not wait to be drafted. In December 1941 he enlisted in the navy, saw combat in the Pacific and missed almost all of the next four seasons. If Feller, who was twenty-three when he went into the navy, had not missed those four years in the middle of his career, he might have won 350 games, and it is likely that

ROBERT W. CREAMER

he would have broken Walter Johnson's strikeout record a generation before Nolan Ryan came along.

Married men and those with dependents or obvious physical deficiencies were deferred from the draft. Unmarried men in good physical condition with no dependents were considered eligible for military duty. Durocher, who was married and also supported his mother, was deferred from the first draft for those reasons. Later on, when more men were needed and more married men and those with dependents were being drafted, a physical examination revealed that Durocher had a perforated ear drum and he was deferred then for physical reasons.

Greenberg apparently had no reasons for deferment, and when he was named Most Valuable Player in the American League a month or so after the draft began, few newspaper stories failed to mention that he had a low order number and was likely to be called up. Greenberg said, "When they want me, I'll be ready to go." Because he was one of the biggest names in baseball, he became an instant symbol of baseball's contribution to what was now being called "the defense effort."

The Greenberg "case," as one newspaper called it, "has made baseball conscription conscious." In a patriotic speech at baseball's winter meetings in December, Commissioner Landis declared that baseball would not seek exemptions from the draft. It would not ask that the required year of military training—which was as long as those peacetime draftees expected to be in uniform—be split so that ballplayers could do their military service in the off season. Nor, Landis said, would baseball ask for some plan to keep valuable, high-salaried stars (an obvious reference to Greenberg) from entering the army until after the season.

Baseball was afraid of doing or saying anything that might antagonize the press, the public or the government, which could order professional baseball to shut down for the duration of the unlimited emergency. Baseball remembered the First World War, when an overzealous quest for manpower in 1918 caused the baseball season to be shut down at the end of August. The famous "green light" that President Roosevelt gave Commissioner Landis to keep big league baseball going in World War II as an aid to public morale did not come about until after Pearl Harbor. The Greenberg "case" came under discussion more than a year before Pearl Harbor.

Club executives were quick to voice agreement with Landis. Jack Zeller, general manager of the Tigers, said, "I've been told by Mr. Briggs to let the draft take its course without any suggestions from us." Warren Giles, by that time general manager of the Reds, said his club's attitude was "hands off the draft."

As it happened, none of Giles' pennant-winning Reds faced an imminent call-up, but his comments, like those of other club executives, served to strengthen the image of baseball tightening its belt and making sacrifices. Baseball would not ask for special treatment.

One dissenting voice was MacPhail's. He said baseball would not know how it stood in the draft until about June 1—that is, until the third wave of inductees were called for military service. He made a plea for players who might be called up in May or June, suggesting that they be given deferments to the end of the season. Remember that this was still peacetime, and that military service was for one year.

"The one year of military service could disrupt two years of their baseball careers," MacPhail said. "They'll be gone half this season and half the next. Missing that much time from two seasons could badly affect their careers. They're not like doctors or businessmen whose earning power increases with age. They have to get theirs while the getting is good."

MacPhail said that draft officials were showing leniency toward men in certain categories—doctors, for instance, and college students—and he argued that the question of deferment should not be left to the individual player and his local draft board. "There should be a national ruling," he said. "Either the ballplayer goes

ROBERT W. CREAMER
‹‹‹‹‹‹‹‹‹‹‹‹‹‹‹‹‹‹‹‹‹‹‹‹

when he's called or, like a college student, he goes when he finishes the season, or semester."

Off the record MacPhail criticized baseball's hands-off policy in regard to the draft. "By doing nothing," he said, "the clubowners are leaving the whole matter up to the ballplayers, getting them to stick their necks out. A ballplayer called up during the season shouldn't have to appeal to his draft board, because that's going to hurt his popularity. Athletes are in a tough spot. They're national heroes, and a hero can't ask to have his military training deferred. It may hurt Greenberg if he has to ask for a ruling that Landis should have asked for long ago.

"What's the judge getting $65,000 a year for?" MacPhail said. "The least he could do is go to Washington and get a ruling, one way or the other, on how a ballplayer stands if he happens to be called in the middle of a season."

But baseball did not ask for a ruling and the responsibility for deferring or inducting men continued to lie with the local draft boards. The local boards had considerable leeway at that time. Later, when the demand for military manpower was much greater, the boards had little choice; they drafted almost everybody they could get their hands on. But in 1941 their responsibility was to supply a certain number of men by the date indicated. They had a large pool to draw from and were often quite receptive to arguments for temporary deferments. Buddy Hassett, who was with the Yankees in 1942, was slated to be drafted that summer but was given a deferment until the day after the World Series ended. "A lot depended on the different local boards," he said. Rizzuto's deferment in 1941 was granted by a local board that understood his family situation. He eventually went into service after the 1942 season, when acceptable reasons for deferment became fewer. Cecil Travis and Buddy Lewis, two top-level prewar ballplayers with the Washington Senators, were both in line for induction in 1941 but were allowed to complete the season before going into uniform. Travis, one of the best hitters in the American League from 1934 through 1941—his .359 was second to Williams' .406 in 1941—missed all or most of four seasons, suffered frostbitten feet in Europe and was no longer effective after the war, his brilliant career ending when he was still in his early thirties. Lewis, who became a captain in the air corps, had only one good postwar year before retiring at the age of thirty-three. But they were able to complete the 1941 season before going into uniform. It seems at least possible that if Greenberg had registered with his local board back home in the Bronx he might well have been deferred until the end of the season.

It's not that he shouldn't have been drafted. He was single, healthy, without dependents and with a low draft number, and others like that were being drafted. It's just that in Detroit he had no chance. He was in the spotlight. He was the symbol of baseball's participation in the defense effort. MacPhail said heroes could not ask for deferment, but Durocher did and Rizzuto did and Hugh Mulcahy, the Philadelphia pitcher, did, with little reaction. Durocher and Rizzuto were granted deferments; Mulcahy was turned down. Publicity was minimal.

Not so with Greenberg. A sort of death watch developed. Early in January a Detroit paper reported that the draft was coming closer to Hank: "His #621 is climbing toward the top of the list of local board 23 . . . [he] should get his questionnaire in three weeks, his call this spring."

Everything having to do with Greenberg and the draft became a news item. Del Baker, the Tigers' manager, was chatting with some baseball writers when he mentioned that Greenberg had flat feet and he wistfully suggested that Hank might be rejected for that reason. That was publicized. Was Greenberg going to try to stay out of the army because he had flat feet? There were overtones of anti-Semitism in the mockery.

In New York it was reported that Morrie Arnovich, a Giant outfielder, was also likely to be drafted in the spring. The Dodgers heard that Lavagetto might be going at the same time. MacPhail

ROBERT W. CREAMER

said that if the Dodgers *knew* that players would be drafted he'd urge that they volunteer before the season began so that they could get their year of military training done without disrupting two seasons. But it soon became evident that the draft was not going to have much effect on baseball in 1941. The reality was not that real. Herb Goren, an alert young sportswriter who called himself "the Old Scout," did a little investigating and found that the big leagues did not expect to lose nearly as many players as they had anticipated. In fact, according to William Mead, historian of wartime baseball, after all the noise only five big leaguers, three of them marginal players, went into the army during the 1941 season.

But early in the year it was obvious that one of them was likely to be Greenberg, and the press stayed on his "case." On February 20, when Greenberg was on vacation in Hawaii, the *Detroit Free Press* said it understood that Greenberg had asked for deferment on the grounds that his presence was of vital importance to his company's business. He was a "necessary man," in draft board terminology. The *Free Press* said the Selective Service Act defined a "necessary man" as one whose civilian activities contributed to the national health, safety or interest and that his removal from his civilian activity would cause material loss of effectiveness in such activity.

The paper said some draft officials had expressed the opinion that Greenberg's presence in the Tiger lineup in 1941 would be "in the community interest." It said the Selective Service System allowed a six-month deferment for a "necessary man," with a second six-month deferment possible. The *Free Press* said draft board officials stressed that both the Tigers and Greenberg would be within their rights in seeking an occupational deferment, and that the board would be equally within its rights in granting it. The story also said, rather quietly, that there was no indication that Greenberg was seeking to avoid service.

The story created a big stir all across the country. Ben Shepard, chairman of Greenberg's draft board, denied that the ballplayer had asked for an occupational deferment, "unless he has done so in the last couple of days. I don't think he's asking deferment on any grounds."

The next day Shepard said he had looked further into the matter and found nothing in the records to show that Greenberg was asking the board for deferment. He said the information given by registrants in their questionnaires was confidential. But he added that he had seen Greenberg's questionnaire and there was nothing in it asking for deferment for occupational reasons.

"I thought there might be something going on in the board that I didn't know about," he said, "but there wasn't. This is all a tempest in a teapot. Greenberg just filed his questionnaire and that's all there is to it."

But the "necessary man" phrase kept popping up—newspapers liked that phrase—and it aroused resentment that anyone, specifically Greenberg, could suggest that playing baseball was essential. At about the same time it became known in New York that Arnovich, who had been headed for military service, had been given a second physical examination by his draft board and had been deferred for "dental deficiencies."

That phrase aroused the mocking criticism of the hanging judges of the sporting press. "Dental deficiencies" seemed a pretty poor excuse for staying out of the army. What was he going to do, bite the enemy? What did he do, have his teeth pulled to avoid going in?

It was explained that the thirty-year-old Arnovich wore both upper and lower dental plates. "Arnovich's store teeth," wrote one wit, "allow him to attack any civilian menu with courage."

Arnovich sought out the baseball writers and pleaded his case. "I have only ten natural teeth," he explained. "I've had bum teeth since I was a kid, and I had some knocked out playing basketball. My old man had a string of gas stations then, which unfortunately do not belong to him anymore, and he paid a lot of dough to get

ROBERT W. CREAMER
〈〈〈〈〈〈〈〈〈〈〈〈〈〈〈〈〈〈〈〈〈〈〈〈〈〈〈〈

these plates made for me. I've had them for ten or twelve years."

He said that when it seemed likely he'd be going in the draft, Stoneham, the Giants' owner, suggested he enlist to get his year's service over with early. "That's why I took the second physical," Arnovich said, "the one that showed the dental deficiencies. The stories that I had my teeth pulled to avoid service are unfair."

The deferment of Arnovich (who, dental plates and all, went into the armed forces a year later and served for three years) intensified the attention paid to Greenberg. The Tigers felt obliged to announce again that they were dead set against asking favors and said that reports of Greenberg seeking occupational deferment were unfounded. Executives of other clubs reiterated their policy of letting the axe fall where it may. Connie Mack said, "Under no circumstances would I ask for a deferment for a player."

In Massachusetts, Mulcahy of the Phillies had been placed in Class 1 by his Newton draft board late in the fall. In February he asked for deferment because he was employed in a necessary occupation and also because he had recently bought a home for his parents which they would be unable to maintain if he were drafted. He said, "I figured that with the nice raise the Phils gave me this season I'd be able to clear up all my commitments and have the house free and clear by the end of the year." His request for deferment was turned down. On March 8, 1941, the twenty-seven-year-old Mulcahy was drafted. He was the first bona fide big leaguer to go into service. He was gone for five seasons, and when he returned he was unable to recapture his old pitching ability.

There was relatively little reaction to Mulcahy's request for deferment or to its denial, and he himself was philosophical about being drafted. He worked out a delay in mortgage payments on the house and said, "I'm ready and willing to go into the army." Doc Prothro, the Phillies' manager, noting that Higbe had beaten the Giants for the Dodgers in Havana, said, "We should have traded them Mulcahy."

18

HOUNDING HANK

Benny McCoy of the Athletics asked for a deferment, was turned down, asked again and was turned down again, carried his request to an appeals board, and what with one thing and another played a full season before he went into the service. Johnny Rigney, a star pitcher for the White Sox, who was engaged to Dorothy Comiskey, daughter of Grace Comiskey, the White Sox owner, also seemed likely to go. His suburban Chicago draft board said his number would be called in April or May. Chicago manager Jimmy Dykes moaned about Rigney's imminent departure. "His absence would put an awful hole in our pitching staff," Dykes said. "I don't know how we could replace him. If we lose John we'll have to give up any pennant hopes we had."

Rigney's case became something of a running soap opera. In March he was ordered to report for a physical examination by the draft board in Pasadena, California, where the White Sox had their spring-training camp. On March 20 the doctors in Pasadena said

Rigney had a perforated right ear drum and recommended that he be given a 4-B classification as unfit for military service. In April Rigney was reexamined in Chicago, was reclassified as physically fit and was slated for induction in May. Then his induction was delayed until June 20.

Early in June Rigney appealed for deferment on occupational grounds and received a sixty-day delay. But there was so much adverse publicity that Rigney recanted, waived the delay and said he would appear for induction on June 20. He reported that morning, went through a physical, and the doctors reaffirmed what the doctors in Pasadena had said back in March. He had a perforated ear drum and was unfit for military service. Rigney finished the season with the White Sox. After Pearl Harbor his physical deficiency, like Arnovich's, was not considered as great a handicap. He went into military service in 1942 and served for three years.

Mulcahy and McCoy and Rigney had asked for deferments. So had Beau Bell, a Cleveland outfielder, whose request for deferment because of dependents was turned down by his draft board in New Braufels, Texas. Rigney was criticized after he was granted a sixty-day delay, but otherwise none of these players aroused a great deal of attention for asking for deferments.

Not so with Greenberg. With him, it was not a question of whether he deserved deferment or not, but whether he had *asked* for one. A couple of days after his draft board chairman denied that Greenberg had asked for a deferment, another member of the board, Floyd T. Smith, said Greenberg in his questionnaire did ask to be deferred. A third board member "tacitly" approved Smith's statement. Smith said the board had discussed the Greenberg case and agreed they'd make no public statement until final action had been taken. Smith also said he did not recall Greenberg's exact words in asking for deferment.

Now there were stories about Greenberg every day. Did he or did he not ask for deferment? Greenberg was on an ocean liner between Honolulu and Los Angeles during the latest fuss. When his ship docked reporters descended on him, asking about the draft and deferment. Greenberg said that if his number was not called until mid-season he might ask for deferment until October. He said he hoped to play the complete 1941 season but so far he had not asked the draft board for deferment. The reporters kept after him, and Greenberg, usually relaxed and cooperative with the press, began to lose his patience.

"My number is 621," he said. "When it's called, I'll be ready. I have no intention of trying to get out of military training."

He flew from Los Angeles to New York to visit his parents for a few days before heading south to Florida and spring training, and more stories appeared. The Detroit draft board placed him in Class 1, which meant he was available for military training, subject to the results of his physical. Now it was reported that a draft board member said Greenberg had "suggested" he be placed in Class 2, which would have given him a six-month deferment. His questionnaire, it was said, listed three reasons: (1) his years of earning power were limited; (2) a year out of action would reduce his effectiveness considerably; (3) he would not be able to resume his present capacity after one year's absence.

GREENBERG'S plane landed at night at La Guardia Airport. It was cold, and the ballplayer wore a topcoat turned up at the collar and a snap-brim fedora. His brother Joe and his father were there to meet him. So was a platoon of reporters. Greenberg, "wearing a deep tan and a deeper frown," was annoyed that so much had been written about his draft status.

"What's all the fuss about?" he said to the reporters. "You'd think I was the only guy going into the army."

What about the draft board's indication that he had asked for a deferment?

"I don't know a thing about it, boys," he said sardonically. "You'd better see the draft board. They're making a statement every day."

He was asked about his questionnaire.

 ROBERT W. CREAMER
<<<<<<<<<<<<<<<<<<<<<<<<<<<<

"Questionnaires are supposed to be confidential," he said.

Had he asked for a deferment?

"There have been all sorts of stories about that. All I'm going to say is that when my number is up, I'm going. My number is 621 and they've reached about 300 out there." He laughed. "All this publicity isn't doing me any good, you know. If there are many more stories about it, you guys will have me in the army next week."

The reporters kept asking the same questions in different ways. What about the contradiction between his stated willingness to go when called and the draft board's indication that he had asked for a deferment?

"Oh, I don't know," he said sarcastically. "I guess the only way to get along with newspapermen is to be like Dizzy Dean and say one thing one day and the direct opposite the next."

Jimmy Durante, the comedian, had been on the same flight. Photographers wanted to get pictures of Durante and Greenberg together. Hank was in no mood to pose, but after he had kissed his father in greeting—the photographers missed that shot—he let Durante, who was quick to sense an opportunity for publicity, pull him into position for photographs. "Never let it be said," wrote one reporter, "that the Durante nose, even when blue with the cold, will avoid the flashlight bulbs."

Greenberg continued pushing his way toward his father's car, which was parked outside the terminal. He was more genial when the reporters ended their questions about the draft and began talking about baseball. But his resentment at the incessant publicity about his draft status remained.

In Florida things were quieter and the stories subsided. He signed his 1941 contract, supposedly for $50,000, the highest salary in the majors and, after Babe Ruth and possibly Ty Cobb, the biggest ever for a major league player up to that time.

Then, toward the end of March, things heated up again. The Detroit draft board announced that it had arranged with the board in Lakeland, Florida, where the Tigers trained, to give Greenberg his physical, a procedure similar to that which Rizzuto was going through at about the same time. The Detroit board added that if Greenberg was physically fit he would be classified 1A, which meant available for immediate military service.

Dr. Grover C. Freeman of Lakeland, who examined Greenberg, reported that he had "second degree bilateral pes planus," or flat feet, which was something that Greenberg, Del Baker, his friends and his family already knew he had, although it was suddenly big news around the country.

Now the stories began again. Would Greenberg be deferred for physical reasons? How serious were flat feet? Would he have to run after the enemy? The Lakeland board said medical deferment for Greenberg was up to the Detroit board. In Detroit there were rumors that Greenberg had been put into Class 1B, available for limited army service only. Selective Service officials around Detroit said nobody with a 1B rating had been drafted in that area.

Greenberg's draft board squelched the rumor. It said he had not been classified yet because the board had not received the medical report from Lakeland. Shepard said it was his unofficial opinion that the board would have to follow the Lakeland medical examiner's recommendation—unless it decided to send Greenberg to a special medical advisory board at Henry Ford Hospital in Detroit for a final decision.

Reporters in Lakeland queried Dr. Freeman, who said his recommendation had to remain confidential until it was released by the Detroit board. But two Detroit newspapers printed stories that said Freeman had recommended Greenberg be placed in Class 1B.

On and on it went. The medical report arrived in Detroit, and a day or so later the draft board announced that Greenberg had been placed in Class 1A. But it also said his case had been referred to the medical advisory board and that it would reconsider Greenberg's classification if he were found unfit for general military service.

In Lakeland, Greenberg, first pulled this way and then pushed that way, said only, "When they want me, I'm ready."

A reporter in Lakeland talked to Dr. Freeman and got a headline story. The doctor said he had indeed recommended a 1B classification for Greenberg and declared that the Detroit draft board did not have the right to overrule him. Other stories said Freeman was wrong and that whether or not Greenberg was deferred was up to the Detroit board.

Almost unnoticed, Buddy Lewis of the Senators took his draft physical in Florida early in April and had it forwarded to his home in Gastonia, North Carolina. He had claimed his mother and father as dependents in his questionnaire but said he expected to be drafted in a month or so. His teammate Cecil Travis, also in class 1A, also expected to be gone in a month. Not much press attention was paid to either, and both played the entire season.

The Tigers returned north to start the season and Greenberg was examined by the medical advisory board. The board found him fit for general military service and on April 18, three days after the season began, Greenberg was put in Class 1A. He said he would not appeal the decision, would not ask for deferment and, once more, said, "I'll be ready when I'm called." On April 23 he was ordered to report for induction on May 7 at 6:30 A.M. The papers noted the irony of the induction date. It was the day the Tigers were to raise the championship pennant they had won in 1940.

Greenberg played nineteen games for the Tigers before entering the army. He was batting only .258 going into his final game and had not hit a home run. Detroit politicians asked the general commanding the 6th Corps area if Greenberg's induction could be delayed until after the game so that he could take part in the raising of the flag he had done so much to win. The general said he had no authority over Greenberg until he was sworn into the army and referred them to Selective Service for a decision. The draft board turned down the request on the grounds that it would set a bad precedent; Greenberg would have to report that morning with the other draftees.

This last bit of push-pull, after four months of unending public attention, was almost too much for Greenberg to handle. He went bitterly into his last game with the Tigers. He refused to pose for photographers as he put on his uniform before the game. Del Baker had him take the Tiger lineup out to the umpires at home plate so that he could receive the applause of the crowd. He received a lot more applause in the second inning when, with the score 0–0, he hit his first home run of the year into the left field seats. In his second time at bat he hit another homer, this one with a man on, to make the score 4–0. The two homers lifted his average temporarily to .281, but he failed to hit in his last three at bats and struck out his last time up.

During the game word came from the draft board that it had changed its mind and that Greenberg could have an extra twenty-four hours before reporting; he could take part in the flag-raising ceremony the next day. Greenberg refused the offer, saying he did not want any special favors. After the game he was still angry, mostly at the press. He didn't want to answer questions. "I don't want the papers to think I'm a good guy," he said, "because I'm not. I think the papers are horseshit."

Later that day he relented. "I guess my attitude is kind of silly," he said, "but I'm bitter. Not about going into the army. I expected that. What I'm sore about is the way the papers hammered away at me, printing untruths and making a heel out of me. I'll be glad when this day is over and I'll be glad to get into the army. This has been an awful strain.

"It's not as if I'm through with baseball for life," he said optimistically. "I'll be back next year and there's no reason why I shouldn't be as good as I ever was."

A newspaper the next day said Greenberg was "the most important big league player to be caught in the draft." In fact, at that point he was, with the exception of Mulcahy, the only one.

ROBERT W. CREAMER
❬❬❬❬❬❬❬❬❬❬❬❬❬❬❬❬❬❬❬❬❬❬❬❬❬

19

DODGERS AND
CARDINALS

The preseason euphoria in Brooklyn ended abruptly when the Yankees swept the three exhibition games in Ebbets Field. On Friday before a noisy, celebrating crowd—balloons bursting, firecrackers going off, people running onto the field, occasional scuffles between fans and park police—the Yankees broke the Dodgers' winning streak by beating them in the ninth inning 7–6. On Saturday they won again, 3–2, when DiMaggio walloped a double in the ninth inning to score Henrich from first base. On Sunday they shut out the Dodgers 3–0.

In Brooklyn optimism subsided, giving way to a sense of foreboding. In the last week of spring training Medwick's batting streak ended, Reese sprained his foot and Reiser, swinging too hard at a pitch, pulled a muscle in his back.

The season began and the hated Giants (it was really one word, like "damn Yankees") opened in Ebbets Field and beat the Dodgers three straight times. The Bums had been home for a week and they'd lost six straight games in Ebbets Field. And all of them to their crosstown rivals. Were the triumphs of 1939 and 1940 just a passing dream? Was Brooklyn back to normal now, down at the bottom of the heap again?

The Giants extended their season-opening winning streak to five straight against the Phillies, while the Dodgers crept off to Boston to play the Bees (who a few days later changed their name back to Braves). In Boston Reiser returned to the Dodger lineup, hit a three-run homer and scored two other runs as Brooklyn finally won a game, and the next day on the anniversary of the battles of Lexington and Concord, Patriots' Day in Boston, the Dodgers crushed the Bees twice, 8–0 and 8–0.

Reinvigorated, they returned to New York and met the undefeated, first-place Giants in a Sunday afternoon game at the Polo Grounds. It was a lovely spring day and 56,314 people pushed their way into the place, supposedly the biggest crowd for a single game in the history of the old ballpark. Fans came early in those days and the stands were filled forty-five minutes before game time. Cars were parked "past the second bridge" on the Speedway, a road that extended away from the ballfield. Every seat was taken, and standees crowded the aisles and the runways, clambered onto railings and the backs of seats, shinnied up pipes, balanced on stanchions. They were everywhere.

It was common practice in those days for smooth operators to buy a couple of general-admission tickets at $1.10 each and then tip an usher half a dollar or so to let them sit in a couple of unoccupied reserved or box seats. On this day a well-dressed man looking for any kind of seat pushed his way through the crowd to an usher, whispered to him and offered the usual bribe.

"A seat?" the usher cried. "A seat? Jesus Christ, I couldn't get my wife a seat today."

It was a tremendous game. The Giants took a 3–0 lead into the sixth inning, but the Dodgers scored four runs to go ahead. The Giants tied it in the bottom of the sixth. Brooklyn scored three more in the top of the seventh to go ahead, 7–4. The Giants tied the score again and added two more runs to take a 9–7 lead. Brooklyn retied it, and in the ninth inning scored on a Giant error to win 10–9. Reiser had four hits in five at-bats and Casey, a Brooklyn favorite, was the winning pitcher. It was a glowing, richly satisfying victory for the Dodgers.

They lost the next day, but then they began a winning streak. Wyatt pitched two successive shutouts. Higbe, in his first win for Brooklyn, also pitched a shutout. But on April 23 a sidearm pitch from a Phillie righthander named Ike Pearson hit the lefthanded-hitting Reiser in the face. There was a sparse crowd in Ebbets Field that afternoon and the noise of the ball hitting Reiser's cheek could be heard all over the field. He spun away from the plate and tumbled to the ground, apparently seriously injured. He was carried off the field and taken to Brooklyn's Caledonia Hospital, where he was X-rayed. There was no fracture and no other signs of damage except for a sore and swollen cheek. He remained in the hospital only a couple of days, but after he rejoined the club Durocher, perhaps thinking of the haste to get Medwick back in the lineup the previous summer, let Reiser sit on the bench for a while.

The Dodgers had another injured player. Medwick, who was really something of a jerk, had come up behind Freddy Fitzsimmons, the portly old pitcher who had won more than 200 games in his career and on whom Durocher was counting for spot starts during the season. Fitzsimmons also functioned as a part-time coach (like most clubs then, the Dodgers had only two full-time coaches) and he was holding Cookie Lavagetto's glove. Medwick playfully tried to yank the glove from Fitzsimmons's grasp, but when he did something seemed to snap in the veteran righthander's pitching arm. The arm hadn't felt right since, and Fitzsimmons did little pitching in the first part of the season.

But the Dodgers kept winning and they beat the Giants again in an odd one-game series on a Sunday in Ebbets Field. The Giants were still in first place, a half game ahead of the Cardinals, a full game ahead of Brooklyn. Casey started but didn't pitch too well and when he came to bat in the fourth inning a rich Brooklyn voice shouted from the stands, "Don't leave him hit, Leo. Get the bum out of there." Leo ignored the advice, Casey made out and two innings later when he fell behind 5–3 the same fan bellowed, "We could have win this one if ya hadn't of left him hit."

In the eighth inning Dixie Walker, who was playing center in Reiser's place, hit a two-run double to tie the game and a moment later scored the winning run when Lavagetto singled. That ended the Giants' dream of revival; they fell from first place to third that day, didn't do much the rest of the season, finished in the second division and didn't take a serious look at first place again until Willie Mays arrived ten years later. So much for the Giants.

While the Dodgers were still behind the Cardinals, who had moved into first place, they were more concerned about the defending champion Reds. The Reds had started off badly, losing their first four games, but they won six of the next seven and seemed as imposing as they had been the previous two seasons. When they came to Brooklyn for four games at the end of April, it was considered an honest-to-god crucial series. Wyatt pitched against Derringer and it was 2–2 in the last of the ninth. Two innings earlier the Dodgers had blown a chance to take the lead when, with the bases loaded, Derringer walked Owen to pitch to Wyatt and Wyatt popped up. In the bottom of the ninth a similar situation developed. The Dodgers had a man on second with two outs and again Derringer walked Owen to pitch to Wyatt, but this time Wyatt singled and drove in the winning run.

That victory moved the Dodgers into first place. The next day, almost contemptuously, they crushed the Reds 13–2 and the day after that, on April 30, the first anniversary of Carleton's no hitter against the Reds, they beat Cincinnati again. They were losing 3–0 but tied the score in the eighth and won it in the last inning for their ninth straight victory, their second nine-game winning streak in April in two years.

Bucky Walters beat them the next day, winning 2–1 in eleven innings. But the Dodgers roused the crowd by mounting a rally in the bottom of the eleventh, filling the bases with one out. Durocher, moving nervously back and forth in the dugout, sent Reiser up to pinch-hit, his first at-bat since he was hit in the face. Leo seemed as excited as the crowd as Reiser worked the count to three balls and two strikes. A fourth ball would force in the tying run. A base hit would drive in the tying and winning runs.

But Walters struck Reiser out. Phelps, back with the team, pinch-hit and Walters struck out him, too, and the Dodgers lost. Walters had stopped their winning streak at nine, as he had done a year earlier.

However, losing three out of four to Brooklyn seemed to deflate the Reds. They went into another slump, fell below .500 and like the Giants faded out of the race. They did rally late in the season to finish a good third, but now in the spring there was no one left to challenge Brooklyn but the Cardinals.

THE Cardinals were a surprise, though not completely so. After the Gas House Gang won the World Series in 1934 St. Louis had gone steadily downhill: second in 1935, third in 1936, fourth in 1937, sixth in 1938. At the end of that year the Cardinals dumped the Gas House Gang manager, Frank Frisch. In 1939, with just about the same ball club, except for a new manager (Ray Blades) and a couple of good rookie pitchers (Mort Cooper and Bowman, Medwick's nemesis), the Cardinals raced up from the second division and finished a challenging second, only four and a half games behind the Reds. Many picked them to win the pennant in 1940, but they started poorly and were floundering deep in the second division when Rickey fired Blades and gave the job to Billy Southworth. It took a while for the team to jell—Medwick was traded five days after Southworth arrived, and young players were taking over—but under Billy the Cardinals played .633 ball in 109 games and finished a promising third.

Although they were still rated behind the Reds and the Dodgers as the 1941 season began, alert observers like MacPhail warned that they were a team to watch out for. The rising Cardinals (they won four pennants in the five years following 1941) were a tribute to Rickey's long-standing faith in his farm system. He controlled more minor league teams than anyone else and, with the exception of the much wealthier Yankees, had the best minor league players. Every year fine-looking rookies popped up on the Cardinals' roster. Some were morning glories who faded, but from out of this rich quantity came spectacular quality: Terry Moore in 1935, Johnny Mize in 1936, Enos Slaughter in 1938, Mort Cooper in 1939, Marty Marion in 1940, Walker Cooper in 1941, Stan Musial in 1942 (to be precise, Musial came up late in September, 1941).

Add to this a seemingly unending flow of strong young pitchers—Ernie White, Max Lanier, Howard Krist, Howie Pollet, Harry Brecheen, Alpha Brazle, Johnny Beazley, George Munger, Ted Wilks, Murry Dickson, Blix Donnelly, Ken Burkhart, Johnny Grodzicki, Hank Gornicki. In 1941 the Cardinals had twenty promising pitchers on their spring-training roster. Bill Brandt, the National League's veteran publicity man, said, "I've never heard of so many pitching prospects coming up to the same club in the same year." The only real veterans were Lon Warneke, who pitched opening day; Ira Hutchinson, a relief specialist; and Fiddler Bill McGee, who early in the season was traded to the Giants for another veteran, Harry Gumbert. McGee was a bust with the Giants, but Gumbert was a valuable member of the Cardinal staff for several seasons, which says something for Rickey's skill in trading.

"If our young pitching comes through," Rickey said, "we'll be in the race." In the meantime he had his charges take three Vitamin B-1 tablets a day for ten days, and two a day thereafter. B-1 was very big in those days; an early singing commercial incessantly piped *"Beewon/Beewon."*

In spring training while everyone was paying attention to the Dahlgren trade, Greenberg, and the Dodgers' adventures in Havana, the Cardinals were quietly putting their team together. Jimmy Brown, a first-rate infielder who had been their second baseman in 1937 and their shortstop in 1939, was put at third base. A rookie named Frank Crespi, who had brief earlier trials with the Cards, was put at second. Crespi, known as Creepy, teamed beautifully with Marty Marion, the long, thin shortstop called Slats who had been a rookie a year earlier and who would soon be recognized as the best fielding shortstop in the major leagues. Crespi, Marion and Brown gave the Cardinals a stability in the infield that the club hadn't had since the pennant winning season of 1934.

Mize, the stolid, unflappable first baseman, held out well into spring training before he signed. He wanted a raise, but Rickey wouldn't give it to him, which says something for Rickey's closeness with a dollar. Mize in 1940 had led the National League in home runs with forty three, led in runs batted in with 137, led in slugging average, led in total bases, and was second in runs scored. But his batting average had fallen from .349 to .314, and that was reason enough to refuse him a raise. "I see no hope in signing Mize at this time," Branch intoned during spring training, which may have been why John signed a week later.

Terry Moore was the best fielding center fielder in the league, and Slaughter in right was almost as good. Slaughter was a strong, slashing hitter who hit doubles, triples and home runs, ran the bases hard and never slowed down; Moore was a quieter hitter but a faster base runner who stole more bases than Slaughter did. They were a pair of gems. Slaughter said of Moore, "He's the greatest center fielder I ever played with. I've never been back to the wall at no time that he wasn't there to tell you how much room there was and what base to throw to."

With Owen gone, the Cardinals were relying heavily on their big rookie catcher, Cooper, who had hit hard in the minors, where he finished third in the American Association's MVP voting behind Rizzuto. The Cardinals also had an experienced old catcher named Gus Mancuso, who had played on five pennant-winning teams in the 1930s, and an inexperienced young one named Don Padgett. One wry observer said, "Padgett can hit, but he doesn't know much about catching. Mancuso knows all there is to know about catching, but he can't hit and he can't run. If Cooper fails Cardinal fans will be howling about Rickey trading Owen."

Padgett was something of a phenomenon—all bat, no glove. A lefthanded batter, he hit .314 in his rookie year in 1937, but he also led all National League outfielders in errors, even though he played only 109 games in the field. In 1938 he hit .271 while splitting his time between the outfield and first base, and in 1939 Rickey decided to transform him into a catcher. Padgett hated catching—a foul tip once broke his finger—but he appeared in sixty-one games behind the plate that year and hit a fascinating .399, although he didn't catch very well. MacPhail tried to get him, offering Rickey $65,000 and two players, but Rickey had high hopes for Padgett and turned MacPhail down. In 1940 Padgett's catching didn't improve and his average dropped to .242. His weight went up as his morale and average went down, and this time Rickey tried to peddle him. There were no takers; Rickey's asking price was too high, and Padgett, a tarnished ballplayer, stayed with the Cardinals. During spring training in 1941 an old-timer watching Padgett said, "Rickey seldom makes mistakes, but when he does it's a beaut. It's a caution how he messed this boy up."

20

GETTING BILLY HERMAN

The Cardinals ran off a winning streak in spring training and they did the same thing early in the regular season. They won their first three games, and then took ten in a row at the same time the Dodgers were winning nine. Southworth was very much a hands-on manager during a game, making changes he felt had to be made, but he often took time to confer with his players when he did. Against the Giants in New York the rookie Sam Nahem had a comfortable lead but gave up a three-run homer in the bottom of the eighth. When the first batter to face Nahem in the ninth doubled, Southworth held a meeting at the mound, a long discussion with pitcher, catcher and all four infielders. (Umpires used to let such meetings run their course until managers like Southworth and Durocher began to abuse the privilege. Durocher would sometimes go out to the mound to talk to his pitcher several times in an inning.)

With a runner on second and no one out, Southworth finally

decided to remove both Nahem and the rookie catcher Cooper, and bring in the rookie pitcher Gornicki and the veteran catcher Mancuso. Gornicki walked the first man he faced, and Southworth held another long conference on the mound. He lifted Gornicki and brought in the veteran relief pitcher, Ira Hutchinson. Now he had it right. The first batter to face Hutchinson tried to sacrifice and popped up, and the next batter hit a sharp bouncer right back to Ira, who started a rapid-fire 1–6–3 double play to end the game.

The Cardinals swept the series from the Giants, helped to some degree by the shaky fielding of the Giants' Joe Orengo, who played third base for New York and played it badly. One writer said Orengo's "limited elasticity at third base let batted balls fly by without interruption." Willard Mullin, the celebrated sports cartoonist for the *New York World Telegram,* did a memorable drawing of Orengo looking through his legs and calling, "Hey you, out there in left field."

The Cardinals moved into first place. In the American League the Cleveland Indians won eleven in a row to take a firm grip on first place there, and in Brooklyn MacPhail completed the fourth and last of the big trades that changed the Dodgers forever.

It happened on a Monday, after rain washed out a game in Ebbets Field. Durocher spent the afternoon closeted with MacPhail in the front office. When he came out he said only that Whitlow Wyatt would be the starting pitcher the next day, but it was clear that Leo and Larry had been talking trade, specifically one for Billy Herman. The Cubs were in New York to play the Giants and MacPhail went into Manhattan to Jimmy Gallagher's suite in the Commodore Hotel. He spent several hours talking with the Chicago general manager and with the manager, Jimmy Wilson, who seemed willing to have the unhappy Herman leave the club. Billy was batting only .194 at the time.

MacPhail kept offering Phelps, but Gallagher said he didn't want Phelps. "For Herman, the best second baseman in the league," Gallagher said, "we're not going to take peanuts."

The talks went on past midnight. Wilson went to bed. MacPhail and Gallagher kept talking. Gallagher was a highly intelligent man, but no one could outtalk MacPhail. In the small hours of the morning they finally came to an agreement, and MacPhail won. The Dodgers got Herman and the Cubs got peanuts—well, $65,000 and two marginal players, Charlie Gilbert and Johny Hudson.

MacPhail went to Herman's room, woke him up and told him the news. The two then phoned Durocher.

"Hello, Leo," Billy said. "This is your new second baseman."

Durocher, elated, started talking. Herman said, "Okay, Leo, listen. I'll see you at the ballpark this afternoon—if your boss will let me go back to sleep."

It was a great coup for Brooklyn. Pete Coscarart, the resident second baseman, was a journeyman and nothing more, but Herman was a future Hall of Famer. He had missed a third of the Cubs' games and was batting poorly at the time of the trade, but he was at second base for the Dodgers in every game for the rest of the pennant race and batted close to .300. Years later Pete Reiser told my friend Fred Opper, "Herman was the key to the 1941 pennant. He made us into a ball club."

He had four hits in his first game in Brooklyn and the Dodgers won. That afternoon Casey Stengel's renamed Braves beat St. Louis to snap the Cardinals' winning streak. Brooklyn was now only half a game back, and St. Louis was coming to town to play two single games with the Dodgers, their first confrontation of the year.

Medwick singled in a run for the Dodgers in the first inning. Crespi tied it with a single in the fifth. In the seventh Warneke sacrificed with men on first and second and was thrown out, but Marion, after advancing from second to third on the sacrifice, didn't stop but rounded third and headed for home. Camilli threw wildly, Marion scored and Crespi, running hard behind him, came all the way from first to cross the plate, too.

Two runs on a sacrifice bunt; that hurt. The Dodgers got a run back in the eighth, but Southworth brought in Hutchinson, and Ira got Medwick to hit his first pitch into an inning-ending double play. Then Reiser, who was back in the lineup again, ran into the outfield wall making what the newspapers called a "gorgeous" catch and had to leave the game.

Brooklyn went into the last of the ninth inning losing 3–2. Hutchinson walked the first man he faced in the ninth and Southworth yanked him. He brought in Max Lanier, who got two quick strikes on Camilli and then walked him. Walker bunted and Lanier threw too late to third. The bases were full with no one out. Southworth took Lanier out ("He's so jumpy," said the New York sportswriters, unused to a manager making so many pitching changes) and brought in McGee. Durocher sent Jimmy Wasdell, his best pinch hitter, to bat for Owen. McGee walked him, forcing in the tying run. The bases were still loaded, no one out, and Leo had Waner, who had been displaced in the Brooklyn outfield by Walker, bat for the pitcher. Waner hit a fly ball to Moore in center field that appeared to be long enough to drive in the winning run, but Moore caught the ball and threw it on a line to home plate to cut down Camilli as he tried to score.

Suddenly there were two out in this game of exhausting emotional highs and lows. But Pee Wee Reese, up next, ended things by calmly stroking a single to left field to drive in Walker with the winning run.

The Dodgers were half a game ahead of the Cardinals, although they were still in second place, percentage points behind. That was the second time in the young season that mathematical vagaries had frustrated Brooklyn. A week or so earlier the Dodgers were in first place, a full game ahead of St. Louis. Each club won its next two games, but as they did the Dodgers fell into a tie and then into second place, even though they were still a game ahead of the Cardinals.

"What is dis shit?" Brooklyn fans muttered. But "Games Behind" doesn't mean anything. It's an artificial stat with no official weight. It's determined by adding the difference in games won to the difference in games lost and dividing by two. Official standings are determined by a team's winning percentage, the number of games played divided into the number of games won. The standings had been:

	Won	Lost	Pct.	Games Behind
Brooklyn	11	4	.733	—
St. Louis	8	3	.727	1

After each team won its next game, the standings were:

	W	L	Pct.	GB
Brooklyn	12	4	.750	—
St. Louis	9	3	.750	1

And when each won again, the standings were:

	W	L	Pct.	GB
St. Louis	10	3	.769	1
Brooklyn	13	4	.765	—

Now, after the Dodger victory over the Cardinals, it was this way:

	W	L	Pct.	GB
St. Louis	15	5	.750	½
Brooklyn	17	6	.739	—

The two clubs went at it again the next afternoon. Reiser didn't play. They had to sew up a two-inch gash on his head, a memento of his catch off the wall the day before.

Both teams scored early and the game was tied in the fourth inning. It stayed that way until the bottom of the twelfth. Medwick started it off by tapping a grounder toward third base. When Jimmy Brown, hurrying in to make the play, threw wildly past first, Medwick ended up at second. Lavagetto hit a grounder between Brown and Marion. Marion might have handled it, but Brown lunged for the ball and deflected it past Marion into left field. Dressen waved Medwick around third and Ducky Wucky cruised unchallenged across home plate, his right fist raised high in triumph. It was the Cardinals' third straight one-run loss, and Brooklyn was now unquestionably in first place.

21

THE REDBIRDS FLY

A fter their sweep of the Cardinals the Dodgers left on their first extended road trip of the year, first to Philadelphia and then on to the "West." In Philadelphia Durocher lay on his bed in his suite at the Warwick Hotel, resplendent in apple-green-and-mauve silk pajamas, and beamed at his courtiers, the baseball writers.

Leo was feeling good. After that pratfall start in Ebbets Field his Dodgers had come back like the champions Brooklyn expected them to be, beating down one challenger after another. They had destroyed the Giants' dream of first place; they had pushed the Reds back into mediocrity; they had faced the surging Cardinals head-on and taken the league lead away from them.

Leo had Herman playing second base for him now, and Herman had six hits in his first seven at-bats as a Dodger. In Philadelphia he had five more hits in one game to lift his batting average to

.352. When Reiser returned to the lineup Leo would have a solid man at every position: Owen catching; Camilli, Herman, Reese and Lavagetto (and occasionally Lew Riggs) in the infield; Medwick, Reiser and the unquenchable Dixie Walker in the outfield.

Leo was feeling good. Reiser was ready to play against Philadelphia, but the Dodgers had been winning with Wasdell in his place, and Durocher was too superstitious to mess with a winning lineup. The Dodgers had a strong bench and Leo liked to use it. As for pitching, now that Walters and Derringer seemed to be bearing out Van Lingle Mungo's prediction, Brooklyn had the best one-two punch in the league in Wyatt and Higbe.

Leo told the writers that morning that he would use both Wyatt and Higbe against the last-place Phils. What kind of strategy was that? asked the writers. The Dodgers were going to Cincinnati from Philadelphia, and despite their early season losses the Reds were still considered the team to beat in the league. Wouldn't it be advisable to hold Wyatt and Higbe for the Reds?

"I know, I know." Leo's great braying voice filled the room. "We have a big series coming up in Cincinnati. Well, let me tell you something. Those two boys are going to pitch every fourth day for me even if we're playing the Bloomer Girls."

The Dodgers swept the Phils and they swept the Reds, and they extended their latest winning streak to seven straight in Pittsburgh. Medwick was on another hitting tear and the newspapers monitored him through seventeen straight before he was stopped.

The Dodgers had won 22 of 25 games since the opening flop in Ebbets Field, and they had a two-and-a-half-game lead on the Cardinals. The rest of the league was nowhere; only one team was above .500. The great 3-year-old colt Whirlaway had just run away with the Kentucky Derby and the Preakness on his way to the Triple Crown, and the Dodgers seemed just as dominant.

But the winning streak ended in Pittsburgh, and in Chicago the balloon burst. The Dodgers were beaten three straight times by the Cubs, the last two games by the crushing scores of 14–5 and

ROBERT W. CREAMER
‹‹‹‹‹‹‹‹‹‹‹‹‹‹‹‹‹‹‹‹‹‹‹‹‹‹‹

9–1, and as quickly as that they fell into second place again behind the Cardinals.

They went from Chicago to St. Louis for another two-game shootout with the Cardinals, and this time they lost both games. The second defeat was particularly galling, because the Dodgers came out of their hitting slump and felt they should have won it. Down 7–2, they scored once in the eighth and three times in the ninth and had the tying run on second base when the game ended. What hurt was that the Cardinals had scored four early runs that the Dodgers felt were undeserved. In the second inning Hugh Casey threw what he and the Dodgers thought was an inning-ending third strike past Terry Moore. But the umpire called the pitch a ball. The Dodgers argued angrily, but Moore walked and Casey, upset by the call, lost his poise. He grooved one to the next batter, Padgett, who hit a three-run home run, and Johnny Mize followed with another homer. The Dodgers were behind 5–0 and were never able to overcome that big lead. It didn't seem fair, but when they boarded the train that evening for the long train ride back to New York they had a six-game losing streak.

Durocher brushed it off. The dapper Leo, who lived in St. Louis, had packed a trunk with clothes for the summer; he brought along six suits, a dozen new ties, ten silk shirts and five pairs of two-tone shoes. Leo liked to look nice.

"Sure, we lost six in a row," he growled at the writers, "but I guess we're entitled to lose a few. It's nothing. The hawks have us, that's all. We'll come out of it. We still have the best team in the National League. Don't tell me you think that's a great Cardinal team we blew two games to. We'll take care of them later."

In the East the Dodgers started another winning streak, taking seven straight games, but the Cardinals had started a streak of their own with the two victories over Brooklyn, and the Dodgers not only failed to gain during their streak, they lost ground. The Cardinals had been rained out of several games early in the season, and now they were playing makeup games and winning them.

Durocher may have dismissed the Cardinals, but they were quite a ball club. They had won ten straight earlier; now they won eleven straight. A gloating Southworth said, "Last winter we got rid of all the dead wood on the club and brought up fresh stock from the farms."

Billy was proud of his youthful squad. Except for Mize and the catchers they all had speed, and Southworth always had them running. Not stealing bases—the Cardinals were fifth in the league in steals (the Dodgers were last)—but in always taking the extra base in a slam-bang, all-out assault on the base paths. The Cardinals routinely stretched singles into doubles and doubles into triples; they hustled from first to third or scored from second on practically every base hit; they tagged up and scored from third on almost every fly ball.

Southworth didn't seem to miss Medwick and his big bat at all. He had put rookie Johnny Hopp in left after Medwick left for Brooklyn, and in 1941 when Hopp had to fill in at first base after Mize broke a finger he used Padgett and two pickup outfielders the Cardinals added to their roster that season. They were the marvelously named Coaker Triplett, a twenty-nine-year-old right-handed hitter who had played only twelve games in the majors before 1941, and the thirty-seven-year-old Estel Crabtree, who played his first game in the majors in 1929 but had been back in the minors since 1933. In one game against the Dodgers Triplett hit a home run, a double and two singles.

The Cardinals were also a superb fielding team. Praising their glove work in May, Casey Stengel of the Braves said, "We might have won two more from them if it hadn't been for that feller in center field." And it wasn't only Moore. Against Brooklyn Crespi broke the back of a Dodger rally when Herman hit what looked like a hard single into center field with two men on. Crespi dived, not as easy a thing to do in those days of pebbly, uneven fields; stopped the ball, not as easy a thing to do in that era of smaller gloves; rolled over onto his back and flipped to Marion for an inning-ending force play at second base. A fairly common play today but not then. "They always give you a battle," Stengel said.

The youngsters Rickey liked in spring training were now showing their stuff, but the main strength of the team lay with players who had been around for a while, or at least for a season or two: Lon Warneke, Mort Cooper, Max Lanier, Johnny Mize, Enos Slaughter, Terry Moore, Jimmy Brown, Marty Marion, Johnny Hopp. Aside from the pitchers, the important rookies were Creepy Crespi, the best-fielding second baseman the Cardinals had had since Frank Frisch, and the catcher, Walker Cooper, Mort's younger, bigger brother. Walker was six feet three inches tall and weighed 195 pounds, and he was clearly a find, a first rate fielding catcher who could hit with power.

So, despite Durocher's disparaging comment and despite his team's impressive .692 winning record through the first six weeks of the season, the Dodgers were three full games behind the Cardinals on Memorial Day morning, with a quarter of the season gone by.

SLUMPS AND CRYBABIES

Back in April when the Yankees and the Dodgers played in Brooklyn just before opening day, both Rizzuto and DiMaggio had carried sixteen-game hitting streaks into Ebbets Field. The papers paid more attention to Rizzuto's spring-training hitting than they did to DiMaggio's. Yankee fans were looking for a renaissance after the failure of 1940, and we were very much aware of Scooter and what he was doing. When a highly publicized rookie comes through the way he did that spring, every-one notices. We noticed his partner, Priddy, too, but we didn't expect as much from him.

Neither of the youngsters had a good day against the Dodgers in their New York debut. Rizzuto went hitless to end his streak, and he fielded poorly. Priddy twisted his ankle so badly that he had to sit out the next two games in Ebbets Field as well as the first three of the regular season. For the first time all spring McCarthy used Gordon at second base and inserted the other rookie, Sturm, at first base. One reporter observed, "Sturm fielded well and had two hits. Gordon looks a lot better at second base than he does at first."

But that wasn't the infield the Yankees had been grooming all spring. Four games into the season, with Priddy healthy again, Sturm was benched, Gordon was returned to first base and Priddy was reestablished at second.

With Rizzuto's streak stopped, attention focused on DiMaggio as the Yankees swept the Brooklyn series. Joe hit in all three games, extending his spring-training streak to nineteen, or every game he played in. The Yankees then opened the American League season in Washington against the Senators, with President Roosevelt on hand to throw out the first ball. In the first inning of that first game of the season DiMaggio hit a triple to score Henrich from first base with what proved to be the winning run in the Yankees' 3–0 victory. It was noted that it was the twentieth straight game Joe had hit in. For the next week we followed this technically invalid stat that combined DiMaggio's spring-training hitting with the regular season. It seemed amazing. He had hit in *every* game he had played in since coming from California to start spring training.

The streak went to twenty-seven games, and his fielding kept pace. In Philadelphia he made what one reporter called "a rare and wonderful play." Sam Chapman hit a long fly ball to left center field, where the wall in Shibe Park canted back slightly. DiMaggio, sprinting full speed, made a backhand grab of the ball just as he was about to crash into the wall. Instead of trying to stop he scared everyone half to death by literally running into the wall and up it, and then lightly dropping to his feet on the outfield grass. At that point, eight games into the season, DiMaggio was batting .525, had nine extra-base hits including four home runs, and had driven in fourteen runs.

The next day in Shibe Park the streak stopped. Batting against a pitcher named Lester W. McCrabb, DiMaggio grounded out all four times he batted. He went hitless again the next day and hitless again the day after that, and even when he broke the drought his fitful slump continued.

The Yankees continued to win for a while without his bat and moved into first place. Rizzuto made people overlook the second of Joe's hitless days in a remarkable game Lefty Gomez pitched against the Red Sox. Gomez had talked the Yankees into keeping him around for another year despite his useless 1940 season, and he was pitching surprisingly well. This day he went eleven innings, giving up eleven hits and eight walks but, surprisingly, only two runs. He let the Red Sox get men on second and third with one out in the third and escaped without yielding a run. In the fourth he walked the bases full and struck out Dominic DiMaggio to end the inning. In the fifth he filled the bases again and struck out Frankie Pytlak, the Boston catcher. It was a charmed-life performance, but Gomez went all eleven innings with it. (In his next start Gomez pitched a three-hitter—and lost.)

In the last of the eleventh Selkirk batted for Gomez and singled. Rizzuto, batting leadoff, was up next. It was getting late that April afternoon, and on the field below the towering Yankee Stadium grandstand it was just about dark. It was apparent that the game would be called by the umpires after the Yankees finished batting. There were no lights in Yankee Stadium then (and would not be for another five years) and there was no provision for suspended games. A game called on account of darkness or unceasing rain was over for good. A tie would be replayed later in the season.

The Boston pitcher was Charlie Wagner, known as Broadway Charlie for his suave good looks and his way with women. He was a pretty good pitcher, too, but Rizzuto got his bat around and sent a fly ball down the left-field line and into the seats. It was a home run, a game-winning home run, the first home run of Phil's major league career. By the time he reached second base jubilant young fans were pouring out of the stands and racing toward him. They surrounded him, pounded his head, shook his hand and formed an unruly escort as he struggled around third base. One kid swiped his hat and ran toward the stand and Rizzuto, barely more than a kid himself, looked for a moment as though he were going to chase him to get his hat back. "In those days we had to buy our own shoes, our own sweatshirts, our own caps," Rizzuto said. "Barrow made me pay for the cap, and that's a fact. I swear to God." Bareheaded, almost lost in the crowd of equally tall or taller kids around him, he forced his way to the plate to complete his home run. His admiring fans half carried him toward the dugout before park police came to his rescue.

But generally Rizzuto was not hitting well and with DiMaggio sluggish at bat the Yankees began to lose. They lost eleven of sixteen games and fell back to second place, then to third, then to fourth. They lost to Lefty Grove and Boston as the famous old lefthander won his 295th game. The next day they lost to Bobby Feller and the Indians—just about everybody called Feller Bobby then, not Bob—for back-to-back defeats by future Hall of Famers.

The Indians beat the Yankees again the next day, and then the White Sox crushed them 13–1. The Yankees were going down Cleveland had won eleven in a row a couple of weeks earlier and now were on a seven-game streak. By the time it ended the Indians had a five-game lead over the second-place White Sox, while the slumping Yankees had fallen to fifth, half a game ahead of sixth-place Washington. They were below .500 and in the second division. It seemed like 1940 all over again.

THE Indians looked like a pretty solid team. Their pitching staff, led by Feller, seemed strong; it had the best team earned-run average in the league in 1940. The infield—Hal Trosky, Ray Mack, Lou Boudreau and Ken Keltner—was excellent. Trosky is one of the forgotten men of baseball, largely because as a slugging first baseman (he hit forty-two homers one year and batted in 162 runs) he was obscured by the titanic performances of Gehrig, Greenberg and Foxx, his American League contemporaries at that position. Also, Trosky's career was short, interrupted by illness before he was thirty.

Mack and Boudreau had established themselves as regulars in 1940 when the Indians challenged so strongly for the pennant. Both made the All Star team that year and had the reputation of being the best keystone combination in the league. Boudreau was the better ballplayer, an eventual Hall of Famer, but Mack was a steady, useful partner.

Keltner at third base was an exceptional fielder and hitter, one of those players who just miss selection to the Hall of Fame. Feller said Keltner was the best third baseman in the game in those days, and history seems to bear him out: He was named to the American League All Star team seven times in eight years.

The Indians also had one fine outfielder, the powerful left-handed-hitting Canadian, Jeff Heath, who batted .340 in 1941 and drove in 123 runs, second in the league to DiMaggio. But despite the presence of hitters like Heath and Trosky and Keltner the Indians had one critical weakness. They couldn't score runs. They finished only a game out of first place in 1940 but were second to last in runs scored. The pennant-winning Tigers tallied almost 200 runs more than the Indians did. Even the best pitching—and Cleveland's *was* the best—found it hard to overcome a handicap like that. The same situation existed in 1941, especially after Trosky was injured in mid-season.

In sum, the 1941 Indians looked better than they were. Two-thirds of their outfield was in the hands of journeymen, mostly Roy (Stormy) Weatherly, a short, squat lefthanded hitter who was a career part-timer, and Gerald (Gee) Walker, a longtime American Leaguer who was in his first and only season with Cleveland. They were supported to a degree by Clarence (Soup) Campbell, who was in his second and last year as a major-leaguer. These three were amiable rather than dangerous hitters. Two of the nicknames in this nickname-heavy trio (Stormy and Soup) are obvious. The third, Walker's, appears obvious but isn't. Walker, a farm boy, was

ROBERT W. CREAMER
<<<<<<<<<<<<<<<<<<<<<<<<<<

asked to coach at first base one day when he was playing for Detroit. A teammate hit a single and with Walker shouting at him from the coach's box tried to stretch it into a double and was thrown out by twenty feet. Asked by his irritated manager why he hadn't told the runner to stop at first base, Walker protested that he had. "I yelled 'Gee!' real loud," he said. Down on the farm, when you were driving a team of mules or horses, "gee" meant turn right, "haw" meant turn left. "Haw" would have meant go on to second; "gee" meant turn back and stay at first. From then on he was Gee Walker.

Beyond their inability to score runs, the Indians were burdened with an unpleasant reputation that had carried over from the previous year. Their manager in 1940, a man named Ossie Vitt, had an abrasive, sarcastic tongue and he used it freely. He had been very successful running minor league teams, notably the 1937 Newark Bears, probably the best minor league club of all time, which won the International League pennant by twenty-five and a half games. Many of Vitt's Newark players went on to successful careers in the major leagues, so presumably he was a capable manager, but the Indian players didn't think so. They were a sensitive lot and they felt put-upon, and they said so. Nineteen forty was Vitt's third year as Cleveland's manager, but in the middle of the season, when the Indians were fighting Detroit for the pennant, a group of players including Feller and Heath went to the Cleveland front office and complained that Vitt's sarcasm and critical comments were upsetting them. They felt his attitude was keeping them from playing their best. In Feller's case this did not seem apparent; Bobby was on his way to twenty-seven victories, the earned-run leadership of the league and the strikeout crown. But Heath, bothered by injuries, missed 60 games in 1940, hit an astonishingly low .219 and was definitely unhappy.

In any case, they went over Vitt's head to management. The story of their rebellion got into the newspapers and the unhappy Indians became indelibly known as "the Crybabies." They were mocked and scorned. It just wasn't part of the ethos of the time for major league ballplayers to complain like that. Argue with your manager, sure. Even yell at him. But to run to mama, so to speak, was considered reprehensible.

When he was informed of the rebellion Vitt expressed surprise at the antagonistic feelings expressed by the players, and he appeared hurt that certain favorites of his, like Feller, were involved. The scandal, for that's what it was in baseball's little world, continued to simmer through the last two months of the season, but Vitt remained the manager and the Indians remained in the pennant race until the end. If they hadn't been such crybabies, everybody said, they probably would have won. After the season, Vitt was fired and was replaced by a former Indian manager, Roger Peckinpaugh. The Indians liked Peckinpaugh much better than Vitt, and when they started the 1941 season so well—they were 28–12 on May 25 and far out in front—everybody was praising ol' Peck and saying they guessed the Indians were right about Ossie Vitt. Heath, hitting .370, parked a home run in the upper deck of Cleveland's enormous Municipal Stadium, the first time anyone had ever hit one up there. Feller won ten games before the end of May. All seemed right with the world.

ROBERT W. CREAMER

23

WILLIAMS AND FELLER
IN THE SPRING

But hard times were coming and, ol' Peck or no ol' Peck, the Indians couldn't cope with them. In mid-May when the Indians were riding high two changes occurred in the Yankees, one that wasn't noticed at the time and one that was. What went unnoticed was that DiMaggio had finally begun to hit consistently again. What was noticed and widely commented on was that McCarthy, after sticking with his prize rookies at second and short through six weeks of spring training and a month of the season, decided to bench Priddy and Rizzuto.

Priddy's batting average had been stuck down around .200 since the season began, and Rizzuto's was sliding in that direction. Crosetti was dusted off and put in at shortstop and Gordon was returned to second base. Sturm was installed at first and took Rizzuto's place as the leadoff hitter. He batted safely in eleven straight games, and the Yankees began to win. Not overwhelmingly; they just began to play better ball. They won seven games during Sturm's little streak and that was enough to send the sports-writers giddy over the young first baseman. His batting streak impressed the press box observers so much that they didn't seem to notice, or care, that after that fine first burst of hitting he settled into a steady .225 gait that slowly brought his average down to the .239 he ended the season with. (In the first thirteen games of DiMaggio's hitting streak Sturm batted .339 and scored a dozen runs; in the last thirteen games of the streak he batted .125 and scored only four runs.)

McCarthy must have noticed, but he didn't seem to mind. Perhaps he felt that Sturm was the catalyst the team needed. Perhaps he realized that Gordon at second base was the catalyst, and keeping Sturm at first base let him play Gordon at second. Perhaps Gordon at first base was all Barrow's idea, and the patient Mc-Carthy went along with it until even Barrow realized it wouldn't work. Whatever, Sturm was now a fixture at first. McCarthy occasionally benched him for a pinch hitter and once in a while batted him eighth, but most of the time he kept his light-hitting first baseman in the lineup at the top of the order as leadoff man. Sturm gave the Yankees about what they would have had if they had kept Dahlgren. He had less power at bat and was perhaps a little more graceful in the field, but he was substantially the same weak-hitting first baseman that Dahlgren was. But somehow it worked better.

Sturm's fine early play also served to obscure the beginning of DiMaggio's hitting streak. Joe's streak started two games before Sturm's did, but it failed to impress anyone at first. Even after Sturm stopped hitting, little notice was paid to DiMaggio. He was doing better, but his hitting was not sensational. His high early season average had dropped sharply during his slump, at a time when Cecil Travis of the Senators, Joe Cronin of the Red Sox and Roy Cullenbine of the Browns were all batting around .400.

As for Ted Williams, he had missed several games with a slight

ROBERT W. CREAMER
<<<<<<<<<<<<<<<<<<<<<<<<<<

injury and his average was around .333 in mid-May. He was fifteenth in the league in hitting at that point; DiMaggio was farther down.

But then Williams started to sizzle, and don't let anyone tell you that no one noticed how well Ted hit during DiMaggio's batting streak. The gangly, goofy-looking kid from Boston *made* people sit up and pay attention. Long before anyone got around to noticing DiMaggio's streak they were marveling at Williams' hitting. He ran off an impressive batting streak himself, starting a day before Joe did and hitting safely in twenty-three straight games before he was shut out in a doubleheader in Chicago early in June.

It wasn't Williams' consecutive-game streak that impressed people. It was the way he was pounding the ball. Hits poured off his bat. He had thirty in fifty-six at-bats. His average soared forty points in one week to put him among the leaders. Then he hit even harder. In ten days his average reached .400. He moved into first place in the batting race. His average continued to climb. On Memorial Day, May 30, he had six hits in a doubleheader and was batting .429, a hundred points higher than DiMaggio. In another doubleheader two days later he had four hits in nine at-bats and raised his average only one point, but another burst of hits pushed him up to a season-high .436 on June 6.

His average dropped off to .416, but it would not be accurate to say he cooled off. By the middle of June attention was shifting to DiMaggio, but Williams' league-leading average stayed well above .400. It rose to .420, subsided to .403, moved back up to .412. Almost every time he dropped down, a cluster of hits brought him back up again. In a doubleheader early in July, on the last Sunday before the mid-season All Star break, Williams had four hits in eight at-bats and went into the All Star game hitting .405. He had a forty-point lead over his nearest challenger, a seventy-point lead over DiMaggio.

Those blazing weeks in the spring and early summer of 1941 were when Williams came of age as a hitter, when he began to be accepted as a great baseball player. Everyone knew by then that he was a lot more than just a pouty juvenile who wanted to be a fireman. He was Ted Williams. He was a force.

WITH Sturm at first, Gordon at second, Crosetti at short and DiMaggio hitting, the Yankees climbed back over .500. On May 25 they were still seven games behind the Indians and only two games above .500, but Cleveland had begun to slow down—the Indians lost more games than they won the last two weeks of May—and if it hadn't been for Feller they might have fallen apart.

Feller was unique. He was only twenty-two, but this was his sixth season in the major leagues. He never played in the minors. He won twenty-four games for Cleveland in 1939 when he was only twenty, twenty-seven in 1940 and twenty-five in 1941. He pitched the first of his three no-hitters on opening day in 1940. He won 30 percent of Cleveland's games in their futile chase after the 1940 pennant, and in 1941 an exact third of their victories were his. He led the league in strikeouts when he was nineteen, twenty, twenty-one and twenty-two, and in each of those seasons only one other pitcher was able to get within one hundred strike-outs of his total. In 1940 he led the league in games started, games completed and innings pitched, and he relieved a few times each year, too.

He was a phenomenon. He was an Iowa farm boy who had been discovered by the Indians and signed to a contract when he was only seventeen. Commissioner Landis found irregularities in the procedure, held a hearing and advised Feller that he had grounds for asking to be made a free agent. By this time the teenage pitcher was famous and other clubs would have showered him with money to sign with them. But Feller, with his father advising him, chose to stay with Cleveland, and the Indians always paid him generously for that period, padding his income each year with bonuses for attendance, appearances in exhibition games and so on. At twenty-

ROBERT W. CREAMER
‹‹‹‹‹‹‹‹‹‹‹‹‹‹‹‹‹‹‹‹‹‹‹‹‹‹

two he was, after Greenberg, the highest-paid player in baseball, with a gross income well above DiMaggio's.

He was six feet tall and weighed 185. He looked shorter because of the chunkiness of his build: thick thighs, a big butt, broad shoulders, a broad chest. Feller was not a graceful pitcher in the manner of Walter Johnson, or Lefty Grove, or Lefty Gomez, or Carl Hubbell, or Dizzy Dean. He just fired the ball, simply and efficiently. Early in his career he added a devastating curve to his over-powering fastball, and those two pitches in combination made him the most feared and respected pitcher in the game. Ted Williams in the 1980s called Feller "the greatest pitcher I ever saw." Joe DiMaggio in 1941 said, "Feller is the best pitcher living. I don't think anyone is ever going to throw a ball faster than he does. And his curve ball isn't human."

Vic Raschi, who later won twenty-one games three years in a row for the Yankees, had a tryout with the Indians when he was a teenager. "I cut loose and threw as hard as I could," he told Don Honig, "and I felt pretty good about myself. Then this kid walked out and started to warm up. You couldn't help noticing him be-cause he had this big flashy windup. He started throwing harder and harder. I had never seen anyone throw a ball like that. Each pitch seemed so much faster than the previous one. Pretty soon it sounded like it was exploding when it hit the catcher's mitt. He was throwing bullets, just plain bullets. It was Feller, of course. 'Good God,' I said to myself. 'No way I'm going to compete with this guy.'" Billy Goodman, who won the American League batting championship in 1950, came into the league as a rookie in 1947 and was sent up to bat against Feller. "Make him throw you a strike," he was told. "I did better," Goodman said. "I made him throw me three strikes. I went back and sat down and I said to myself, 'Man, you're in the wrong league.' I had never seen anything like that."

He was the best pitcher in the game and he tried his best to carry the Indians almost single-handedly. In 1941 he pitched six shutouts and won five games by 2–1 scores. From May 26 through June 6 the Indians lost six of nine games; the three they won were complete games by Feller, two of them shutouts.

Nonetheless, the Indians had slowed down, and the Yankees were winning, nine of their first twelve games after the revamped infield was put in place on the day after DiMaggio started hitting. When the Yankees won the first game of a Memorial Day doubleheader in Boston, they were still in third place but only three games back of Cleveland.

The second game in Fenway Park that day sobered them up. They were awful. They lost to the Red Sox 13–0. They were shut out for the first time all season. They let the Red Sox pull off a successful triple steal. DiMaggio had the worst day of his career in the outfield; he made four errors in the doubleheader, three of them in the 13–0 second game. His one bright note was a double in the fifth inning, the only hit the Yankees made until they added a single in the ninth. A third Yankee reached base when Dominic DiMaggio dropped a fly ball. It was not a good day for the DiMaggio boys.

Except that, all but unnoticed, Joe's double meant he had now hit in sixteen straight games.

24

ROOSEVELT AND THE WAR

On May 27 in the Polo Grounds a strange thing happened. The Giants were playing the Braves in their first night game of the year. It was a hot, sticky night, very warm for May, and there were threats of rain. Attendance was only 17,009, much lower than expected for a night game, particularly the first night game of the season, but it wasn't the weather that kept so many fans at home.

It had been announced for several days that President Roosevelt would make a very important speech that night about the war, and many people, especially husbands and wives, fathers and mothers, those with an intense, worried interest in what world events might do to them, stayed home to listen to the president on the radio.

In the Polo Grounds, with the score tied at the end of the seventh inning, the umpires waved their arms and stopped the game, the way they would have halted play if it had started to rain. It was almost ten-thirty. Both teams left the field. A few moments later a voice on the public-address system said, "Ladies and gentlemen, the President of the United States," and for the next forty-five minutes the 17,000 people in the Polo Grounds listened as Franklin Roosevelt spoke. It was the first and, as far as I know, the only presidential address ever piped into a ballpark in the middle of a game.

The war was going badly for Britain. Although the German air attacks of 1940 had eased somewhat, and the immediate threat of a German invasion had passed, England was still under continuous, almost constant attack. Its factories and ports were repeatedly bombed. The blitz was destroying homes and killing civilians.

On the European continent the German army, after sitting still for more than half a year since the fall of France, had moved into the Balkans. Political pressure and the threat of armed invasion brought Nazi sympathizers into command in Hungary and Romania, and both those countries reluctantly entered the German fold. Bulgaria soon followed. Yugoslavia resisted, and in April Germany invaded that country and quickly overran it. Guerrilla bands formed in the hills and harassed the Nazis until the end of the war, but practically speaking Yugoslavia was another conquered nation.

Italy was still struggling in Albania with the difficult Greeks. Now the Germans moved southward from Yugoslavia into Greece, and despite the presence there of Australian and New Zealand troops and guerrilla forces similar to those in Yugoslavia, the Nazis soon captured Athens and crushed the last active ally of Britain in Europe. It had taken the Germans only three weeks to complete the conquest of the Balkans, another blitzkrieg. Soon the Germans pressed onward and attacked the large Greek island of Crete, using paratroopers—a new military tactic—in the invasion, and in ten days of hard fighting routed the Greek and British troops there. Max Schmeling, the German heavyweight fighter who had knocked out Joe Louis five years earlier, was reported to have taken part in the invasion of Crete.

Now the Nazis had a jumping-off place for a move toward Egypt, the Suez Canal and the oil fields of the Near East. In North Africa, where the Italians had made their halfhearted invasion of Egypt, German troops and armor replaced the Italians. While the other German army was gathering up the Balkans, these troops, known as the Afrika Korps and commanded by the military genius Erwin Rommel, stopped the British advance and forced them back into Egypt. Now the Germans had two forces aimed at the Suez Canal.

To my naive mind the Nazi triumphs had been balanced by two recent defeats, or what seemed like defeats—although despite the big headlines they were only setbacks. In May Rudolf Hess, Hitler's number-two man, climbed into a small German plane, took off, flew across the North Sea to Great Britain and parachuted into Scotland. That was a startling event, a sensation when it hit the newspapers. Here was the second most important man in Germany defecting to our side. What did it mean? Was the war going to end? Did Hitler want peace?

The speculation went on for the next fifty years, but Hess, who seemed to live forever, never explained his motives and when he did die, at the age of ninety-three, even his death—by suicide— was mysterious. My uninformed assumption is that Hess was a loony in a nest of dangerous loonys, with Hitler on top of the heap. His flight to Britain at perhaps Germany's highest point in the war and Britain's lowest didn't make much sense. If the Germans wanted to approach England with a peace offer there were easier and more practical ways to do it.

But Hess made the flight, and it was great news. A week or so later the newspapers were tracking the British pursuit of the German pocket battleship *Bismarck*. After the war the British made a gripping movie called *Sink the Bismarck!* but in May 1941, when I was a freshman reading headlines on the newsstand in the college store, it wasn't a movie; it was happening at the moment, day to day, hour by hour.

The *Bismarck* had been bottled up in a German port, but after the Nazis took Norway it moved out of Germany to the Norwegian port of Bergen. The British tried to keep the *Bismarck* penned in there, but one dark night it slipped out of Bergen and past the northern tip of Great Britain into the open Atlantic. The powerful German battleship loose in the North Atlantic scared hell out of the British. Their navy frantically chased it, lost it, found it again. The *Bismarck* sank one of Britain's biggest warships but was itself hit and damaged. It tried to run to the safety of a port in German-occupied France, but before it could get there it was caught and sunk by the pursuing British.

That was some story to follow in the newspapers, as exciting to me as the pennant race. More to the point, those two events—Hess and the *Bismarck*—served in my innocent mind, and in the minds of other half-thinking Americans, to counterbalance the Nazi victories in the Balkans and North Africa.

But not in Roosevelt's. At this low point of the war for Great Britain, he decided it was time to call for stronger action by the United States. I was getting ready to come home from college after a fairly disastrous freshman year. I had dropped one course and failed another and wasn't going to be returning in September. I was saying good-bye to friends and had gone with a fellow named Harry Schmidt to have dinner with his father, who had come to the college to drive Harry home. After dinner we went back to Mr. Schmidt's hotel room to listen to Roosevelt's speech. I doubt that Harry and I would have listened if we hadn't been with Mr. Schmidt. At eighteen who worries about those things? We might instead have gone to Wysocki's, where you could get a sixteen-ounce glass of beer for a nickel. But we listened, and I still recall the impact of Roosevelt's talk.

In the speech heard in the Polo Grounds and the hotel room and almost everywhere else, Roosevelt said that because of the bad way the war was going he was declaring that the United States was now in a state of unlimited national emergency. He made it clear that he would not hesitate to wage war against Germany, Italy and Japan if he felt it was necessary for the defense of the United States and the Western Hemisphere. "We are placing our armed forces in strategic military positions," he said. "We will not hesitate to use our armed forces to repel attack." He said U.S. Navy ships were already doing patrol duty in the North Atlantic and that their number was increasing.

He dramatized the seriousness of the situation, saying the blunt truth was that British and Allied ships carrying food and supplies to Britain and her overseas outposts were being sunk by Nazi U-boats and surface vessels at a rate more than twice as fast as British and American shipyards could replace them. He wanted stepped-up production, and he demanded that capital and labor have no disputes that would interfere with that production. He said our armed forces would resist attack, and he also said the navy would take all necessary steps to make sure that ships going to Britain got through. Presumably that meant the United States might attack Nazi submarines that were threatening Allied shipping.

Roosevelt said the United States would fight to stop a Hitler move toward the Western Hemisphere and warned, "We in the Americas will decide for ourselves whether and when and where our American interests are attacked or our security threatened." He did not ask for a declaration of war, as some had feared he might, but he did bring America much closer to involvement in the war.

He spoke for a long time, and it was estimated that 85 million people, or more than half the population of the country in 1941 listened to him. NBC said at the time that it was by far the largest audience ever to listen to a radio broadcast in America. The number of telephone calls made while he was speaking was half the normal number at that hour. Attendance at movies and stage plays was way down. In many cities traffic came almost to a standstill as people with car radios pulled to the side of the road and parked in order to listen without distraction. In busy Times Square in New York—in those days every street in midtown Manhattan was alive and swinging at that time of night—pedestrian traffic all but stopped as passersby paused to listen to Roosevelt's voice coming from radios in newsstands or from the open windows of taxicabs and cars halted along Broadway. A traffic cop—they had those on every busy corner in New York in those days—stood with his arm resting on the roof of a taxi as he bent his head to listen to the cab's radio.

There was mixed reaction to the speech. The isolationists didn't like it; interventionists and middle-of-the-roaders did. The Right Reverend William T. Manning, the most prominent Episcopal bishop in the country, said, "The president's speech is a great historic event. All true and clear-thinking Americans will support him." New York's Mayor La Guardia called it "a statement the world will understand." But Hamilton Fish, an anti-Roosevelt congressman, said it promoted "war hysteria," and Alf Landon said the speech marked "the end of democratic government in the United States, temporarily at least. The power is now in the president's hands. . . . Whether that means war is something else, but it does look like we're on our way."

In the Polo Grounds there was applause from the crowd at various points during the speech and rich applause at the end. Fred Opper, who was my age, was in the bleachers and he heard no anti-Roosevelt comments. "Maybe there were some in the box seats," he said, "but the bleachers were Roosevelt country. Nobody had money out there. That's why we sat there. Why spend $1.10 to sit in the grandstand? Money was still scarce, and you could see two games in the bleachers for that."

The two teams came back on the field. Carl Hubbell resumed pitching for New York. The Giants won, and baseball went on.

ROBERT W. CREAMER

Brooklyn Dodger baseball was dead in the water in the mid-1930's. Then the loud, flashy Larry MacPhail took over the club and made the loud, combative Leo Durocher the manager. The Dodger renaissance began.

MacPhail hired Red Barber to broadcast Brooklyn's games. The gifted young announcer captivated his New York audience with colorful Southern locutions like "tearin' up the pea patch" and "sittin' in the catbird seat." A grimmer note was sounded (below) when Joe Medwick, the great hitter the Dodgers had just obtained from the Cardinals, was knocked unconscious by a pitched ball thrown by a former St. Louis team-mate, Bob Bowman.

The New York Yankees dominated baseball from 1936 through 1939 when Joe McCarthy (left) became the first big-league manager to win four consecutive World Series. But in 1940, the season after the death of the Yankees' aristocratic owner, Col. Jacob Ruppert (right), the team stunned its loyal fans by playing poorly and falling to third place.

In 1941 the Yankees were counting heavily on Joe DiMaggio, even though the star of the Yankees had suffered injuries and ailments that had caused him to miss opening day four times in his first five seasons. Here, Doc Painter, the Yankees' trainer, examines DiMaggio's sometimes recalcitrant knee.

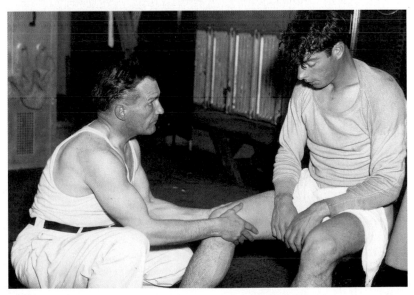

The Yankees had two prize rookies just up from the minor leagues in 1941. Second baseman Gerry Priddy (right) ended up on the bench, but little Phil Rizzuto, known as Scooter even then, batted .307 in his rookie year and went on to a brilliant career in which he played on nine pennant winners in thirteen seasons.

Despite the serious expression on his face, DiMaggio (left) was, as always, vastly amused by the quips and sallies issued by his gregarious roommate, Lefty Gomez. Gomez, a Yankee star for a decade, was fading in 1941 but still managed to win fifteen games for the Yankees.

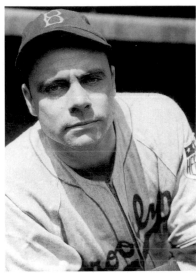

The rising Dodgers rode to the pennant on the arms of their two right-handed pitching stars, Whitlow Wyatt (left) and Kirby Higbe (right). Each won 22 games.

Brooklyn's most glittering star in 1941 was the 22-year-old center fielder, Pete Reiser, playing his first full major league season. Reiser won the league batting championship, was a daring outfielder and ran the bases with a furious abandon that delighted Dodger fans.

Another 22-year-old star in 1941 was Cleveland's Bobby Feller, who was in his sixth big league season at that young age. Feller used an overpowering fast ball and an intimidating curve to win 25 games and lead the majors in strikeouts for the fourth straight year.

The most powerful hitter in the major leagues at that time was Hank Greenberg of the Detroit Tigers. But in May 1941 Greenberg was drafted into the army and spent all or most of the next five seasons in military service.

Ted Williams came to baseball maturity in 1941. At the beginning of the season he was considered just a tall, skinny kid with a talent for hitting well and behaving irresponsibly. But in May he lifted his batting average over .400 and seldom let it fall below that exalted mark for the rest of the year. He finished at .406, the best anyone has hit in the past sixty years, and earned the respect of everyone in baseball.

Gordon (Babe) Phelps was a hard-hitting but eccentric catcher for the Dodgers. In June, saying he was ill, he refused to go on a road trip with the Brooklyn club and was suspended. In New York he and his wife packed his bag before leaving for their home in Maryland, where Phelps remained for the rest of the season. In December, just after Pearl Harbor, the Dodgers traded him to Pittsburgh.

Lou Gehrig, the great Yankee first baseman, died in June 1941. A month later the Yankees erected a monument to his memory in center field in Yankee Stadium. Manager Joe McCarthy (right) and catcher Bill Dickey, Gehrig's roommate and close friend, unveiled the plaque. Gehrig's widow, Eleanor, watched the ceremony with New York City's feisty little mayor, Fiorello La Guardia.

25

THE LAST OF THE
DAFFINESS BOYS

On Memorial Day, three days after the President's speech, the Dodgers played the Giants in the Polo Grounds in one of those great holiday doubleheaders. It was a lovely, sunny day in New York. Bunting was hung around the old ballpark and a crowd officially counted at 59,487 jammed into the place, the biggest major league crowd of the season. Bleacher fans were on line before sunrise. Miss a Giant-Dodger doubleheader? Never.

By noon the ballpark was full, and the police on duty in the streets outside were given orders to turn would-be spectators away from the park unless they could show reserved or box-seat tickets, but even those people with tickets had trouble getting earlier arrivals out of their bought-and-paid-for seats. "They couldn't squeeze another person in here," said an usher.

Brooklyn was three games behind St. Louis, and optimistic Giant fans pointed out that a New York sweep of the doubleheader would trample the Dodgers' pennant chances and put the Giants right on Brooklyn's heels again. Alas, Whit Wyatt shut out New York in the first game, and after the Giants led 2–1 into the ninth inning of the nightcap, Brooklyn rallied for five runs to triumph 6–2. Higbe the Giant Killer came out of the bullpen in the last of the ninth to stifle the Polo Grounders' last hope. The Dodgers beat the Giants again the next day for their eighth straight victory, and when the Cardinals lost, Brooklyn moved to within one game of first place.

On June 1 the Cardinals came into Ebbets Field for the second of the four visits they made to Brooklyn that season. Max Lanier pitched against Higbe and the Dodgers got to him for three quick runs, held on and won 3–2. It was their ninth in a row, their second nine-game winning streak of the season, and it tied them with St. Louis for the lead, the first time in that tangled season that the two clubs were in a flat tie.

The Cardinals were hurting. Mize had broken a finger and was out for thirty games. Crespi dislocated a finger and missed a week. Walker Cooper broke his right shoulder blade and was sidelined for two months. Hopp played first base, while Padgett and Triplett alternated in left. Old Gus Mancuso did most of the catching.

Crespi returned to the lineup in Brooklyn, and in a scrambling, back-and-forth game the Cardinals snapped the Dodger streak and regained a one-game lead. The Cardinals scored first, the Dodgers tied it up. The Cardinals went ahead again. The Dodgers scored three runs to lead 4–2. The Cardinals tied the game in the eighth and won it in the ninth when Hopp, who had tripled, contemptuously challenged Medwick's throwing arm after Ducky caught a short fly to left field. Hopp took off and didn't appear to have a chance to score, but Medwick's throw was well off line, and Hopp crossed home plate with the winning run.

Now the two clubs had played each other six times. Brooklyn had won the first two, St. Louis the next two and they had split the next two. On June 3 they played their first rubber match of the year, with each team's star pitcher on the mound—Wyatt vs. Mort Cooper. But Reiser hit a two-run homer off Cooper in the

ROBERT W. CREAMER
‹‹‹‹‹‹‹‹‹‹‹‹‹‹‹‹‹‹‹‹‹‹‹‹‹‹‹

first inning, Camilli hit another in the fourth, Wyatt pitched a shutout, and the Dodgers won 6–0. Once again the teams were tied for first place, each with a 32–13 record, a .711 winning percentage. Only one other team in the league was above .500.

The Dodgers took sole possession of the lead when they had an off day while the Cardinals lost in Boston. Both clubs were rained out the next day, and both won the day after that. The Cardinals regained first place when they beat the Giants while the Dodgers were losing to the Reds, but then the Cardinals lost two while Brooklyn was losing one and the Dodgers backed into first place. They backed out a day later when they lost and the Cardinals won.

It was the seventh time the lead had changed in nine days, but now the Cardinals held onto it for a while, and by June 12 the Dodgers were two games behind.

It was not a good time of the year for Brooklyn. The Dodgers lost four of their last five home games, and as they left on another road trip that began in St. Louis against the Cardinals, they had a one-man rebellion on their hands. When the team assembled at Pennsylvania Station in New York to board the train that would take them to St. Louis, Babe Phelps was not there. The Blimp had been doing some of the catching lately and had batted cleanup the day before. But now he was missing.

The Dodgers delayed the train's departure for five minutes or so while Durocher and John McDonald, the all-purpose aide, made some hurried phone calls. MacPhail was making the trip with the club and was already on the train, but he stayed in his compartment. Phelps did not appear, and the train left. Durocher, lying breezily, told the baseball writers that everything was okay and that Phelps was catching the second section of the train. In those days it was common practice for a second train to follow the first to accommodate overflow bookings.

Durocher's explanation seemed reasonable enough until one of the reporters asked a trainman what time the second section would arrive in St. Louis. "It'll arrive before we do," the trainman said. "It left before us. We left late."

Now the Phelps story was a hot item. Why was Durocher lying? Where was the missing catcher? Why wasn't he with the Dodgers? It was the second time in four months that the plump eccentric had jumped the club; everybody remembered the time in Miami when he refused to go to Cuba and went back home. It was a funny story—Phelps was looked upon as a comic figure—but it was a serious one, too. The Dodgers were hurting in the catching department. Herman Franks, the number-three catcher, had been sent to the minors and Owen was the only other one on the squad. And Medwick, who had been fighting a fever, had been diagnosed as having a mild case of the mumps and had been left behind to recuperate.

It was rough. The Dodgers were facing four games in St. Louis— one Friday night, another Saturday afternoon, a doubleheader on Sunday—and they were short-handed. Everyone agreed that the next seventy-two hours might be the most important of the year for Brooklyn. Damn, they needed Phelps.

MacPhail was uncharacteristically quiet during the long train ride, as was Durocher. The two huddled with Leo's coaches, Dressen and Red Corriden, and with a former big league pitcher named George Uhle, whose job with the Dodgers was scouting the other National League teams. Uhle was not an advance scout who gathered tactical information for use in upcoming games but an appraiser, evaluating the current abilities of players on other teams that the Dodgers might want to trade for. A rule in effect then prohibited player deals after midnight, June 15, which was the coming Sunday. Apparently, MacPhail and Durocher were trying to work out a deal for Phelps and were sending wires or making phone calls whenever the train made a station stop.

They had no luck. The writers on the train waited and wondered but nothing came of the meeting of Dodger minds except an obvious decision to recall Franks from Montreal. Durocher finally lifted his veil of silence and talked to the press about Phelps.

"He's fined $500," he announced, "and he's suspended. He didn't want to catch the game on Wednesday against Pittsburgh. I told him I needed him. I told him Owen had to be rested because he'd been catching so much. And with a righthanded pitcher for Pittsburgh, I said to Phelps [who was a lefthanded batter], 'You might hit a couple for me. This is an important ballgame.'

"He told me he was worried about his heart, but he said he'd give it a try. Shit, you fellows saw him catch. Next thing I know he's not at the railroad station."

Durocher said in his autobiography that Phelps was the worst hypochondriac he'd ever seen. Babe had a theory, Leo claimed, that if your heart missed a beat or two it was okay but if it missed four in a row you were dead. "He'd come dragging into the clubhouse," Leo said, "and tell us he hadn't slept a wink. Why not? He'd been up all night checking his heart beat."

In New York Phelps told a reporter that he did not make the trip to St. Louis because he was ill. "I've had the misery in my chest all spring," he said, "and I've had pains in my head, too. I packed my bags and was ready to go when I got to feeling worse, and I couldn't make it. I tried to call MacPhail in the office but nobody answered." Phelps said he'd spent three hours in a hospital on Thursday, the day the Dodgers left for St. Louis.

Asked what he planned to do Phelps said, "I can't do nothin' now. I've been suspended. I guess I'll pack up and go home and try to get well." He glanced slyly at the reporter. "And when I get back down there they won't be able to find me."

In St. Louis Durocher grew angrier. "I'm through with him," Leo said. "I'm completely disgusted with him. I don't want him on my ball club."

Apparently, Durocher and McDonald had reached Phelps on the telephone before the train left, but the big catcher could not be budged. He simply refused to leave. Later, according to the Dodgers, he was examined in his hotel room by two Brooklyn doctors who submitted a statement saying there was nothing physically wrong with Phelps. He had a history of sinus headaches, but the doctors said his sinuses were clear and he had no temperature.

The report also said that Phelps was apparently a "neurasthenic," which the newspapers of the day defined as "a person who imagines things." That seemed pretty funny to us sports-page readers. However, neurasthenia is more precisely described as an emotional or psychic disorder, characterized by fatigue, lack of motivation, feelings of inadequacy and psychosomatic symptoms. Phelps seemed to be a comic figure; apparently he was also a genuinely sick man.

But that didn't go in those days. Phelps was faking, dogging it, letting the team down. Durocher, no worse in his attitude toward emotional illness than most baseball men in those days—or, for that matter, most Americans in any calling—was still fuming when the club got to St. Louis.

"First, he doesn't go to spring training," Leo said. "Then he has a sore arm. Then he gets his finger in the way of a pitch and he's out for four weeks. Now this thing. Imagine going off and leaving us with only one catcher when we're on one of the most important road trips in years.

"I repeat, I'm through with Phelps. I don't want him on my club. Franks is here now, and he's my kind of player."

Phelps remained at his home in Maryland for the rest of the season and the following December was traded to the Pirates. He was the last man on the club who had played under Stengel when Casey managed the Dodgers, the last of the Daffiness Boys.

ROBERT W. CREAMER

DEATH AND REVIVAL

A day or so after I got home from college early in June Kaiser Wilhelm, Larry MacPhail's former target, died in Holland. And Alabama Pitts was stabbed to death down South somewhere. Alabama Pitts was one of the glamorous names of my boyhood, a by-product of the country's fascinated interest in crime and sports. In the early 1930s he was a convict, an inmate of Sing Sing, the big prison on the Hudson River a few miles north of New York City. Being "sent up the river" meant being sent to prison. The man in charge of Sing Sing was the aptly named Warden Lewis Lawes, who became as well-known as the infamous crooks and killers he had in his charge.

We were always reading and hearing about a fabulous athlete Warden Lawes had at Sing Sing who was the star of the prison's football and baseball teams. The stock joke, of course, was that Sing Sing teams played only home games, but good football and baseball teams went inside the prison walls to play the convict teams, and Alabama Pitts' fame spread.

When it came time for Pitts to be released from Sing Sing after five and a half years behind bars, Warden Lawes led a vigorous campaign to make Organized Baseball give Pitts a chance to play professionally. There was a hell of a debate for a while—vigorous arguments for and against, and it became something of a cause célèbre—but Lawes won, and when Pitts was released from Sing Sing in 1935 he was signed to a minor league contract with the Albany Senators of the Class A Eastern League. I remember feeling disappointed because I thought a big league club would snap him up and he'd be an instant star. However, as it turned out, Pitts couldn't cut it. He showed fine fielding ability, but he was unable to hit good professional pitching consistently, and after a season or two he slid out of sight. He worked in mills in the South and now, half a dozen years later, he had gotten into an argument, was stabbed, and had bled to death. I remember the grim note of injustice in the stories that I read in 1941 about his demise: Pitts had spent five and a half years in Sing Sing for stealing $72.50.

Andre Laguerre, my boss at *Sports Illustrated,* used to say that death comes in threes, and, sure enough, there was a third death early in June. On the night of June 2 Lou Gehrig died at his home in the fashionable Riverdale section of the Bronx. The Yankees were in Detroit, and all the stories touched on the irony—or co-incidence—that Gehrig's last game had been played in Detroit two years earlier. His death shook the Yankees, even though it was not a surprise. Ed Barrow said, "We all knew it was coming, but I'm still deeply shocked."

In Detroit the hushed Yankee players murmured the usual things. "He was a great guy," DiMaggio said, and the others said the same. Bill Dickey, who had roomed with Gehrig and who was closer to him than anyone else on the team, said almost nothing beyond "He was my friend." After the game Dickey flew back to New York on "the night plane," the only player on the club given license to leave the pennant race for the wake and the funeral. McCarthy, the manager, had flown back earlier in the day, leaving the team in the hands of his third-base coach, Arthur Fletcher. Before he left for the airport McCarthy stood in the lobby of the Book Cadillac Hotel in Detroit, talking with reporters.

McCarthy recalled, "It was here that he came to me—May 2, two years ago. He said, 'Joe, I always said I'd quit when I felt I was no longer any help to this team. I don't think I'm any help. When do you want me to quit?'

" 'Today,' I said. I was afraid he'd get hurt. His reflexes were gone. He couldn't get out of the way of the ball."

That day in 1939 was when Gehrig took the batting order out to the umpires and then went back to the bench and stayed there. He played only once more for the Yankees, in an exhibition game a short time later in Kansas City against the Blues, the Yankees' farm club. He grounded out in his one time at bat, fell down fielding a ball and left the game in the third inning. It was after that that he went to the Mayo Clinic and found out he was fatally ill.

In Detroit in 1941 McCarthy said, "What can I say? I'm all filled up."

AFTER the disastrous game in Fenway Park when DiMaggio made all the errors, the Yankees traveled to Cleveland to play the Indians. At that point they were in third place, behind both the Indians and the White Sox, and were only four games above .500.

It was June, and it was time to move, and they did. On Sunday, June 1, before 52,000 fans in Municipal Stadium in Cleveland they beat the Indians twice and knocked them out of first place. Chicago moved into the lead, with the Indians close behind. Red Ruffing and Lefty Gomez, the old war-horses, pitched the doubleheader and squelched the Indians. DiMaggio had a single in each game. In the eighth inning of the second game Johnny Sturm hit a two-run homer that was the start of an extraordinary team achievement. Beginning with Sturm's clout on June 1 the Yankees hit at least one home run in every game they played for the entire month. For a time later in June the team's home-run streak attracted as much attention as DiMaggio's hitting streak.

It was a rousing afternoon for the Yankees, but the next day Feller beat them, the Indians regained first place, and the Yankees went into another slump. The Indians strengthened their grip on the lead. The White Sox more or less collapsed, and the Red Sox, even with Williams hitting so beautifully, couldn't mount a serious challenge and didn't all year.

By June 5 the Yankees were only three games over .500 and were only a half game out of sixth place in the bunched-up standings. About the only fun Yankee fans had was seeing how far DiMaggio could extend his new batting streak, which was now at twenty-one games. That was a nice streak, second best to Williams in the majors so far in 1941, but that was about all. No one was very excited about it.

The Yankees moved on to St. Louis and on June 7 were losing to the lowly, last-place Browns in the ninth inning when, all of a sudden, everything came into focus. I don't know why that is, why a certain moment can in retrospect seem so significant. It was probably DiMaggio who did it. Mike Seidel, in his splendidly detailed book, *Streak*, says that DiMaggio had been suffering from a stiff neck and a sore shoulder on Memorial Day when he made his four errors. By the time the Yankees reached St. Louis he was feeling fine again. As a fan I wasn't aware of that. I just knew he had made four errors in Boston. I also knew that even though his streak had moved past the twenty mark, he had not been hitting particularly well. In eight of the nine previous games he had made only one hit, which is a tenuous way to keep a batting streak going. He'd hit only two homers in his last nineteen games and had batted in only two runs in the last nine. Where Williams at this time was terrorizing pitching staffs (or pitching staves, as a whimsical Cincinnati writer once called them), DiMaggio had batted a mild .323 since the fifth game of his streak.

But that afternoon in St. Louis he seemed to shrug off the wraps that had been holding him down. He had hit a bases-empty home run in Detroit the day before. Today he rapped out three hits, drove in a run and made a great throw to cut down a base runner, and the Yankees, as though on cue, rallied for five runs in the ninth inning and an 11–7 victory.

The next day the Yankees routed the Browns twice. DiMaggio had two homers in the first game, a single and a double in the second, and batted in seven runs in the doubleheader. The Yanks moved on to Chicago and beat the White Sox twice, Joe getting two hits in one of the games and a long home run, and then they headed home to New York for another three-game series with the Indians.

By now the Yankees had streaks all over the place. They had won five straight, DiMaggio's string was up to twenty-six and the club had hit home runs in nine straight games. Yet when Cleveland came to town riding a six-game winning streak themselves, with Feller, who had not lost since May 9, scheduled to open the series, the Yankees were still four full games behind the Indians.

Atley Donald from Louisiana, known as Swampy, pitched for New York against Feller, and it turned out to be no contest. No, not for Feller. The Yankees won handily 4–1. Henrich hit a homer in the first, DiMaggio jumped on a three-and-nothing pitch for a run-scoring double in the third, and Keller drove in two more runs in the fifth. The Yankees snapped Feller's eight-game winning streak and the Indians' six-game streak while extending all three of their own streaks. They had won six in a row; the newspapers noted that they had hit home runs in ten straight games; and everybody was aware that DiMaggio had reached twenty-seven straight and was within two of equaling the Yankee club record of twenty-nine. That had been set in 1919 by Roger Peckinpaugh, the Indians' manager, who was the Yankees' shortstop back then. His mark had been equaled in 1931 by Earle Combs, a DiMaggio predecessor in center field.

Joe was beginning to excite people. A crowd of 44,000 saw the first Cleveland game. One just as big came out the next day, a Sunday. The Yanks beat the Indians again, and there were great cheers when DiMaggio belted a gigantic home run into the third deck of the left-field stands. That hit extended the team home-run streak to eleven and moved Joe to within one game of Peckinpaugh's record.

On Monday, in the final game of the series, the Indians were tougher. They scored in the first inning, and after the Yankees tied the game in the third the Indians came right back to take a 3–1 lead in the fourth. Gordon hit a two-run homer in the bottom of the fourth to tie the game again and push the team home-run streak to eleven.

Then came the very odd fifth inning. The Indians put men on first and second with no one out. Trosky hit an easy fly ball to right field, too short to advance the runners. Henrich, always thinking, dropped the ball on purpose, with the idea of forcing the lead runner at third base and maybe getting a double play on the other runner at second. When Henrich dropped the ball Heath, the man on second, took off for third, but Henrich's throw beat him easily and Rolfe tagged him out.

The other runner had stayed at first base because as soon as Henrich dropped Trosky's fly umpire Bill McGowan called the batter out. In the ensuing argument he explained that the baseball rulebook stated that with a man on first, or with men on first and second, or first, second and third, if in the umpire's judgment a fielder intentionally drops a fly ball, the umpire shall immediately rule the ball has been caught. The rule was a cousin to the well-known infield fly rule, which prohibits infielders from deliberately dropping pop flies to begin double plays. The same principle applied here.

Okay, the Indians said, so Heath, who had been tagged out at third, goes back to second, right? No, said McGowan, Heath is out. The Indians screamed. Why can't he go back to second, since

ROBERT W. CREAMER
‹‹‹‹‹‹‹‹‹‹‹‹‹‹‹‹‹‹‹‹‹‹‹‹‹

that's where he was when the ball was ruled to have been caught?

Because, said McGowan, the base runner is on his own. If he wants to tag up and try for the next base after the ball is caught, or ruled caught, he can do so at his own risk. Same thing applies in the infield fly rule.

Technically, Heath had tagged up and tried for third base after the catch and had been thrown out. If Rolfe had not tagged him but had stepped on the base for an apparent force out, Heath presumably would not have been out. But he had been tagged, and the shrewd Henrich had his double play after all.

The inning was not over yet. There were two out now and a man on first base, and the next batter sent a hard ground ball past second. It looked like a certain base hit, but the agile Gordon dived for the ball, stopped it and flipped the ball toward Crosetti at second. The desperate, hurried throw was off-line and Crosetti had to grab it near the ground to make the out, which he did to end the Indians' half of the inning. But as he did the runner coming into the base accidentally spiked him. Crosetti had to leave the game—his finger required two stitches and a splint—and Rizzuto was called into action to take his place at shortstop.

Crosetti had played shortstop for exactly one month since May 16, the day Rizzuto and Priddy were benched, the day after Di-Maggio started his streak. During that month Rizzuto made only four pinch-hit appearances (one walk, no hits), was a pinch runner once and was a ninth-inning fielding replacement for Crosetti on three occasions. Otherwise, he just sat, a failed rookie. Now, with the Yankees trying to get back into the pennant race, he was suddenly the regular shortstop again.

The memorable fifth inning still wasn't over. DiMaggio had gone hitless so far, and now there was a rain delay of more than an hour. For a while, the rain threatened to wash out his chance to bat again and tie Peckinpaugh's record. But it finally stopped and Joe promptly whacked a double, which excited the crowd far more than Gordon's home run, Henrich's double play or Crosetti's injury.

At twenty-nine straight, his streak was becoming bigger than the game.

The Indians, still gamely battling, went ahead in the seventh inning, but the Yankees scored twice in the eighth to win the game, sweep the series and move to within a game of first place.

Despite the crucial setback the Indians refused to give in. They won their next three games while the Yankees lost two to the White Sox. That gave Cleveland a good grasp on first place again, but hardly anyone noticed. The press, the fans, the Yankees themselves were far more interested in DiMaggio's hitting streak and the home-run streak than they were in the pennant race. The two games the Yankees lost to the White Sox were deemed a success because Joe singled in each of them to break the old Yankee record and extend his new one to thirty-one straight. And Keller homered in each game to keep the home-run string going.

Joe's lively bat became livelier. He had reached his goal—the Yankee record—and in retrospect it seemed as though he had been just a little cautious as he approached it, not swinging quite as freely as he might. Seidel points out that DiMaggio struck out only five times during his hitting streak, which is pretty amazing. He never did strike out much—trivia fans know that he had 361 homers in his career and only 369 strikeouts—but in 1941 he struck out only thirteen times all season, much the lowest for a season in his career. If he wasn't being cautious, he certainly was paying close attention at the plate.

In any case, now that he had broken the Yankee record Joe seemed to swing more freely. We fans knew that the major league record for hitting safely in consecutive games was forty-one, set by George Sisler in 1922. We were also aware that there was an ancient record of forty-four set by the almost legendary Willie Keeler before the turn of the century. In later years DiMaggio said he didn't know about Keeler's record until he reached his fortieth game, but in 1941 he had to be aware of it. Sportswriters weren't quite as record-happy then as they are today, when computers

ROBERT W. CREAMER
‹‹‹‹‹‹‹‹‹‹‹‹‹‹‹‹‹‹‹‹‹‹‹‹‹‹

help to keep every last detail updated, but they wrote and talked a lot about both Sisler's record and, to a lesser degree, Keeler's.

Nonetheless, at this point the Sisler mark, which everyone felt was the real record, seemed a little remote. DiMaggio had reached his primary goal, the Yankee team record, and now he appeared to relax. Exuberantly, he made ten hits in his next seventeen at-bats, including two home runs, and took off from there. In the first thirty-one games of the streak, DiMaggio batted .363; in the last twenty-five he batted .461, almost one hundred points higher.

Lifted by DiMaggio, the Yankees made their big move. On June 18, the day Joe hit in his thirty-first straight, they were still three games behind the Indians. They won six of their next seven while the Indians faltered, and on June 25 edged past Cleveland into first place. The Yankees fell back momentarily when Feller won his sixteenth game—he was 16–3, and it was only June 26—but on June 28 they moved into first place to stay. A weary Feller was routed by the Browns on June 30 when he seemed to be breezing toward his seventeenth victory, and the Yankees held a two-game lead entering July. By the All Star break a week later they were three and a half games ahead.

They were back. They were on top again. My baseball world had been restored to order.

PART III

27

JOYCE, JAZZ AND
JOE LOUIS

omeone asked me if I were trying to do a "social history" in writing this book. Good lord, no. I tend to be put off by books and articles on social history that talk about such things as the songs "we" were singing, the books "we" were reading, the clothes "we" were wearing. Who is "we"? I mean, I began reading James Joyce in 1941 and I fell in love with his stuff. I've been reading and rereading *Ulysses* and *Portrait* and *Dubliners* ever since. I may even get through *Finnegans Wake* before I die. I liked reading Joyce, but most of my friends who enjoyed reading didn't care for him at all. They liked Faulkner. I didn't. I still don't.

Almost all of us read Hemingway, however. *For Whom the Bell Tolls* was published at about the time I entered college, and we relished the scene in which Robert Jordan makes love to the girl ("once again to nowhere") and afterward asks her if she felt "the earth move." Those were boffo lines among college comics for a long while afterward.

Popular music—big-band stuff—didn't mean that much to me then. I couldn't play an instrument, couldn't sing, could barely carry a tune. But I had a fair sense of rhythm and I loved to dance, and I liked listening to music. I had liked swing music when I was in high school and now I was beginning to savor jazz, mostly through my friendship with Arnold Benson, although he was always a stage or two ahead of me. When I liked Tommy Dorsey he liked Benny Goodman. When I grew to like Goodman, he had advanced to Count Basie. When I caught up with Basie, he had found the old recordings from the 1920s of Louis Armstrong and Bix Beiderbecke. When I began to appreciate the incredible musical artistry of those two—we used to sandwich 78-rpms by Louis and Bix on an automatic record changer and listen to them alternately—he was falling in love with Wild Bill Davison and George Brunies and Eddie Condon. Still, I learned about jazz, and I remember fondly going with Ben and Fred Opper to Cafe Society Downtown in lower Manhattan to listen to Albert Ammons and Meade Lux Lewis and Pete Johnson, the great boogie-woogie pianists. In small jazz clubs I heard Hot Lips Page sing "There Was a Old Woman" and Billie Holiday do "Them There Eyes."

What I liked to listen to was seldom what most of my contemporaries liked to listen to. Not many of the people I knew when I was young liked jazz, and I was surprised as I grew older to find so many new friends my age who did. I was delighted to learn that Philip Larkin, the English poet who was an exact contemporary of mine—I wish I had known him—loved jazz and wrote about it. There were a lot of jazz fans around in my later years, but I had known only a few when I was a kid. Other tastes prevailed. My wife-to-be, for example, liked Glen Miller's "Tuxedo Junction" and "String of Pearls." That was okay. I didn't mind dance music. Dancing with a girl was always fun, and dancing to something like Artie Shaw's "Begin the Beguine," the best dance record ever made, was sheer delight.

ROBERT W. CREAMER
≪≪≪≪≪≪≪≪≪≪≪≪≪≪≪≪≪≪≪≪≪≪

But popular music, the cliche of social history, was different from jazz—what they now call classic jazz, or traditional jazz. When Andy Crichton, who liked jazz, and I were senior editors at *Sports Illustrated* we went out one night after work with a bunch of the young people on the magazine. They took us to an upscale hamburger joint on the Upper East Side where, the kids said, we'd love the music in the jukebox. "They have your tunes in it," they said. So they poured quarters into the jukebox and pop recordings of the early forties poured out, and they couldn't understand why Andy and I didn't go bonkers with pleasure at hearing our old favorites again. But it was just stuff like Dorsey and Miller and Harry James and other big bands. Andy and I listened politely enough, I thought, but that wasn't enough for our young benefactors. What was wrong? Finally and quite gently for him, Andy said, "You don't understand. We didn't like this music."

From memory, I couldn't pinpoint a pop song from 1941, except for "Frenesi" and "Jeanie with the Light Brown Hair," which were played incessantly through the first half of the year because of the memorable contract dispute between ASCAP and the radio networks. ASCAP, the American Society of Composers, Authors and Publishers, which represented the songwriters and their allies, controlled popular music, and it would not permit any of its songs to be played over the radio until the dispute was settled. For five or six months the only tunes we heard were those in the public domain, like Stephen Foster's "Jeanie," or songs like "Frenesi" that were sponsored by the broadcaster's puppet organization, BMI. I can still hear—and flinch inwardly when I do—the relentless lilt of "Frenesi"; and the standard gag about Jeanie was that by the time the dispute was settled her hair had turned gray.

I recall one other bit about popular music in 1941. Tommy Dorsey and his orchestra came to my college to play at the Senior Ball, and what I remember about that was a small item in the college paper. As a freshman journalism student I worked on the paper, doing menial things, and so did a pleasant girl from New Jersey named Marian Buzzone. The item said, "The singer with the Tommy Dorsey orchestra, Frank Sinatra, is a cousin of Marian Buzzone of the *Daily Orange* staff." We thought it only fair to give Marian's cousin a little ink.

I suppose Joe Louis was social history. He fought his famous thirteen-round fight with Billy Conn in June of 1941. DiMaggio was at the fight. I think Louis paralleled DiMaggio in gaining public respect. He came across as such a decent, admirable man.

There were the usual racist pinheads who wanted Conn to beat him just because Conn was white and Louis was black, but nowhere near the number who were so adamantly opposed to Jack Johnson thirty years earlier. I know that I rooted hard for Louis to beat Conn, to knock him out early, and I was no race-conscious liberal then. I just liked Louis because he was such a good fighter and because he handled himself so well. He never mouthed off, but he could make succinct comments that hit home. You never know for certain if a quote credited to an athlete or a politician is really his (or hers). Look at Yogi Berra, who has been quoted so often that he is no longer quite sure which of the many pithy remarks attributed to him are actually his. But early in the war someone commented piously that God was on our side, and Louis is supposed to have said, "No, we're on God's side." When someone said he might have trouble in the ring catching a quick-footed opponent like Conn, Louis replied, "He can run, but he can't hide."

I was stunned in 1936 when Louis was knocked out by Max Schmeling. I was thirteen and I lost a quarter on that fight to my grandmother, who admired the way Schmeling kept in shape by chopping down trees. A quarter was a lot of money to me. I listened to the fight on the radio—she didn't—and when it was over I went up to her room and paid her the quarter, which, to her everlasting credit, she accepted. I mean, a bet's a bet. And I still liked Louis.

When Louis destroyed Schmeling in the first round of their

ROBERT W. CREAMER

return bout two years later I was delighted, and I never stopped rooting for Louis. I had started following boxing in the sports pages and on radio in the early 1930s when heavyweight champions tried to keep their titles as long as they could by the simple process of not fighting anybody—or not fighting anybody for as long as they could get away with it. When they did fight they usually lost. The title was held by five different men in five years.

Louis was a welcome change. He fought everyone, he knocked out each of the five previous champions and defended his title regularly. From January 1939 to March 1942 (after which he went into the army) he fought and won seventeen times, sixteen times by a knockout. He was a pleasure to root for.

I CAME home from college early in June to find the war in my brother's face. My brother was good-looking, taller than I and better built. Where I was pale with lank blond hair that never stayed combed, he had skin that tanned and thick dark hair that was always perfectly groomed in the correct Robert Taylor, movie-star way. He was a handsome fellow, but when I arrived at the house with a friend from college he was a mess. One side of his mouth was twisted and swollen, and his cheek was puffed up to the size of a small grapefruit. I was shocked by his appearance— he looked like a gargoyle—and a little embarrassed in front of my college friend. But my friend, who was never embarrassed, looked Jerry straight in the face and said, "What in the world happened to you?"

"Air corps," Jerry said. "Tooth."

Instead of waiting to be drafted he had decided to enlist in the air corps. He told me later about his preliminary interview with an examining officer.

"Why do you want to join the air corps?"

"I want to fly," Jerry said fervently. "I love airplanes. I've always been interested in airplanes."

"I see. Describe what an aileron does."

"An aileron?" Jerry said. "Is that the little thing on the wing?"

But he passed the preliminary examination only to find during the physical that he had an abcess under one of his front teeth that would have to be cleared up before his teeth met the stringent air corps standards. He had to have root-canal work done, which in those days was like being tortured. Thus his battered face.

His appearance made the war seem closer. It had been only marginal before. I didn't *know* Hugh Mulcahy or Hank Greenberg. The only man I knew personally who had been inducted at that point was a fellow my older sister had gone out with a few times, and I didn't really know him. I think I met him once. I read about him at college in my hometown paper, which came in the mail once a week. We had a fellow in our dormitory named George Prokupek, one of the two or three Democrats who had been pro-Roosevelt in the 1940 election in the face of all us Willkie Republicans. Prokupek knew a lot more about the country's problems than we did, and he had been fiercely in favor of Roosevelt. He was fierce-looking anyway, blond and red–faced with intense blue eyes. He was passionate about politics, as he was about everything. He was the catcher on our dormitory baseball team (we played honest-to-god hardball in an intramural league) and I played third base. Our games were scheduled in the late afternoon, with the sun low in the sky behind home plate. In infield warmup before each inning Prokupek, who took infield practice seriously, would fire the ball out of that sun down to me at third. I can remember almost nothing else about those games except the shiver of terror I felt each time George blazed the ball toward me. That spring I was sitting in the common room of the dormitory when I read about my sister's escort going into the army. Without thinking, I said aloud, "Well, I'll be. My sister's boyfriend was drafted." Prokupek, his blue eyes blazing, leaped up and cried, "Hah! Even the rich get drafted!" God knows we weren't rich, and neither was

ROBERT W. CREAMER

my sister's friend, but as far as George was concerned Roosevelt had stuck it to the Republicans again.

My brother's dental problem was solved and he passed his next physical. He was accepted by the air corps, was sworn in and was instructed to report for duty in the middle of September. That gave him the summer.

28

THE INCOMPARABLE
PETE REISER

The Phelpsless Dodgers detrained in St. Louis and lost to the Cardinals. Wyatt pitched another beautiful game, but Max Lanier threw a 1–0 shutout for the Cardinals. The next day the Dodgers were shut out for five more innings and were losing 4–0 when they suddenly came to life. They hammered five straight hits in the sixth inning, including a homer by Camilli, and scored seven runs. An inning or so later Pete Reiser, who was leading the league with a .364 average, hit a 400-foot homer to the roof of the right–center field stands, and the Dodgers won 12–5.

In the Sunday doubleheader with the Cardinals the Dodgers continued to hit in the first game, which they won 8–1, but were shut out in the second game 3–0. The accident-prone Reiser was hit twice with pitched balls and also twisted his ankle. Reese and Crespi had a difference of opinion at second base. Hopp was so sore after Babe Pinelli called him out on strikes that he kicked dirt in the umpire's face when Pinelli bent over to dust off the plate. It was a tough series, and a standoff. The two clubs had now played each other eleven times, half the twenty-two they were scheduled to play during the season, and they had split the games as evenly as possible, the Dodgers winning six, the Cardinals five.

They were evenly matched, which was frustrating for Durocher and even more so for MacPhail, who in making his seemingly extravagant deals for Medwick, Higbe, Owen and Herman had put together a club designed to be stronger than the defending-champion Reds. The Reds had been disposed of, and the Dodgers should have been riding high. In one sense they were: They had won thirty-seven and lost only nineteen for a winning percentage of .661, a pace that would give them 102 victories for the season or more than any National League team had won in twenty-nine years. But they were in second place behind the irritating Cardinals, a team Rickey had assembled cheaply from his farm system. The Cards were playing even better ball than Brooklyn and were doing it in the face of repeated misfortune—Crespi hurt, Mize hurt, Walker Cooper hurt. How could a team keep winning with such injuries?

The Cardinals sagged after Mize got hurt and lost seven of ten games early in June. But they perked up and won eight of ten, their only defeats the two to Brooklyn in St. Louis. The Dodgers trudged on to Chicago, where they won two out of three only to fall another game behind the resurgent Cardinals. On the morning of June 22 Brooklyn was three full games behind St. Louis.

That was a Sunday, the day Hitler invaded the Soviet Union. It was a momentous day in the history of the world, and I feel a little silly coupling what happened in the National League that day to the beginning of the biggest battle in history, one that spread over thousands of square miles and lasted nearly three years.

In actual fact, I can't relate the two. The mind is selective, compartmentalized. When you comb through old memories you are sometimes startled to discover that one unforgettable event occurred at the same time as another unforgettable event. I was surprised in reading about World War II to find that the *Bismarck* sinking occurred the same day as Roosevelt's unlimited-emergency speech. I remember both vividly, but separately. They have no relationship to each other in my mind. I distinctly remember the newspaper headlines blaring the news that the Germans had invaded Russia, but that doesn't connect in my mind to the baseball events of that same day, which I remember just as vividly.

The Dodgers were in Cincinnati for a doubleheader with the Reds, who after falling hopelessly behind were beginning to play like the champions they had been for two years. They had beaten the Dodgers the day before while the Cardinals were winning in St. Louis, and with the Cardinals playing a doubleheader at home against the compliant Giants, Brooklyn fans had uneasy visions of the Cards sweeping the Giants and their team being swept by the Reds and falling five games behind.

Wyatt faced Paul Derringer, who was having an in-and-out season but who was still a strong pitcher on his good days. This day he was superb, but so was Wyatt, and neither allowed a run for ten innings. It was a hot, draining day, and in the Dodger dugout in the eighth inning Wyatt took a salt tablet and washed it down with what he assumed was a glass of water but which turned out to be mouthwash. He gagged and spit out what he could but seemed all right and continued to pitch shutout ball.

In the top of the eleventh Wyatt stunned Derringer and the Reds by hitting a home run, and Brooklyn was ahead 1–0. Wyatt circled the bases triumphantly. Well, he began circling them triumphantly, but by the time he finished jogging the 120 yards after pitching ten innings on that hot day, with mouthwash and salt rocking around in his belly, he got sick. He began vomiting and he was unable to stay in the game.

Durocher ordered Casey to warm up, and on short notice Hugh took the mound and almost cost the Dodgers the game. Lonnie Frey, the Dodgers' bête noire, hit a drive to deep center field for

ROBERT W. CREAMER

a double and possibly a triple. Frey tried for three, but Reiser made a magnificent throw to Reese, who threw a perfect relay to Lew Riggs at third to get Frey sliding. That saved a run and probably the game, because after getting a second out Casey gave up a double to Frank McCormick and singles to Ival Goodman and Mike McCormick (no relation to Frank). One run was in, the score was tied, the potential winning run was on third base and Ernie Lombardi, the massive catcher and a dangerous hitter, was up. There was a man on first base, but Durocher ordered Casey to walk Lombardi anyway and pitch to Eddie Joost. Joost grounded into a force play, and the game went on, tied 1–1, for four more innings.

The Dodgers put men on first and third with one out in the thirteenth inning, but Herman hit a line drive to Frey, who picked the runner off first for a double play. The Dodgers filled the bases in the fourteenth, but Lavagetto popped up to end the inning.

Reiser led off the sixteenth. He had been to bat six times in the game without a hit, but now he singled. Riggs laid down a bunt and was safe on a bad throw, with Reiser going all the way to third. Camilli struck out. Walker came to bat and Durocher signaled for a squeeze bunt. Walker dropped the bunt toward Frank McCormick at first base as Reiser raced for the plate. McCormick fielded it cleanly and threw the ball to Lombardi in an attempt to get the flying Reiser, but as a reporter described it, "Pete was almost in the dugout when Lom swung his glove around to tag him."

Now the Dodgers led 2–1, but the Reds had another turn at bat. In the bottom of the fifteenth Billy Werber led off with a single into the gap in right center and made the mistake of trying to stretch it into a double. Reiser's second great throw of the game nailed him at second base. Casey retired the next two batters and the Dodgers had an unforgettable victory.

In the second game the Reds scored two quick runs off Higbe in the first inning, but after that he settled in and did not allow a hit the rest of the game. The Dodgers tied it and Reiser drove in the winning run. He had only two hits in twelve at-bats in the doubleheader, but he scored the winning run in the first game after his first hit, drove in the winning run in the second with the other, and made two superior throws to help Brooklyn sweep a most dramatic doubleheader.

What made it particularly significant and the day so memorable was that in St. Louis the Giants beat the Cardinals twice, and the Dodgers moved to within a game of the lead. Fewer than 16,000 people came to see the league-leading Cardinals play—there were more than 36,000 at the doubleheader in Cincinnati—and maybe the disappointing attendance depressed the Cardinals. Their morale had to be low anyway: Mort Cooper, their best pitcher, had to have surgery on his elbow for the removal of a bone chip "as large as a lima bean." The Cardinals blew a lead in the ninth inning to lose the first game, and blew a lead in the seventh inning to lose the second game. Mize was back in the lineup and had a run-scoring single, but he also struck out three straight times.

The next day, after Herman Franks, the restored catcher, hit a three-run homer to beat the Pirates, the Dodgers were only half a game behind. They swept the Pirates, came home for a night game in Ebbets Field, won that one and moved into a tie for first place. That was when DiMaggio was closing in on Sisler's record, and except for passionate Brooklyn and St. Louis fans no one paid much heed to the Dodgers and Cardinals as they continued their scramble for first place. The Cardinals won on Friday when the Dodgers didn't play; the Dodgers won on Saturday when the Cardinals didn't. They each split a doubleheader on Sunday. On Monday, June 30, the Dodgers won while the Cardinals lost, and their hectic month ended with the two tied for first place, exactly as they had been on June 1.

Reiser hit the first pitch to him in the June 30th game for a triple and scored on a ground ball to the infield. The throw home was in plenty of time, but Reiser dropped away from the catcher at

ROBERT W. CREAMER

the last instant and slid past home plate to one side, just touching the plate with an outstretched hand as he passed. When he came to bat the next time he hit the first pitch for a home run. Two pitches, two hits, seven total bases, two runs scored. A few days earlier in Pittsburgh he nubbed a little squib hit past Arky Vaughan at shortstop and before Vaughan could run the ball down Reiser was on second base with a double.

Everyone was talking about him. He'd been leading the league in batting since May. He was hitting with power, hitting for average, getting the extra base, scoring unanticipated runs with his explosive speed. He was chasing down fly balls all over center field, and throwing out runners with his splendid arm. He was chunky, maybe five foot ten and 185 pounds. He had a smooth, remarkably compact swing. He batted lefthanded, although when he came up to the Dodgers he was a switch hitter.

Old Brooklyn fans still speak with awe of Reiser's debut in 1939. He was twenty, with only two years of experience in the low minors, but the Dodgers brought him to spring training for a look. They had gotten him on a fluke a year earlier. Reiser (everybody in baseball called him Reezer, although the correct pronunciation of the name is Rizer) grew up in St. Louis and was signed by the Cardinals as a teenager in 1937. In his first season in the Cardinals' system he was moved around among three Class D minor league teams. Commissioner Landis, in one of his periodic raids on what the newspapers called Rickey's "chain gang," declared eighty or ninety of the Cardinals' low-level farm hands free agents. Reiser was one of them.

Most of the freed Cardinal minor leaguers proved to be just that: minor leaguers. But there were a few prizes. One was a shortstop named Frank Croucher, who later played for Detroit, but a scout told MacPhail he ought to sign a kid named Harold Reiser.

The Dodgers gave the youngster a hundred dollars as a signing bonus and in 1938 sent him to Superior, Wisconsin, in the Class

D Northern League. In 1939 Durocher was so impressed by Reiser's hitting and fielding early in spring training that he was raving about him two weeks before Reiser ever played a game.

"I'm telling you," Durocher said to the press. "This boy is a whiz."

In the latter part of March Leo put him in a game for the first time, and in his first time at bat Reiser hit a three-run homer. He walked the next time up and then hit two singles, the only hits the Dodgers had in the last six innings. The next day he hit a single, hit another three-run homer, beat out a drag bunt and hit yet another home run. He had another base hit in his first at-bat the next day to make it eight hits in eight at-bats, but he strained his thigh scoring from first base on a double and Durocher sat him down for a couple of games.

By now everybody thought he was a whiz. He was called "Hal Reiser, the wonder boy," although soon everyone was calling him by his nickname, Pete. He went 0 for 3 in his next game—"REISER STOPPED!" a headline said—but walked twice and scored twice, and the day after that he hit another home run.

Pictures of Reiser began to appear in the newspapers. He was described as "Larry MacPhail's wonder child" and "the Frank Merriwell of the Brooklyn camp." Joe McCarthy said, "You need only one look at that boy to know he's a hitter." The Cardinal scout who discovered him said he'd be a National League regular by 1940, and there was conjecture that he would stick with the club in 1939.

When Durocher asked him one day if he thought he could hit the pitcher the Dodgers were about to face, Reiser said ingenuously, "I can hit any pitcher that ever threw a baseball." Durocher, who was in his first year as manager, wanted to put him on the Dodgers' major league roster, but MacPhail said no, the boy was too young, he needed experience; Larry said he was going back to the minors for at least one more year. Leo and Larry started

ROBERT W. CREAMER
‹‹‹‹‹‹‹‹‹‹‹‹‹‹‹‹‹‹‹‹‹‹‹‹‹

yelling at each other and MacPhail fired Durocher again, but Reiser was sent down to Elmira in the Class A Eastern League.

Some say it was Rickey who tipped MacPhail off to Reiser, and that he and Larry had a deal under which MacPhail would sell Reiser back to Rickey after two years, the length of time during which the commissioner barred the freed players from rejoining the Cardinals' system. A myth holds that MacPhail was furious when Durocher played Reiser and exposed him to public view, thereby endangering Larry's deal to return the rookie to St. Louis. That seems rather farfetched. If MacPhail was trying to keep Reiser hidden, why in the world would he bring him into a major league training camp?

MacPhail did get sore at Durocher, but it was over the question of sending Reiser out for more seasoning. At Elmira he had a good but not extraordinary year, and after spring training in 1940 he was sent down to Elmira again. This time he was sensational, and in midsummer he was called up to the Dodgers. He hit .293 in fifty-eight games, played a few times at shortstop after Reese broke his heel, but divided most of his time between third base and the outfield. In 1941 Durocher put him in center field and left him there, and Pete was everything Leo expected him to be until a sad talent for getting hurt ruined him as a great ballplayer. He was always running into walls, pulling muscles, getting beaned. Once he snapped a bone in his ankle running hard to first base. His worst injury, the one that really destroyed him, came in 1942 when he ran full tilt into the concrete outfield wall in Sportsman's Park in St. Louis, but up to then he was a dream, the perfect player.

"There will never be a ballplayer as good as Willie Mays," Durocher said in his autobiography, and then added, "but Reiser was every bit as good as Mays. He might have been better. Pete Reiser might have been the best ballplayer I ever saw. He had more power than Willie. He could throw as good as Willie. You think Willie Mays could run in his hey-day? You think Mickey Mantle could run? Name whoever you want to, and Pete Reiser was faster. And knew how to run the bases. Willie Mays had everything. Pete Reiser had everything but luck."

THE Cardinals edged into the lead again for a day or so at the beginning of July, but then fell back into a tie and on the Fourth of July lost another sickening doubleheader, this one to the Cubs. Brooklyn's Fourth of July doubleheader with the Giants was rained out, but with the Cardinals' double defeat the Dodgers found themselves alone in first place. They won the next day as the Cardinals lost and on Sunday, July 6, the last day before baseball closed down for three days for the All Star game, they won as the Cardinals lost again. Just like that, it seemed, Brooklyn had a solid hold on first place, three games ahead of the molting Red Birds.

29

DIMAGGIO, CHALLENGING

Although DiMaggio was the key to the Yankee revival other Yankees were swept along by his infectious force. Keller was particularly powerful, hitting more home runs than DiMaggio during the season and batting in only three fewer runs. Henrich and Gordon were almost as dangerous. Dickey, reviving after his terrible 1940 season, was remarkably productive, even though his backup, Rosar, caught about a third of the team's games. Rolfe, the third baseman, nearing the end of his short but impressive career, was about the only one of the old guard who didn't improve on 1940.

And then there was Rizzuto, back in the lineup because of Crosetti's injury. He immediately began hitting sharply and continued at a vigorous rate, batting .432 in the twenty games the Yankees played from the time of his return until the All Star game, and he went on to finish the season at .307. Crosetti didn't get his job back until Rizzuto went into service after the 1942 season, but contrary to the horror stories of how cruelly veteran players treated rookies in those dark days, Crosetti went out of his way to help Rizzuto.

Five days after his return Rizzuto was the slugging hero of the day. With DiMaggio now past the Yankee record and with Sisler's major league mark still several games ahead of him, interest in Joe's streak subsided just a little. Batting safely in his thirty-second, thirty-third, thirty-fourth games seemed pleasantly routine. The fans whooped just as loudly for Joe, but the team's other streak, the parade of home runs, was the big novelty now. A year earlier the Greenberg-led Tigers hit home runs in seventeen straight games. The Yankees' streak had reached sixteen, and they were playing Detroit in Yankee Stadium. In the first inning DiMaggio kept his hitting streak going with a single, which took the suspense out of his subsequent plate appearances. The Tigers took a commanding 7–1 lead behind Dizzy Trout, who stifled the Yankee home-run bats. DiMaggio had just the one single. Keller, who had hit a homer in each of the four previous games, went hitless. So did Gordon. So did Henrich.

When Rizzuto came to bat in the seventh inning he had hit only one major league home run, the game winner in the dark against Boston back in April, but now he hit a long fly ball that carried into the left-field seats. That tied the Tigers' record and, in a sense, surpassed it, since the Yankees had hit twenty-eight homers in their seventeen games, the Tigers only twenty-six in theirs. The crowd let out a huge roar of surprise at Rizzuto's blast, and the dugout cheered raucously as little Phil, a broad grin on his expressive face, trotted around the bases.

The next afternoon DiMaggio resumed the hero's role. He broke a 2–2 tie in the sixth by hitting a home run to the opposite field—Joe didn't always pull the ball down the third-base line or into the far reaches of Yankee Stadium's Death Valley in deep left–center field. That blow extended the home-run string to a record-breaking eighteen games and his own streak to thirty-five.

ROBERT W. CREAMER

Rolfe kept the home-run record going the next day with a poke in the second inning, and Henrich and Gordon also homered. But DiMaggio grounded out, fouled out and hit a fly to deep left. Finally, in the eighth inning, with the small crowd (the paid attendance of 9,081 was the lowest in Yankee Stadium since May 23) yelling rhythmically, "We want a hit! We want a hit!" Joe singled to left to keep the streak alive. The fans cheered, and then most of them got up and went home. Why wait around? The Yanks had a big lead, they had already hit a home run, and Joe had his hit for the day. His single was the biggest moment of the afternoon for the spectators, but it wasn't the newspaper story of the day. I have a clipping of that game with a headline that reads "YANKS EXTEND HOMER STREAK TO 19 GAMES." Under it, almost as an afterthought, a subhead says, "DiMaggio Hits in 36th Straight with Single in Last At Bat."

He hit a home run the next day to push his streak to thirty-seven and the home-run skein to twenty, and now the excitement and the attention shifted his way again. On June 26 before an even smaller Yankee Stadium crowd—8,602—he went through the most precarious day of his streak. Henrich hit a home run to prolong that string. Marius Russo pitched a no-hitter through six innings and had a 3–1 lead in the eighth. But DiMaggio had flied out in the second inning, was safe on an obvious error in the fourth and grounded out again in the sixth. With the way Russo was pitching it appeared unlikely that the Yankees would have to bat in the ninth. DiMaggio was the fourth man due up in the eighth. If the three Yankees ahead of him went out in order, he was done. The streak would end.

Sturm popped up for the first out, but Rolfe walked, and the crowd cheered. Now DiMaggio would at least get a chance to hit. But Henrich, the next batter, the thinking man, the one who preferred classical music to pop songs, the player the Yankees depended on so much in critical situations that in time he became known as "Old Reliable," thought of something. If he hit a sharp grounder or a line drive, it could be turned into a double play and DiMaggio would never get to bat. Before he moved into the batter's box Henrich went back to the dugout for a moment and spoke to McCarthy. Would it be okay if he sacrificed? Henrich, a power hitter, seldom bunted, but this way he could be reasonably certain of not hitting into a double play and DiMaggio would get his chance to hit.

McCarthy nodded. Sure, go ahead. Henrich laid down a perfect sacrifice and was thrown out, with Rolfe moving to second. An ecstatic cheer went up. DiMaggio was getting another shot.

What DiMaggio did then impresses me still, even after all these years. You'd think he would have waited at bat, taken a pitch or two to get his timing just right, to sound out the pitcher a little. Not at all. He swung at the first pitch and rifled the ball down the left-field line for a double. Oh, the cheers then!

His streak had reached thirty-eight, and the melodramatic last-minute hit gained a lot of attention, outside baseball as well as in. Sisler's record was now only three games away.

The Yankees had two games coming up with the Athletics in Philadelphia on Friday and Saturday and then a doubleheader with the Senators in Washington on Sunday. Playing at home is considered an advantage, but it wasn't so for DiMaggio. At home, with the Yankees winning almost every day now, they seldom came to bat in the ninth inning. On the road he wouldn't be cheated out of those ninth-inning at-bats.

DiMaggio acted with dispatch in Philadelphia on Friday. He hit the first pitch to him for a clean hit to center, and he later hit a home run to keep the team's homer streak going. Now he had thirty-nine straight, and the next day everybody in the country, it seemed, was paying attention. If he hit safely it would be forty straight, and forty had a nice historical sound. The Philadelphia pitcher, a righthander named Johnny Babich, had said that if he got DiMaggio out once he was not going to give him anything to hit, meaning he would keep his pitches away from the plate. He got DiMaggio out in the first inning on a bad pitch, and in the fourth he went to a three-and-nothing count. The next pitch was outside, a certain fourth ball, but DiMaggio reached across the plate and drove the ball on a line into right–center field. He had hit in forty straight.

The Yankees went on to Washington for the doubleheader with the Senators. Attendance the two previous days had been good for Philadelphia, whose fans were numb from watching terrible teams (the A's were in the process of falling into last place for the fifth time in seven years; the Phillies were finishing last for the fourth season in a row); but even so, Shibe Park had been little more than half filled. In Washington it was different. Old Clark Griffith had been ballyhooing the doubleheader for weeks. He must have prayed every night that the weather would be good and that DiMaggio's streak would still be alive when he got to Washington. If so, the Old Fox's prayers were answered. It was miserably hot and sultry, close to a hundred degrees and humid, a typical summer afternoon in the nation's capital, but there was no rain, nothing to keep an extraordinary crowd from filling Griffith Stadium. People from the North were there, people from the South, people from all over. DiMaggio's arrival in Washington was front-page news, and the stands filled early. People wanted to see DiMaggio take batting practice. There were newsreel cameramen and reporters from dozens of papers clustered around him before the double-header.

In the first game, he faced Emil (Dutch) Leonard, one of the best knuckleball pitchers of all time. He won twenty games in 1939 and 191 games in his career. Leonard got DiMaggio out the first two times he batted, but in the sixth inning Joe hit a liner to left–center field that bounced and rolled all the way to the fence for a double. He had hit in forty-one straight; he had tied Sisler's record. No, they didn't stop the game and give him the ball—they didn't do sentimental things like that in those days—but there were great cheers. When he scored from third a few minutes later on a passed ball, Gordon, the Yankee batter, reached out and shook his hand, which at the time seemed a remarkable thing for Gordon to do.

Between games the big crowd chattered and moved around, and in the confusion one of the spectators stole DiMaggio's bat from the rack in the Yankee dugout. Joe had other bats, of course—you never knew when you were going to crack or split one, although the thicker-handled bats of that era lasted longer than the thin-handled wands of today—but losing a favorite bat is upsetting to a ballplayer. DiMaggio was superstitious, as almost all major leaguers are, mostly in the matter of doing certain things the same way each day, especially if things are going well. Durocher, the natty dresser, would wear the same tie or the same slacks day after day during a winning streak.

As with children, routine is important to ballplayers; upsetting the routine is disturbing. Having such a violent change—the theft of his bat—just before a game in which he hoped to set a new major league record must have been shattering, but DiMaggio shook it off. His teammates seemed more shocked by the loss of the bat than he was.

He found another one to use, not one of his own reserve but an old bat of his that Henrich had borrowed early in the season. It wasn't identical to the bat he'd been using; ballplayers shave handles and bone the wood and rub them and make subtle changes in them. Nonetheless, the bat felt good when Henrich urged it on him, and he decided to use it.

He went hitless in his first three at-bats. He flied to right, lined out to shortstop, flied to center. In the seventh inning, against a big burly righthander named Arnold (Red) Anderson, he took the first pitch in tight for a ball and hit the second one on a line to left field for a single. He had done it. He had set a new record,

ROBERT W. CREAMER

forty-two straight games in which he had batted safely. They didn't stop this game either, but the Washington crowd, even though it was suffering through defeats in both ends of the doubleheader, roared its acclaim.

He scored later in the inning, and when he approached the dugout the Yankee players came out en masse to greet him. That's done every day now, but it was a rare thing to see in that more conservative age, a real departure from the manly ideal of not showing emotion. The stoical DiMaggio almost always kept his own feelings under control, but he aroused extraordinary displays of affection in others. The Yankee players later gave him a sterling-silver humidor with all their signatures etched on its cover as a tribute to him and his streak.

In the excitement over DiMaggio's achievement it was hardly noticed that home runs by Henrich in the first game and Keller in the second extended the Yankees' home-run record to twenty-five straight games. The homer streak ended in the next game, but fifty years later that remarkable example of sustained power was still the major league record.

In the clubhouse DiMaggio talked about his new record. "Sure, I'm tickled," he said. "Why wouldn't I be? It's swell." He praised McCarthy. "You've got to give him some of the credit. He let me hit at those three-and-nothing pitches. Ordinarily, you know, I couldn't do that, but McCarthy was with me all the time."

He was asked when he really became aware of his chance to catch Sisler. "I never really gave the record much thought," he said, "until I had hit in about thirty-three or thirty-five games. The first time I think I really worried was yesterday in Philadelphia."

As the game ended some of the players coming in from the bullpen spotted DiMaggio's stolen bat being carried out of the park by a spectator. There was no way he could hide it; it wasn't the kind of day you wore a coat. The players shouted for someone to stop the man, but the thief slipped through the crowd and got away. Less than a week later a friend of DiMaggio's named Jim Ceres heard from a man who said he had the bat. A ransom was asked. It was paid, the bat was handed over and Ceres returned it to DiMaggio.

ROBERT W. CREAMER

30

WILLIAMS' HOME RUN

iMaggio broke Sisler's mark on June 29, and he tied Willie Keeler's ancient record when the Yankees played again two days later, although at the time it seemed to take much longer than that for him to get to Keeler. Sisler happened on a Sunday and the Yankees had Monday off, so for two full days the morning and evening papers were filled with stories about DiMaggio breaking the one record and starting after the other.

Then, too, Keeler's record was so old and indistinct that it seemed a little unreal. Sisler's record of forty-one straight was the big one, the one Joe had to break. In those days, and up to the publication of the first edition of *The Baseball Encyclopedia* in 1969, little concrete attention was paid to baseball statistics from the nineteenth century. They seemed ethereal rather than factual, the stuff of "the Old Orioles" and Cap Anson, who were gone before 1900 arrived. Even Cy Young's 511 victories, more than half of which occurred before 1900, didn't seem quite valid. When we spoke of the great pitchers of the past we cited Christy Mathewson and Grover Cleveland Alexander and Walter Johnson, none of whom came anywhere close to Young's victory total but all of whom pitched exclusively in the 1900s. Young was back there in the mist, and so was Willie Keeler.

We heard about Keeler's forty-four straight several days before Joe reached Sisler's forty-one, though Dominic DiMaggio, in recalling 1941, said its existence came as a late surprise. I can't believe it was a surprise as much as it was a nuisance. Here Joe had broken the real record, and there was this nagging old one still to get by.

In any case DiMaggio and the Yankees returned from Washington to Yankee Stadium, where on July 1 a huge weekday afternoon crowd of 53,000 came out to welcome him home and to see if he could catch Keeler in the doubleheader the Yankees were playing that afternoon. The Yanks were only two games ahead of Cleveland in the pennant race, their still viable home-run record was up to twenty-five, and they were playing the Red Sox and Ted Williams, who was batting .408, but no one really cared. They were there to see DiMaggio.

There were great anticipatory cheers when Joe came to bat in the first inning of the first game, and great groans of disappointment when he fouled out to the first baseman. Next time up he hit a hard smash to third but was thrown out on a fine play by the Boston third baseman, Jim Tabor. In the fifth inning he hit a high bouncer to third and reached first just as Tabor's hurried throw pulled the first baseman off the bag. The scorer ruled it a hit but relatively few people in the big crowd knew that. There was no public-address announcement about it and nothing on the old-fashioned scoreboard to show that it was a hit. DiMaggio batted again in the sixth inning and rifled a clean single to left, and now the crowd roared in triumph. Even DiMaggio smiled with satisfaction as he stood on first base. He had hit in forty-three straight. One more to go.

ROBERT W. CREAMER
<<<<<<<<<<<<<<<<<<<<<<<<<<<<

The Yankees won the first game; the home-run streak ended; Williams had only one hit in four at-bats; and still no one cared—the only thing that mattered was what Joe would do in the second game. It was getting late when it started, and the hot, sultry day had turned dark, with clouds moving in and rain threatening. It was unlikely that the second game would go the full nine innings.

So DiMaggio ended the suspense by hitting a line single to center in the first inning to tie Keeler. The cheering from the exultant crowd lasted a long time. The game didn't. It was called by the umpires after five innings, just long enough to make it a legal game. The hit counted.

The next day DiMaggio went after Keeler's record aggressively. In his first at-bat he hit a long drive to deep right–center field and was out only because Boston's right fielder, Stan Spence, made a beautiful catch. In his second at-bat he hit a foul home run to left field, then hit another blistering ground ball to third base. Tabor made a superb backhand stop and threw to first base in time for the out.

In his third at-bat DiMaggio hit a line drive high over Williams' head in left field, and there was no question about this one. The crowd rose at the crack of the bat and yelled as the ball soared toward the seats. Williams turned all the way around and stood watching as it disappeared into the stands for a home run. Joe had broken Keeler's record.

With the crowd cheering, DiMaggio circled the bases and returned to the bench where everyone in the dugout, including the batboy, shook his hand. When the game was over he trotted in to the dugout from center field and a youth (or yout', as a New York fight manager used to call the type) jumped from the stands, grabbed DiMaggio's hat and raced toward the exit gate in right field. An usher and a park policeman went after him. During the game the exit area functioned as the visiting team's bullpen and Mike Ryba, a Boston relief pitcher, was walking in toward the dugout when he saw the chase. He threw a body block on the thief, "the likes of which you usually see in professional football," according to a newspaper account. The usher grabbed the cap and returned it to DiMaggio, and the cap snatcher left quietly.

DiMaggio now had forty-five straight, and he was in the clear, ahead of everybody. He was out there alone, flying. He ripped out seven hits in his next three games, including two doubles, a triple and a home run, and by the time the season paused for the All Star game he had extended his streak to forty-eight.

It was an exhilarating time for him and for everyone. I don't mean to be carping, but the idea has been presented that America's great interest in DiMaggio and his streak in 1941 was to a considerable extent an escape, a welcome diversion from the fearful news of war and America's increasing involvement in it. I don't agree. I think it was just the sheer joy of sharing in DiMaggio's achievement.

It was a wonderful feat, maintained over a long period. Whenever anyone does something marvelous, something truly admirable and endearing, other human beings feel a sense of pride and exaltation. We are pleased that someone human, someone who eats and breathes like us, who has arms and legs and ears and eyes like us, has done this splendid thing. It gives us a vicarious sense of accomplishment and even self-satisfaction. *We* did that. When we applauded DiMaggio we were applauding ourselves.

When Pete Rose, so sadly brought down later on, ran his hit streak to forty-four straight in 1978, attention was beginning to focus on him as it had on DiMaggio, and we weren't trying to escape reality then. If Rose had maintained his streak, if he had reached forty-eight straight and fifty straight and fifty-two straight, the attention would have bordered on the hysterical. If he had broken DiMaggio's record— Well, I don't know. What DiMaggio had going for him beyond the sheer impressiveness of his streak was his personality. His reticence might only have been a product of shyness, but it came out like dignity. And class. He looked so damned good. Pete Rose looked like the bosun's mate on a pirate

ROBERT W. CREAMER
<<<<<<<<<<<<<<<<<<<<<<<<<<<

ship in a Hollywood movie of the thirties; DiMaggio looked like the sea captain who captures the pirates. He never lost his poise. He was excellence.

IN Detroit, where the All Star game was to be played, a rumor spread that DiMaggio had been hurt in an auto accident, and there was audible relief before the game when he appeared on the field in uniform, the rumor dispelled. Many of the All Star players had "candid cameras," as the newly popular 35-mm cameras were called, and some had movie cameras. All of them took pictures of DiMaggio. When the All Star teams were introduced he and Feller received the greatest applause from the Detroit crowd (except for Rudy York, the lone Tiger in the American League lineup).

DiMaggio batted third for the American League while Williams hit fourth. Feller pitched the first three innings and shut down the National League with only one hit. Williams drove in the first run of the game with a double off Paul Derringer in the fourth, and after six innings the American League led 2–1.

Then the presumptive hero of the game emerged. He was Arky Vaughan, the renowned shortstop of the Pittsburgh Pirates, who was being bumped from his job that season by the Pittsburgh manager, Frank Frisch, who favored a young and not very promising infielder named Alf Anderson. Vaughan hit a two-run homer in the seventh inning to put the National League ahead 3–2, and in the eighth he hit another two-run homer to make the score 5–2.

The American League, the dominant league in those days, had won six of the first seven All Star games, but the Nationals had won the year before when they shut out the Americans 4–0. Then the Nationals won the World Series for the first time in six years, and now they were winning the All Star game again. People gave credit for this success to Bill McKechnie, the Cincinnati Reds' manager, who piloted the National League All Stars in both 1940 and 1941. All Star pitchers usually worked three innings, as Feller had, but in 1940 McKechnie had used four top pitchers for only two innings each and a fifth pitcher for one inning and came away with that shutout victory. He was using the same technique in 1941, pitching Wyatt, Derringer and Walters two innings each before turning to Claude Passeau of the Cubs in the seventh inning.

DiMaggio had not yet had a hit, not that it mattered as far as his streak was concerned. The All Star game was an exhibition, not a regular-season game. But the crowd wanted a hit from Joe and yelled for him to get one each time he batted, and it felt let down each time he failed. In the eighth inning, to the joy of the crowd, Joe doubled, and a moment later, after Passeau struck out Williams, he scored on his brother Dominic's double. But that was all the American League could do. The Nationals still led 5–3 going into the last half of the ninth.

McKechnie then abandoned his pitching pattern and let Passeau stay in the game for a third inning. The big righthander (he was six foot three and 200 pounds) got the first man out on a pop-up to Billy Herman, who was playing second base for the Nationals. But Ken Keltner hit a hard ground ball to short that took a bad hop and hit Eddie Miller, who had taken over for Vaughan, on the shoulder. Keltner was safe. Joe Gordon followed with a clean single to right. Passeau went to a three-and-two count on Cecil Travis and walked him, filling the bases with one out, and the great DiMaggio came to bat.

Detroit's American League crowd rose, yelling with joy. What a setting. The tying runs were on second and third, the winning run was on first, DiMaggio was up. The fans buzzed with anticipation.

But DiMaggio hit a bouncing ball to the shortstop, a grounder made to order for a fast, game-ending double play. Miller fielded it, hurried his throw and tossed the ball a little off-line to Herman at second base. Herman, veteran of a thousand double plays, caught the ball just as Travis slid in hard and relayed it a little awkwardly to first base. They missed the double play. Herman's throw pulled the first baseman off the bag and DiMaggio, running

ROBERT W. CREAMER

hard as always, was safe. The run scored. The game, which seemed over, was not over. The American League still had life.

Gordon was on third base, DiMaggio on first. There were two out, the score was 5–4 in favor of the Nationals, and Williams was up. He was a lefthanded hitter opposing the righthanded Passeau, who was facing his sixth batter in this third inning of pitching, and yet McKechnie stayed with him. He remembered that Passeau had struck out Williams in the eighth.

"Passeau was always tough," Williams said in his autobiography. "He had a fast tailing ball he'd jam a lefthanded hitter with, right into your fists, and if you weren't quick he'd get it past you. He worked the count to two balls and one strike, then he came in with that sliding fast ball around my belt, and I swung."

The first pitch was low for a ball. Williams fouled the second down the first-base line. The third was high and inside for ball two. The fourth was the tailing fast ball Williams spoke of, in on the fists. Obviously, Williams was waiting for it. "Be quick," he said to himself. "Be quick."

He hit the ball. Briggs Stadium in Detroit was famous as an easy home-run park, but Williams' towering blast down the right-field line was a home run the instant it left his bat. It would have been a home run anywhere. It soared on a high arc and hit against the green woodwork at the front of the roof high in right field. Three runs scored. The game was over now, but the American League had won, 7–5. Williams, laughing, clapping his hands, leaping like a young colt, bounded his way around the base paths and touched home plate. The All Stars on the American League bench ran toward home plate like small boys to pound Williams on the back, pat him, shake his hand. Feller, who had changed out of his uniform after his three innings of pitching, ran out on the field in his street clothes to greet Williams.

There had been dramatic moments in earlier All Star games— Ruth's home run in 1933, Carl Hubbell striking out five great hitters in a row in 1934, Feller coming on in relief in 1939 with the bases loaded and one out and ending the uprising with one pitch that was hit into an inning-ending double play. But Williams' homer, coming after Vaughan's two, made this the first truly exciting All Star *game,* and in half a century since there hasn't been another to top it.

Never before was so much emotion shown by All Star players after the game. The National Leaguers swore, kicked over stools, ripped off their uniforms. There was angry second guessing. McKechnie should have relieved Passeau. He should have walked Williams. He shouldn't have let humpty-dumpties play in the late innings. But managers stayed longer with good pitchers in those days; walking Williams would have put the winning run on second base; and those weren't humpty-dumpties; they were major league All Stars. After all, if Herman's throw had been just a little better the National League would have gotten the double play on Di-Maggio's grounder, and it would have won.

"How can you beat a team when you let them have five outs in the ninth inning?" McKechnie complained. "That's what we did."

Durocher, who coached first base for the Nationals, said, "There's no excuse for missing a double play like that."

Herman muttered an apology to McKechnie.

"Forget it," McKechnie said. "It's over."

Passeau seemed dazed.

"I threw him one inside about chest high," he said. Then, with an honest self-analysis seldom heard in baseball before or since, he added, "It must have been the wrong thing to do."

The Nationals were sad and angry, but the American League clubhouse was a roaring maelstrom of happy noise. Williams was the center of attention, grinning happily as the other players shook his hand, ruffled his hair, hugged him, patted his shoulder affectionately. If there was a precise moment when Williams was fully accepted by the baseball fraternity, this was it.

"I'm delighted," he kept saying. "Boy, was I glad to beat those guys this way. That's a moment I'll never forget."

ROBERT W. CREAMER

He never did. He played another sixteen seasons, batted .400, won six batting titles, won the Most Valuable Player award as his team won the pennant, hit three more homers in All Star play, hit another 450 homers in regular-season play, and was elected to the Hall of Fame. When it was all over he said the home run in Detroit was "the most thrilling hit of my life. It was a wonderful, wonderful day for me."

31

THE SUMMER BEFORE
THE WAR

The Germans invaded the Soviet Union on my brother's twenty-fifth birthday, and Hitler began his long slide into the toilet. It didn't seem so at first. The Germans used the blitzkrieg techniques that had been so successful in crushing Poland, Denmark and Norway, France and the Low Countries, Yugoslavia, Greece and Crete. In a week they were a hundred miles inside Russia with huge newspaper arrows showing Nazi armies headed toward Leningrad, Moscow, Kiev. Hitler's strategy was to divide, surround and wipe out the Soviet army, as he had done to other armies in earlier campaigns. After that he could continue on against nominal opposition to occupy the entire country and gather in all the wheat and oil and other resources he wanted. When he finished occupying all of the Soviet Union he would be in position to aid the Japanese in their conquest of China. After that—well, today Europe, tomorrow the world.

It didn't work out that way. Hitler's earlier campaigns had been a breeze, with the ultimate collapse of his enemies obvious after only a few days, or a week or two at the most. In Russia Hitler gained more territory in the first ten days than he had in any earlier campaign and he killed and captured Russians at an appalling rate, but catching and destroying the Soviet armies was like trying to punch his way through a sheet of soft plastic. The sheet gave way, but it didn't break. The Germans continued to advance, and the Russians continued to retreat, suffering defeat after defeat. But they rebuilt their armies from their vast population reserve, and as they withdrew they burned their fields, destroyed their factories, blew up their bridges, tore up their railroads—a scorched-earth policy designed to leave the conquering Germans with not much more than the dirt their tanks and troops were sitting on. The Germans swallowed great chunks of territory, but hundreds of thousands of Soviet troops still confronted them along an enormous line of battle that ran from the Baltic to the Black Sea.

After a while it became apparent that this would be no lightning war. For the first time since Hitler took power the German army was suffering extensive casualties. The conquest of Russia was going to be long, difficult and expensive, and the Germans were in it up to the ass. Now it was a month since the invasion, now two months, now three, and winter was coming. People were beginning to compare Hitler to Napoleon in 1812, and as it turned out they were right. Alexander de Seversky, an American aircraft designer and manufacturer, said in the spring of 1941, before Russia was invaded, that the part of the world under Nazi control would be increasingly plagued by shortages of critical materials, would be under increasing attack by enemy aviation and in large part would be using an increasingly undernourished labor force working sullenly and under coercion. At the low point of the war he indicated that Germany's defeat was inevitable.

Hitler's invasion of Russia was the turning point of the war. It eased the pressure on Britain, even though the devastating air attacks continued. A German invasion of England had been a dreaded possibility, even a probability, for a year. Now prospects for such an invasion had all but disappeared. Hitler had to take care of Russia first, and Britain breathed easier. America began sending help to Russia as it was already sending help to England. For those middle-of-the-road Americans who had been wondering whether a negotiated peace between Britain and Germany might not be a good idea, Hitler's double cross of Russia was final evidence that you couldn't do business with him. He could not be trusted. America, despite continued bleats from the America Firsters, became more united behind Roosevelt.

American Communists, noisily antiwar and anti-Britain since Stalin's 1939 pact with Hitler, did an abrupt about-face, stopped being isolationists and became interventionists. This second easy switch of allegiance just about finished Communism as a serious political influence in America, which it had been in the 1930s. Many bright, concerned people had embraced Communism as a way to a more equitable society and had looked upon the Soviet Union as an almost perfect state. M. R. (Morrie) Werner, a wonderfully irascible old man who worked for *Sports Illustrated* when I was there and who was markedly liberal in politics, told me that he traveled to Russia in the early 1930s to see for himself what it was like. When he came back, he discussed what he had seen with Edmund Wilson, the literary critic, an old friend who shared Morrie's concern about social and economic inequities. Werner and Wilson had both been born in an age when Russia was ruled by the czars, and Morrie dismissed the Soviet Union by saying "It's the same old tyranny." Wilson, who had not been to Russia, scoffed, saying, according to Werner, "Pish. Tush. Bullshit." A few years later Wilson visited the Soviet Union himself and when he returned he said to Werner, "Morrie, you were right."

Such disillusion with Communism spread slowly, and not until the Nazi-Soviet pact did many abandon their now-shattered ideal. Hard-core, hard-line Communists accepted the pact, criticized

Britain, called Roosevelt a warmonger for wanting to help Britain and encouraged labor unrest in defense industries. Their loyalty to Stalin impressed some wavering followers, but when they did their second about-face in 1941, the change of heart to a pro-British, pro-Roosevelt, prowar stance was so transparently servile that few intellectuals and labor activists took them seriously anymore.

Communism in America never had the appeal that socialism did. In the Depression years the Socialist Party had a much broader following than the Communists, with surprising strength in the Midwest and Southwest. Debs Garms, the National League batting champion in 1940, who was from Bangs, Texas, was named for Eugene V. Debs, a Socialist candidate for president five times in the early decades of the century.

What the Communists had was a ruthless understanding of the mechanics of political control. They understood how a small group of skillful people could run a group in which they were a distinct minority. When I was a junior in high school a delegation of seniors went into New York City to attend a meeting of the National Youth Association, a group that was supposed to rally the kids of the nation behind good causes, or whatever. A credo of anti-Semites at that time was that Jews were Communists. Perhaps that's why I was so impressed when Maurice Kurtz, a Jewish kid from our school, came back from the NYA meeting and said it was lousy and told me why. "The Communists took it over," he explained. "Nobody else could say a word. They rammed through everything they wanted."

The double switch from opposing Hitler to accommodating him to opposing him again castrated American Communism. We cheered for the Russians, rooted for them to stop Hitler, turned them into gallant heroes in our movies and even hummed the stirring Soviet anthem, "Meadowland," but only a handful of political automatons continued to follow the Stalin line. The party tried hard, but Communism as a political force was dead long before Joe McCarthy—the senator, not the manager—began waving papers around in the 1950s as he accused everyone he didn't like of being a Communist. A witch hunt is looking for something that isn't there, and that's what McCarthy did. Our country's shame is that so many paid attention to him.

IN the summer of 1941 I rooted for DiMaggio, the Dodgers and the Russians, and I played stickball on the beach. We used to go to a club on Long Island Sound called Milton Point. There were little huts, rather grandly called cabanas, that families rented to use as dressing rooms, and ours was next to that of the Boland family. I was in love with Claire Boland, who was about a million years older than I and already married to a big, strong, pleasant Swede named Arne Bleiberg. I wasn't really in love with her; I just thought she was great, and she was. The younger members of the families, along with friends that happened to be there, would choose up sides and play stickball on the sand. My brother and Jack Boland, as the oldest in each family, usually did the choosing up. The girls played. In that era when relatively few women played the so-called male sports, the girls were given an advantage. They were allowed to hit the tennis ball we played with as far as they could, but we boys had to make sure the balls we hit touched the ground before they passed a line drawn in the sand between first base and third. No fly balls for us, no long taters. The most effective hit was a well-hit grounder past third base that would reach the hard sand near the water and keep rolling.

Lord, those games were fun. My sister Martha once pitched a perfect game, gently laying the tennis ball over the plate while everybody tried to kill it. The greatest moment of all came one day when my stepsister Eleanor played. My father had married again a few years after my mother's death to a widow with three children, Eleanor, Elizabeth and Bill. Eleanor, who was about my age, was a cheerful, pretty girl, but she'd been overweight all her life. A few years earlier she had been very sick with rheumatic fever, and she wasn't supposed to do too much physically, which was a shame because she was a good athlete. She played golf, she was good at Ping-Pong, and she could swing a bat surprisingly well. But at the beach she usually just swam a little and sat on the sand.

On Labor Day, our last day at the beach that summer, Jack and my brother began to choose up sides. Eleanor came over and said she'd like to play. Jack had already picked me, and when he and Jerry started choosing the girls I whispered to Jack, "Take Eleanor! Take Eleanor!" He was startled that I wanted an overweight invalid on our side, but he picked her, and when the game started he put her at first base. Eleanor didn't have to run around there. All she had to do was catch the gentle lobs we tossed when one of us managed to field a grounder in the cuppy sand.

The game went along for an inning or so without incident. Then around the top of the third they got men—well, women—on second and third with two out and my brother coming up. I was playing an all-purpose short field behind second base. Jack was playing shortstop/third base, in close when the girls batted and deeper when the boys did. My brother hit a vicious shot that touched the sand legally before it passed the line and seemed on its way toward the hard sand and extra bases. Jack dove to his right and to his surprise, as much as to mine and everyone else's, came up with the ball. I think it was still spinning in his hands as he did. It was a great play, but for the barest moment he didn't know what to do with it. The female base runners were flitting safely toward third and home, and he knew he couldn't get either of them for the third out. My brother, who could run—he'd been a track man at Penn—was sprinting through the soft sand toward first base, where Eleanor stood, one foot on the base, leaning toward Jack with her hands out ready for the throw. A lot of the runs in our beach game were scored when throws got past inept fielders, and ordinarily Jack would have eaten the ball, held the second base runner at third, given up the run and let Jerry have the hit.

But he had made such a great play that it seemed a shame to stop there, and so with an "Oh, what the hell" attitude he fired the ball across his body toward first base as though he had Keith Hernandez there waiting for it. The throw was low and skipped off the sand about two feet in front of the base, but Eleanor calmly leaned down and scooped it out of the sand on the short hop for the third out of the inning. Jerry didn't have his hit, the run didn't score, the inning was over, and Jack Boland dropped to a sitting position on the sand and stared open-mouthed at my stepsister.

Then she came to bat for the first time. There were a couple of runners on base. Eleanor was a lefty thrower but a righty hitter, like Rickey Henderson. She wasn't allowed to run, so one of the other girls stood near, ready to pinch-run for her if she hit the ball. I think Jerry or another male must have been pitching because I remember the throws to the plate as being rather fast. Maybe it was Jerry, steaming a little over being robbed of his hit. Eleanor took one pitch, took another and then put coordination and her ample weight into a beautiful, powerful swing that shot the tennis ball far beyond the most distant outfielder. Her runner scooted gleefully around the bases behind the others, and Eleanor had a three-run homer that José Canseco would have been proud of. Jack, shaking his head in admiration, said to me, "Kid, you can pick 'em."

Later that afternoon I sat on the steps of the cabana with my sister Jane and my stepsister Elizabeth. I was listening to the Dodger game and watching Jerry and Jack and a couple of other older guys playing touch, using a knotted beach towel for a football. They'd been playing games on the beach all afternoon, but it was as though they couldn't get enough. Jerry had less than three weeks before he had to report to the air corps, and Jack was leaving at the same time for the navy. It was probably the influence of novels I had read about England on the eve of the First World War, but watching them I said aloud, "The summer before the war." Jane remembered the moment, and when I phoned Elizabeth in North Carolina to tell her I was writing a book about 1941 she said, "The summer before the war. Remember when you said that?"

Yes, I remember. And I remember the summer and the last day of the summer. Before this gets too hokey, let me add that Jerry came back and Jack came back and we all lived happily ever after—or for a long while anyway.

32

DIMAGGIO, TRIUMPHANT

After the All Star game DiMaggio resumed his position at the center of things. He and the Yankees left New York for what was in effect a triumphal tour of the West. The St. Louis Browns advertised his imminent appearance in the newspapers as though he were a circus coming to town. The Chicago White Sox drew 50,000 people to see him play in a Sunday doubleheader, the largest crowd in Comiskey Park in eight years.

DiMaggio responded like the superb performer he was. He had seventeen hits in his first thirty-one at-bats after the All Star game, the glory of his streak rising to a crescendo in its last eight games. He had four hits, including a home run, in his fiftieth straight game, and four hits in eight at-bats before the big crowd in Chicago when he extended the string to fifty-three. He had only one hit, a single, on my birthday, July 14, but the next day he had two and the day after that, in Cleveland, in his fifty-sixth straight game, he had three more.

It was so extraordinary. It was so satisfying. It filled some sort of human need to learn each day that DiMaggio had done it again, that he was still hitting, that his streak was still alive.

Then it ended, and the strange thing about that is that the game in which he was stopped, the one in which he failed, is far more famous that the game before it in which he reached the now almost sacred figure of fifty-six. It was as though the death of the man, so to speak, was more fascinating than his life, like the killing of Kennedy. The details are repeated, hashed over, relished.

In his first at-bat DiMaggio hit a smashing ground ball down the third-base line, almost directly over the base. Keltner was playing deep and near the line and he stabbed at the ball backhanded as it went by. He was in foul territory when he set himself and threw hard to first, just in time to get DiMaggio. Al Smith, the Cleveland starting pitcher, a lefthander, walked DiMaggio the second time he batted, but on his third at bat, in the seventh inning, DiMaggio pulled another hard grounder down the third-base line, and again Keltner made a fine play, grabbing the ball and nipping DiMaggio at first by less than a step.

DiMaggio came to bat for the fourth and last time in the eighth inning, with one out and the bases loaded. Jim Bagby, a right-hander, was the Cleveland pitcher now, and DiMaggio hit another hard grounder, this one to shortstop. It was like the ball he had hit in the All Star game, except that this time it *was* a double play. That ended the inning and apparently the streak.

People savoring the game remember that the Cleveland fans booed Smith when he walked DiMaggio. They did because while they wanted to see the Indians win they wanted to see DiMaggio hit safely and they were getting neither. In the last half of the ninth the Indians, behind 4–1, rallied to score twice and had the tying run on third base with no one out. Everyone figured if the Indians could get just the runner on third to score, and no more, the game would be tied and would go into extra innings and DiMaggio might get another chance to bat. The Indians could win the game later.

But the runner stayed on third while one batter grounded out, and when the second batter hit back to the pitcher the runner got hung up between third and home and was tagged out. The next man grounded out, the game was over and so was the streak.

The fond rendering of detail about that game helps explain something to me. I used to wonder why there were so many saints in the Christian hagiology, so many men and women who were exalted after their deaths to near-mythic proportions. Some, like St. Christopher and St. Philomena, were later demoted when Church officials investigating past records could find no factual verification of the deeds and virtues that had supposedly lifted them to sainthood. We can be amused in our superior modern way by the naivete of the medieval saint-makers. But in our own secular times Western civilization, proud of its pragmatic Enlightenment, has created its own saints—secular saints, to be sure, but saints nonetheless. Lenin in Russia. Kennedy in our country. Churchill in England. Elvis Presley. Maybe even Frank Sinatra in some circles. The reality of the life is softened and obscured by what people choose to believe, by what we say and think and believe about our heroes and heroines. Why was Joan of Arc—a soldier, a killer—a saint?

In baseball DiMaggio is surely a saint, and his downfall, his martyrdom, so to speak, at the hands of Keltner and Smith and Bagby fascinates modern America as much as Joan being burned at the stake fascinated medieval Europe. They both behaved so well.

As Mike Seidel writes, "DiMaggio spoke very carefully after the game." Pete Rose, you will remember, angrily accused the pitcher who stopped him of pitching "like it was the World Series," as though Gene Garber should have laid one in there for Pete to hit. DiMaggio on the other hand was outwardly gracious, although years later he was still simmering at the way Keltner had played his position that night. "Deep?" he said to Seidel. "My God, he was standing in left field." At the time he swallowed his disappointment, spoke carefully to the press and said he was relieved it was over.

But, he added, "I can't say I'm glad it's over. I wanted it to go on as long as it could."

So did we, Joe.

And it has.

DiMAGGIO'S streak obscured not only the pennant race in the National League but also his own team's remarkable charge toward the American League flag. We fans knew that the Yankees had knocked off Cleveland in mid-June and had taken a firm grip on first place in July, but we were so taken with what Joe was doing that we didn't really appreciate the magnitude of the Yankees' advance. What they did in baseball was what the Germans had hoped to do in Russia—destroy all opposition. Beginning on June 6 (two weeks before Hitler crossed the Soviet border) the Yankees moved in twenty-two days from a weak fourth to permanent posession of first place. Their drag-ass 25–22 record jumped spectacularly to 48–26 by the All Star game, and that was only the beginning, the breakthrough. A winning streak that started before the All Star game reached fourteen straight after it, and by July 17, when Joe's streak ended, the Yankees had won seventeen of eighteen and held a seven-game lead.

But they weren't through, and neither was DiMaggio. The day after his streak ended he banged a single and a double off Bobby Feller and was off on another run, a carefree, rampaging hitting binge that carried through sixteen games and lifted his average to within twenty points of Williams'. I saw one of those games. DiMaggio hit a homer. I watched him closely each time he got ready for a pitch. He was very still in the batter's box. He stood with his legs wide apart and took almost no stride when he swung. Andy Crichton, in a contrary mood, insisted it was a lousy stance, that it was too restricted, and that DiMaggio would have been an even better hitter if his feet had been a little closer together. Maybe. I don't know. I just remember watching as he stood in the batter's box waiting for a pitch, his hands back, his bat held rather high, though not as high as Jackie Robinson held his bat. DiMaggio never took his eyes off the pitcher. The only thing that wasn't still was the end of his bat, slowly moving like the tip of a cat's tail. When the pitcher began his delivery, the bat stopped moving and everything seemed to lock in with a click as DiMaggio got set. When he swung it was a smooth, graceful thrust of power. I thought it was a beautiful swing. No wasted motion, no fidgeting, no flash.

When the second streak ended early in August, DiMaggio was batting .381 and had hit safely in seventy-two of seventy-three games. Feller said in later years with disarming frankness, "You know, Joe had a little luck in his streak." Sure he did, but in seventy-two games out of seventy-three? In 1938 when Greenberg hit his fifty-eight home runs to come within two of matching Babe Ruth's then-record sixty, a consoling sportswriter said, "Hank, an awful lot of fly balls you hit just missed going over the fence." Greenberg replied, "Yeah, and a lot just barely got over. It all evens out."

It evened out with DiMaggio, too: a scratch hit here, but a brilliant defensive play that took away a hit there. Luck or no luck, he hit safely in fifty-six straight games, and seventy-two of seventy-three—and the luck went the other way in the one game he missed.

DiMaggio had an affinity for streaks. He had that twenty-seven-game run earlier in 1941 that began in spring training, and a year earlier he hit safely in twenty-three straight. In 1933 when he was an eighteen-year-old rookie with the San Francisco Seals he set a Pacific Coast League record by hitting in sixty-one straight. There had been some mention of that when he was nearing fifty-six games, but not too much was made of it. If he had reached fifty-nine or sixty, there would have been. And if he had passed sixty-one, someone would have dug up the all-time professional record of sixty-nine, made in 1919 by Joe Wilhoit of Wichita in the Class A Western League.

Possibly the most impressive measure of the validity of DiMaggio's streak is the realization that in all the years that professional baseball has been played in all the leagues from the nethermost minor circuit to the majors, there have been only five batting streaks that lasted fifty games or more, and DiMaggio has two of them. Here are the ten longest streaks of all time (major league performances are in capital letters):

69   Joe Wilhoit, Wichita, Western League, 1919
61   Joe DiMaggio, San Francisco, Pacific Coast League, 1933
56   JOE DiMAGGIO, NEW YORK, AMERICAN LEAGUE, 1941
55   Roman Mejias, Waco, Big State League, 1954
50   Otto Pahlman, Danville, Three-Eye League, 1922

49   Jack Ness, Oakland, Pacific Coast League, 1915
49   Harry Chozen, Mobile, Southern Association, 1945
46   John Bates, Nashville, Southern Association, 1925
44   WILLIE KEELER, BALTIMORE, NATIONAL LEAGUE, 1898
44   PETE ROSE, CINCINNATI, NATIONAL LEAGUE, 1978

The Yankees won nine straight during Joe's second streak and by August 2 had won forty-four and lost only eight of their last fifty-two games. Their three and a half game lead at All Star time had burgeoned to twelve over the Indians and to eighteen over the third-place Red Sox. They had blown the league apart. It was still almost two months to the end of the season, but the pennant race was over.

The Yankees appeared to know it, for they and DiMaggio more or less closed up shop until the World Series. The club blew both games of a Sunday doubleheader on August 3, and Joe went 0 for eight in the two games. He stopped hitting—his average plummeted twenty-five points in seventeen days—and the Yankees lost more than they won over the next few weeks. DiMaggio sprained his ankle on August 19 and was sidelined for twenty days. He wasn't even with the club (he had stayed back in New York, and so had Joe McCarthy) when the Yankees officially clinched the pennant in Boston on September 4, the earliest a major league team has ever locked up a championship.

Despite their indifferent play in August the Yankees kept expanding their lead and had a twenty-game margin when they clinched. This was because the Indians, after trying for two months to resist the Yankee onslaught, collapsed. Trosky broke his thumb, Feller won only two games in a month, and the Indians lost eighteen of twenty-one games.

I was pleased by the Yankees' twenty-game lead. I may have passed my nineteenth birthday, but I was still a little kid when it came to rooting, and a kid would rather have his team win 15–1 than 2–1 in ten innings. Excitement you could have; what I wanted was domination. I wanted the Yankees to win big, the bigger the better, and I relished the twenty-game lead and hoped it would grow larger. The 1927 Yankees had won by nineteen, the 1936 Yankees by nineteen and a half, and I wanted the 1941 team to win by more than that, by the biggest margin in American League history.

Alas, they went through the motions in September, and I resented it. I didn't like them using benchwarmers in the starting lineup and second-string pitchers on the mound, and I wasn't mollified when I read McCarthy's explanation: "I have some fellows here who need work. The others have won the pennant."

The Red Sox, after barely staying above .500 all season, staged a salary drive in September—or maybe at long last they were inspired by Williams' splendid hitting—and finished with a rush to end the year with a respectable 84–70 mark that cut the dawdling Yankees' final margin to only seventeen, which disappointed me. It wasn't much consolation that the Indians finished fourth, twenty-six games behind.

ROBERT W. CREAMER

33

THE DUEL BEGINS

I t was lovely the way the 1941 season meshed. DiMaggio had his turn, Williams had his and then DiMaggio took over again. When both DiMaggio and Williams were in the background in August and September the Dodgers and the Cardinals took their dazzling pennant two-step to the center of things, and then Williams finished up.

In talking about the National League race I begin to feel like the Ancient Mariner; I keep telling the same story over and over. But the National League pennant race was that way—a constant, unceasing battle between Brooklyn and St. Louis from April to the end of September. There were nine days very early in the season when neither team was in first place, but after that it was either one or the other in the lead with no one else close, all the way to the finish. The Cardinals were alone in first place seventy-three days, the Dodgers seventy-eight; there were seven times when the two were tied and eighteen other occasions when the two were in a virtual tie, separated by only a few percentage points.

The league lead changed hands seven times early in June, six times around the first of July, five times in the middle of August, three times around Labor Day. Almost all year long they were within two games of one another. There was a period just after the All Star game when the Cardinals fell three and a half and then four games back, for one day, but that changed in a hurry. Never were two big league teams more evenly matched. They played one another twenty-three times in 1941; Brooklyn won eleven, St. Louis won eleven, and the odd game was a twelve-inning 7–7 tie.

The two clubs had scrambled one way and the other through a hectic June before finishing the month as they started, in a tie, but the Cardinals entered July in a woozy state. They lost five in a row and eight of eleven at a time when the Dodgers were winning ten of thirteen and riding high.

The highest moment came in Ebbets Field against the Cubs. Higbe pitched nine shutout innings, but the Dodgers were unable to score against Vern Olsen, a good lefthander who had won thirteen games for Chicago the year before, and the teams went to the last half of the ninth still in a scoreless tie.

Medwick led off the inning with a single. Camilli, the slugger, laid down a sacrifice bunt. Walker was safe when Dahlgren, the ex-Yankee who was now with the Cubs, messed up a play. Medwick moved to third base on the error and the Dodgers had the winning run ninety feet from home with only one out.

Olsen walked Mickey Owen intentionally to fill the bases. The Cubs were looking for a force-out at the plate—or, with Higbe up, possibly a double play. The Cubs expected Higbe to bat. In those days you did not hit for your pitcher at a moment like that, not when the game was tied and the pitcher was throwing a shutout.

But Durocher was not conventional. He took Higbe out for a pinch hitter, and the pinch hitter he chose was himself. That was a daring thing for him to do. Although he was still technically an

ROBERT W. CREAMER

active player Leo appeared in only eighteen games all season, and even in his prime he was a terrible hitter, known throughout baseball as the All-American Out. Mark Belanger, the elegant fielding shortstop of the Baltimore Orioles in the sixties and seventies, was infamous for his poor hitting, but Durocher was worse than Belanger. Compare their batting averages each season with the overall league average and you'll see what I mean. In 1937, for example, Durocher hit sixty-nine points below the league average. The worst Belanger ever did was sixty points below, and Durocher matched that in 1930. There must be something about great fielding shortstops of French-Canadian extraction from western Massachusetts (Belanger was from Pittsfield, Durocher from Springfield) that makes them shy away from bats.

Nonetheless, Durocher put himself in to hit with the bases loaded, one out, a 0–0 score. Olsen's first pitch was a ball. On the second pitch Durocher laid down a perfect squeeze bunt between the mound and the third-base line. Olsen had no chance. By the time he picked up the ball Medwick was across home plate with the winning run. Olsen was so angry he threw the ball over the Ebbets Field grandstand.

Two days later the Cardinals, four games behind, came to Brooklyn for two games. For a team that had been in a slump for more than two weeks the Cardinals were remarkably chipper, regaling reporters before the game with stories about their victory over the Phils the day before. They had blown a game to the Phils two days earlier after leading 4–3 in the eighth, and they had almost blown this more recent one when the Phils tied the score in the ninth and filled the bases with no one out in the eleventh. But the Cardinals held the Phils off and won the game in the sixteenth when Jimmy Brown hit a fly ball to drive in Hopp with the winning tally.

That heart-stopper did wonders for the Cardinals' morale, because in Ebbets Field they burst into base hits. Slaughter doubled, Marion tripled; Crespi, Moore, Hopp and Mize singled in succession; Brown came through with a two-run base hit. They ran the bases with abandon and beat Wyatt 7–4. Then they routed Higbe the next day to sweep the two-game series from Brooklyn and move right back into it.

As they rose the Dodgers sank. Brooklyn lost the two to the Cardinals, two of three to Pittsburgh and another to Cincinnati. The last one was particularly disheartening. They were beating the Reds 4–1 in the ninth when Casey gave up a triple with the bases loaded and a long, scoring fly, and Brooklyn lost 5–4.

With the Dodgers' stumble the Cardinals moved into first place. Rickey's young pitchers were doing well enough, but it was the Cardinals' hitting that lifted the club. Crabtree, almost thirty-eight and used mostly as a pinch hitter, was batting .477. Mize was at .326, Hopp .324, Slaughter .320, Walker Cooper .310, Moore .309, Brown .308, Crespi .303, Triplett .299. It was a fearsome lineup of hitters, and most of them could run like the wind. Marion and Crespi were the best shortstop/second-base combination in the league, even better than Reese and Herman, and Moore and Slaughter seemed to make game-saving catches in the outfield every day.

The battered Dodgers crept into St. Louis near the end of July after losing both games of a Sunday doubleheader in Pittsburgh. (There were an awful lot of doubleheaders that season.) They were now two games behind, having lost six games in the standings in eleven days. They had three games with the Cardinals, the first on a hot, sticky St. Louis night with the temperature close to a hundred degrees. The oppressive heat was not eased by rain that delayed the start of the game for an hour. The Dodgers took a 6–1 lead but lost it when the Cardinals routed Higbe again. Durocher, making a rare start at shortstop in an effort to rouse his club, couldn't get to a pop fly along the left-field line that fell in for a double and later threw a ball wildly past third to let two runs score.

That moment was the pit of the season for Brooklyn. But they managed to tie the score, and the game went into extra innings. Casey pitched excellent ball in relief, but in the twelfth the Cardinals put men on first and third with one out. Walker Cooper tried to squeeze the run in from third. It was exactly the situation the Dodgers had against the Cubs, except that Cooper couldn't pull it off. Casey pounced on the bunt, threw the runner out at the plate and retired the next man to end the inning. By that time, under the curfew rules then in effect in baseball, it was too late to start another inning. The umpires called it a night and the game ended in a tie.

Although St. Louis beat Brooklyn again in their next game, the spirited tie seemed to revive the Dodgers. MacPhail had flown to St. Louis to see the Cardinal series and he presented Durocher with a new pitcher, the notoriously bad-tempered Johnny Allen, whom MacPhail had bought on waivers from the Browns. Allen had been a fine pitcher, but he was almost thirty-seven, a veteran of ten American League seasons. Yet he pitched well for Brooklyn, winning five games in the last two months of the season, which was as many as Feller won for the Indians.

Allen was also a presence, a very angry man, particularly on the ballfield. He'd flare up at opposing players, umpires, even his own teammates. You didn't dare play lackadaisically with Allen on the mound. Bill Grieve, a longtime major league umpire, was asked in an interview many years later who was the worst-tempered ballplayer he ever had to deal with.

"*Ohhh, Johnny Allen!*" he cried, as though there could never be anyone else.

In any case, after Allen arrived Brooklyn righted itself. Fitzsimmons, a pleasanter man than Allen, could get angry himself when he pitched and was just as tough a competitor. When the Cardinals knocked Wyatt around early in the third and final game of the series—Leo started his ace with short rest—Fitzsimmons was sent to the mound in the fourth inning. Freddie was a starting pitcher—

this was his only relief appearance in 1941—but Durocher's relievers had been losing too many games. Fitzsimmons pitched six fine innings, squeezed in a run with a bunt (as though to show the Cardinals how it was done) and won 9–5.

That was a big one. Instead of leaving St. Louis four games behind, as they would have if they lost, the Dodgers were only two back, and when they won the next day and the Cardinals lost, they were only a game behind. The extraordinary duel between the two teams that carried through August and September was about to begin. For the next five weeks, while the league lead changed eight times, neither team fell further than a game and a half behind (except for one day when the margin soared to two). Both clubs were over their mid-season slumps, and the Cardinals were at full strength for the first time since the early days of the season.

"Barring further injuries," said a confident Billy Southworth, "the Cardinals will win the pennant."

He had good reason for his optimism. He was in first place despite a casualty list few managers ever had to cope with. Most clubs suffer illnesses and injuries during a season, but the 1941 Cardinals were savagely hit. Second-baseman Crespi dislocated a finger. First-baseman Mize broke a finger. Third-baseman Brown broke his hand. Pitcher Mort Cooper had an operation on his elbow. Catcher Walker Cooper broke his shoulder. Left-fielder Padgett had tonsilitis. Center-fielder Moore sprained his shoulder. Relief pitcher Clyde Shoun jammed his ankle sliding. Right-fielder Slaughter had missed several games with various ailments. Catcher Mancuso, filling in for Cooper, had sprained fingers and aching legs.

Now everyone was healthy again, and the Cards felt ready to move. But so were the Dodgers, who won seven straight early in August. They were brimming with the new confidence that was theirs as the toast of New York. All eyes were on them. DiMaggio was quiescent, the American League pennant was in the bag, the rival Giants were floundering in fifth place. The Dodgers were now the city's team.

On a Saturday night in August, when the Dodgers were on the road, an evening of classical music was presented at Lewisohn Stadium, an arena in upper Manhattan (a long way from Ebbets Field) where open-air concerts were held regularly in the summer months. The featured work that Saturday was a new symphonic creation by the eminent American composer Robert Russell Bennett. Bennett called his piece "Symphony In D, for the Dodgers."

He said it was "a good-natured musical frolic, not to be taken too seriously," but it was nonetheless a symphony, set in four formal movements: Allegro con brio ("Brooklyn wins"); Andante lamentoso ("Brooklyn loses"); Scherzo ("MacPhail tries to give Cleveland the Brooklyn Bridge for Bobby Feller"); and Finale ("The Giants come to town").

The final movement was a chorale, an "Ode to Joy" type, according to Bennett, except that the featured soloist was Red Barber. Barber, of course, was not on the road with the Dodgers but in New York to do the re-created wire-report broadcasts of out-of-town games. His presence insured a packed house at Lewisohn Stadium. Arturo Toscanini's grandson persuaded his mother to take him to the concert not because of Bennett's composition but because Barber was going to be there.

Red's "solo" was a brisk imitation of his broadcasting technique, presented against a musical background. He began, "Here we go in the top of the ninth . . . ," described a Giant rally, a Brooklyn counter-rally, and ended ringingly, ". . . and it's a home run! That's the ballgame! The Dodgers win!"

I had been to Lewisohn Stadium with my aunt Gertrude to hear a Gershwin concert. (During one piece my aunt said, "This must be 'An American in Paris.' I can hear the Paris taxi horns," which impressed hell out of me. At that point I had never been farther from home than Buffalo.) But I didn't attend the Dodger symphony concert. What I remember about it was Stanley Woodward's comment in the *New York Herald-Tribune*. The concert had been originally scheduled for the previous Wednesday but had been canceled because of rain, and Woodward said the Saturday concert should have been a doubleheader.

THE Dodgers took first place on August 6 when Walker hit a ninth-inning triple to beat the Giants. St. Louis took it back the next day by beating the Reds 3–2 in eleven innings; old Estel Crabtree put the Cardinals ahead in the top of the inning, and Mort Cooper, recovered from his elbow surgery, kept them there when he got the last two Cincinnati batters to hit foul pop-ups with the bases loaded.

The Dodgers regained the lead by winning when the Cardinals were off, and held onto it when both lost the next day, both won doubleheaders the next, and both won single games the day after that. For five days they were in lockstep, only percentage points apart, and then both ran into trouble.

In St. Louis, Slaughter raced back into right center field for a long fly ball and tripped over Moore, who had run over from center field to make a diving catch. In trying to avoid Moore, Slaughter bounced off the outfield wall and fell awkwardly. He landed heavily on his shoulder and broke his collar bone. It was only August 11, but he was through for the season.

Even without Slaughter (Coaker Triplett took his place) the Cardinals won that day and the next, which was when disaster of a different sort hit Brooklyn. The Dodgers had a Tuesday doubleheader with the Giants and an impossibly large crowd of 39,135 pressed into Ebbets Field to see it. That means there were five thousand standees in the ballpark. There was joy in Brooklyn when the first game started; the Dodgers had beaten the Giants nine times in ten games since those three humiliating defeats at the start of the season, and the crowd expected the dominance to continue. Wyatt was pitching, Reiser was only one point behind in the batting race and Camilli was leading the league in home runs. What could go wrong?

What went wrong was the Giants knocked Wyatt out of the box in the first inning, Reiser went to bat nine times in the doubleheader without getting a hit, and the Dodgers lost both games and fell into second place.

34

THE DUEL GOES ON

For several days Brooklyn remained close behind. Then in mid-August in Boston Wyatt pitched a near-perfect game, retiring the first twenty-five Braves before giving up a single with one out in the ninth. That was the only base runner. The Dodgers won and when the Cardinals lost the standings were reversed. St. Louis fell behind.

As the Cardinals followed Brooklyn into Boston, Durocher and his men returned home for four games with Pittsburgh. The last time the Dodgers met the Pirates, they lost four out of five games. This time they won all four, while in Boston the Cardinals suffered yet another destructive injury. Terry Moore tried to duck away from a high pitch and was hit behind the left ear. He was carried off the field on a stretcher and taken by ambulance to a Boston hospital. Baseball was inured to beanings, and at first everyone assumed Moore would be in the lineup again in a day or so, but he suffered dizzy spells and was kept in the hospital when the

Cardinals left town. It wasn't until ten days later that he was released and flown from Boston to St. Louis. Taking the train was the standard manner of travel then, but the doctors were concerned about Moore's condition, and in St. Louis he was hospitalized for several more days.

It seemed incredible that the Cardinals should have suffered another injury. Every man in their starting lineup except Marion and Hopp had been badly hurt during the season, and two days after Moore was beaned Hopp jammed his wrist diving into a base and had to leave the game. He was back in a day or so, apparently okay, but his batting average, which was .333 when he hurt his wrist, dropped thirty points in the five weeks left in the season. And Max Lanier, one of the good young lefthanders, developed an inflamed elbow that kept him off the mound for a couple of weeks.

Four days after Moore was hurt the Cardinals and Dodgers met in Ebbets Field—St. Louis' last visit there in 1941. It was a peculiar series—a doubleheader Sunday and a doubleheader Tuesday, with a day off in between. Becase of the importance of the games four umpires were assigned to work the series instead of the usual three, but that didn't help much. Durocher beefed about everything, and so did Southworth. A sportswriter commented, "The four umpires kept getting in each other's way. Three umpires is company, but four is a damned nuisance."

The Cardinals won the first game of the first doubleheader and moved to within half a game of the lead, but the Dodgers stopped them in the second game when Wyatt outpitched Howie Pollet, a graceful lefthanded rookie the Cardinals had called up a week or so earlier from their Houston farm club. Pollet had won twenty-one games and lost only three at Houston, and he had pitched a four-hitter to win his major league debut on the day Moore was beaned. Pollet had a successful big league career—he would have won the Cy Young Award in 1946 if there had been such a trophy then—but he became almost a cult figure among baseball fans because of the way he threw the ball. He was the epitome of the cliche "a stylish lefthander." If you wanted a perfect statue of a pitcher, it was said, you would use Howie Pollet as the model. I didn't disagree with that. He was a lovely pitcher to watch. The fans in Ebbets Field, seeing him for the first time, were entranced by the rhythmic perfection of his pitching motion and began chanting, "One, two, *three!*" each time he threw the ball. They did the same thing after the war with Warren Spahn, although with Spahn the chant went, "One, two, three, *four!*"

Against Wyatt, Pollet pitched splendidly. The game was tied 2–2 in the ninth. If the Cardinals won they would move into first place again despite the loss of Slaughter and Moore and the injuries to Hopp and Lanier. But Reese beat out a bunt, Owen sacrificed him to second, and Wyatt hit a ringing single through the middle box to drive in the winning run. "Whitlow Wyatt for president!" yelled an ecstatic man coming out of a Brooklyn bar a couple of hours afterward.

The Dodgers won the first game of the Tuesday doubleheader but lost the second one to stay one and a half games in front. Of course, the Dodgers felt they should have swept the doubleheader. Fitzsimmons pitched shutout ball against Cooper for six innings. Brooklyn loaded the bases twice and couldn't score. In the seventh inning Reese let a ground ball go through his legs. A second ground ball, a double-play ball, was hit to Reese, and Pee Wee threw this one into the dirt. Fitzsimmons stomped around angrily. Now there were runners on first and third with no one out. Fitzsimmons, who had given up only two hits, growled at Reese and slammed the resin bag to the ground. The next batter hit a fly ball for what should have been the third out, but it drove in the first run of the game. Another man got on base, Hopp doubled, and Fitzsimmons and the Dodgers were three runs behind. Brooklyn scored in the seventh and again in the eighth, but the Dodgers lost 3–2.

The tight race went on. The Cardinals ran off a seven-game winning streak, but the Dodgers held on to first place until they played the Giants in the Polo Grounds near the end of August,

ROBERT W. CREAMER

when for the second time in three weeks they were shocked as the Giants beat them in both ends of a doubleheader. Just as the Giants took the lead in the second game the scoreboard showed that St. Louis had beaten Cincinnati. The Polo Grounds was two-thirds filled with Giant fans, and a huge shout of glee went up. The Giants finished the sweep of the doubleheader and Brooklyn was down in second place again, with September about to begin. To top it off the Dodgers learned later that Lon Warneke had pitched a no-hit, no-run game for the Cardinals.

IT was such an odd race. The Cardinals were clearly the outsiders, a young, injured team fighting bravely against the odds, but most people thought of Brooklyn as the underdog. The stigma of its losing past was too strong to dismiss. St. Louis had won five pennants and three world championships since the Dodgers last had a flag. The Cardinals were the rich kids on the block, the Dodgers the poor ones. Poor Brooklyn. Now their lovable Bums were stumbling again, in second place, faltering, while the Cardinals were winning every day. Warneke's no-hitter felt like the coup de grace.

It seemed almost a miracle on September 1 when Camilli repeatedly saved the day for Brooklyn in a fifteen-inning game with Boston. Dolph hit a home run with two out in the eighth inning to tie the game; he hit a double with two out in the bottom of the tenth to tie it again; and he hit a single with two out in the fifteenth to win it. That was the game I was listening to on Labor Day afternoon, our last day at the beach that summer. The war in Europe was two years old.

St. Louis played the same kind of extra-inning game a few days later with the Cubs—and lost it when Padgett dropped a fly ball in the eleventh. That was another miracle, from the Brooklyn standpoint.

After the Cardinals' winning streak ended they lost four out of five. After the Dodgers' doubleheader loss in the Polo Grounds they won seven of eight and recaptured first place. They played the Giants again and this time beat them three in a row. Camilli hit three homers. Reiser drove in the winning run in one of the games. Durocher stormed at the plate umpire after a called third strike on Camilli and was ordered off the field. The Ebbets Field crowd cheered Leo, booed the umpire and threw pop bottles at him. The game was held up until the mess was cleared away.

Brooklyn's lead lengthened to a fat three games by September 9 when the team left on its last road trip of the year. The trip began with a doubleheader in Chicago before the Dodgers moved on to St. Louis for three games with the Cardinals. After that they would play in Cincinnati, Pittsburgh, Philadelphia and Boston before returning to Brooklyn for two final games with the Phillies on the last weekend of the season.

Nineteen games left, seventeen on the road. This was the showdown, the trip that would settle the pennant race. As it turned out, all the tension and excitement of the first four and a half months of the pennant race were nothing compared to the next sixteen days.

ROBERT W. CREAMER

35

SHOWDOWN IN ST. LOUIS

In Chicago on September 10 the Dodgers lost two games to the Cubs, in St. Louis the Cardinals won two games from the Phils, and, that quickly, Brooklyn's fat lead was cut to one game. The Dodgers went into St. Louis the next day under the same pressure they had felt all season, except that they were facing the Cardinals for the last time in 1941 and had to win two of the three games just to stay in first place.

Durocher picked Fitzsimmons to pitch the important first game of the series. The old righthander had won only five games all season, but he had lost only one. The year before in a similar spot-starting role he had won sixteen and lost only two. That 21–3 record in twenty-seven starts impressed Durocher. Old Freddie was a money pitcher, and Leo wanted him.

Fitzsimmons was in a feisty mood as the game started, his ire directed at the Cardinals. He bad-mouthed them from the mound, called them names, threw at their feet, kept them loose at the plate. He was a knuckleballer, and he was not as sharp as he had been in the last game he pitched against the Cardinals, the one he lost to errors in Brooklyn, but he managed to get through the first two innings without yielding a run.

In the third he gave up a single to Jimmy Brown, who went on to second base when Medwick bobbled the ball. Camilli fielded Hopp's grounder cleanly, but Fitzsimmons, running toward first base to take Camilli's throw, slipped and fell, and Hopp was safe.

Fitzsimmons was an excellent fielding pitcher and he was angry at himself for falling down. He grew even angrier when Padgett followed with a hit that drove in the first run of the game. The next Cardinal batter was the dangerous Mize, and Fitzsimmons cursed him, saying something to the effect of "You fat melon head. *You're* not going to get a hit off me. You're going to end up flat on your ass."

He threw pitches inside, out on the corner, back inside again, yammering at Mize, who seemed a bit discomfited by Fitzsimmons' anger. Mize was a big, easygoing man who was so laid back that it earned him a lasting nickname some years later when he was hitting home runs for the Giants. A teammate said, "John, you got to hit fifteen homers to break Babe Ruth's record." Mize said, "I don't got to do anything but die." Bill Rigney noticed him one day sitting placidly on the bench before an important game. "Look at Mize," Rigney said. "Nothing bothers him. He looks like a big cat sleeping in the sun." The description fit, and from then on Mize was known as "the Big Cat."

Muttering and swearing on every pitch, Fitzsimmons fanned Mize and got Crabtree, who was playing center for Moore, to fly out. But he couldn't get Crespi, who singled to drive in another run, and the Cardinals led 2–0.

Fitzsimmons steamed his way to the bench and sat there fuming. His teammates had gone down in order through the first three innings, and five of them had struck out. Ernie White, the best of the Cardinals' rookie pitchers that season, had great stuff. As

ROBERT W. CREAMER

though to placate Fitz, Reese broke the string of outs by hitting a single to lead off the fourth inning and went to second on an infield out. Reiser was hit by a pitch, but with men on first and second and no one out, White got Medwick to hit a double-play ball to Marion. Marion, the nonpareil shortstop, fumbled the ball and the bases were loaded. A run came in on a fly ball, and then Camilli, the clutch hitter, belted a three-run homer to put Brooklyn on top 4–2.

Fitzsimmons held the Cardinals scoreless through the fourth, the fifth and the sixth. In the seventh he hit Brown, but Camilli made a great play on Hopp's hard-hit ground ball to force Brown at second. Padgett singled Hopp to third and again Mize came to bat with a runner in scoring position. Again, Fitzsimmons swore at Mize, insulted him.

"Fitz didn't like Mize," Durocher said. "I don't know why he didn't, but he didn't. He was on him all day."

The rotund Fitzsimmons had an idiosyncratic pitching motion in which he rotated completely away from the batter before spinning back and releasing the ball. In today's high-stolen-base era such a delivery wouldn't work with men on base, but in those days steals were infrequent. Few teams attempted more than two or three steals a week. Fitzsimmons spun away from the plate, wheeled back and threw, and Mize tapped the ball back to the box. Hopp was headed home, but Fitzsimmons ignored Hopp and threw to Reese at second, anticipating a brisk pitcher-to-shortstop-to-first double play to end the inning. Reese dropped the ball. Hopp scored, Padgett moved to second, Mize was safe at first, and Fitzsimmons was enraged.

He gave up a single to left field by Crabtree and Padgett tried to score from second on Medwick's arm. This time Joe made a perfect throw home to Owen, who tagged Padgett. Al Barlick, a rookie umpire that year, called Padgett out, but when the ball popped out of Owen's mitt Barlick reversed himself and called the runner safe. Fitzsimmons swore. Durocher made a long, loud, futile complaint to Barlick. Southworth came out to make sure Barlick didn't back down. The decision stood. The run counted. The score was tied 4–4.

Now Fitzsimmons was really angry, and Durocher went to the mound to soothe him. Fitzsimmons got Crespi to hit into a double play to end the inning. Gamely, he shut out the Cardinals in the eighth, the ninth and the tenth. White pitched scoreless ball after Camilli's home run, but in the eighth he gave up a two-out triple to Reiser and with Medwick at bat did something that had Medwick, Durocher and the other Dodgers screaming, "Balk! Balk!" Barlick, one of the few umpires elected to the Hall of Fame, disagreed. Durocher raised hell again, and again Southworth came out as amicus curiae. The argument ended, Medwick made out and the inning was over.

In the tenth inning, when Barlick called a borderline pitch to Marion a ball, Fitzsimmons shouted angrily and tossed his mitt high in the air in disgust. A pitch or two later Barlick called Marion out on strikes, and now Marion screamed at the young umpire. Southworth came flying off the bench like Durocher to join in the scolding.

The score was still tied in the top of the eleventh when Medwick led off with a line drive over the third baseman's head. Brown leaped and got his glove on the ball, knocked it down, picked it up and threw wildly to first base. White walked the next man to put Dodgers on first and second with no one out. Camilli came to bat and, as a sportswriter commented, everyone in the ballpark knew he was going to bunt. Except, apparently, Mize. The big first baseman came in hurriedly to field it, slipped, sat down and kicked the ball back toward home plate for an error.

The bases were loaded and no one was out. Southworth called the infield in to cut off the run at the plate. Casey Stengel said that when you pulled your infield in you turned a .200 hitter into a .300 hitter. Dixie Walker, who was already a .300 hitter, slapped a ground ball through the left side of the drawn-in infield to drive

ROBERT W. CREAMER
‹‹‹‹‹‹‹‹‹‹‹‹‹‹‹‹‹‹‹‹‹‹‹‹

in two runs and give Brooklyn the lead. Durocher sent in a pinch hitter to bat for the weary Fitzsimmons, and Hugh Casey retired the Cardinals in order in the last half of the eleventh. The game was over. The Dodgers had held onto first place.

BEFORE the game the next day Ford Frick, the league president, called the four umpires and the two managers into conference. He told Durocher and Southworth that the incessant hounding of the umpires had to stop. (It wasn't until later that the rule barring a manager from arguing about balls and strikes was instituted, but it had its genesis with Durocher.) Frick said Barlick and the other umpires had leaned over backward to keep from throwing people out of the game, but that that was going to change. Durocher started to say something, but Frick stopped him.

"This is not an argument," he said. "We are *telling* you that we are going to run the ball game. We are going to treat you as though you were eighth-place teams, and if a man's actions call for his dismissal from the game he will be dismissed. If it hurts either club, that's just too bad."

The game that day was quieter. Southworth yelled at the umpires a little, but he was more upset by his left fielder. With the Cardinals leading 2–0 in the fifth inning Padgett played a single into a triple and another single into a double. His misplays helped the Dodgers score twice, and Camilli hit a clean single to put them ahead. But in the sixth Crabtree drove in a run with a triple to bring the Cardinals even, and he scored a moment later on Crespi's fly ball. That was it. The Cardinals won 4–3.

The final game of the series, the last of the season between the two teams, was as good as baseball can get: two superb teams, the class of their league, fighting for a pennant, with their best pitchers, Wyatt and Cooper, facing one another. Wyatt allowed only three hits, Cooper the same, and Cooper had a no-hitter into the eighth inning. Even so, both pitchers had trouble. In the second inning Mize hit a long drive off Wyatt that Walker snared with a leaping catch against the outfield wall. In the fourth the Cardinals worked the Dodger pitcher for two bases on balls but were unable to score.

In the fifth Crespi led off with a base hit to right center and, as was his custom, stretched it to a double, diving headfirst into the base just ahead of the tag. Marion, the next batter, hit a ground ball to Reese. Crespi daringly raced for third base, and Reese threw the ball to Riggs, the Dodger third baseman, in an attempt to cut him down. The ball hit Crespi's shoulder just as the Cardinal base runner started to dive toward the bag. It bounced off him and past Riggs, far enough past so that even a slow runner should have been able to score. But Crespi didn't. He lay sprawled on the ground next to the base, unable to move. Reese's throw had knocked him off balance and he had landed heavily on top of the base and had the wind knocked out of him.

It was a startling tableau: the ball dancing away with Riggs chasing it, and Crespi lying inert, one hand resting on the base. Marion had reached second, and the crowd was in an uproar. Southworth was coaching at third and it must have taken all his self-restraint to keep from picking Crespi up bodily and pushing him toward home plate. But, of course, he couldn't touch him, couldn't help him until the play was over.

Riggs retrieved the ball, time was called, and Crespi was helped to his feet. After a few minutes he felt okay, and the game went on. It was still a scoreless tie, but the Cardinals had men on second and third with no one out. Wyatt stayed calm, taking plenty of time before each pitch. He struck out Mancuso, struck out Cooper and got Brown on a tap back to the mound. He was out of the inning.

When the Dodgers came to bat Cooper retired the first batter but walked the next two. Reiser was up, with Camilli to follow. Like Wyatt, Cooper rose to the challenge. He threw two strikes past Reiser and got him on a fly ball to left. He lost Camilli on a three-and-two pitch to fill the bases, but fooled Riggs, who topped the ball down the third-base line. Brown scooped it up and fired it to first in time for the third out.

It was still 0–0.

With two out in the Cardinal sixth Mize singled and Wyatt hit Crabtree on the foot with a low pitch. Franks, the Brooklyn catcher, claimed the ball hit his mitt first and caromed off it to Crabtree's foot. Wyatt ran to the plate to argue, and Durocher hurried from the dugout to join in. Babe Pinelli, the umpire, was quickly surrounded by shouting ballplayers. Press photographers, who were allowed on the field then, clustered around home plate to shoot pictures of the dispute. It was another long wrangle, but when it ended Crabtree was given first base.

A pitch got away from Franks, and the runners moved to second and third. Wyatt then issued an intentional walk to fill the bases. Marion hit a bounder through the middle that looked like a base hit and two runs for St. Louis, but Reese made a great play to stop the ball and tossed it to Herman at second base for a force-out to end the inning.

The scoreless tie continued through the seventh, and Cooper still had his no-hitter going into the eighth. Then it ended with a bang. Dixie Walker had popped up his two previous times at bat, but this time he stung Cooper for a double to right center. The St. Louis crowd groaned, and groaned again a moment later when Herman hit a double in the same direction, all the way to the wall. Walker scored easily and the Dodgers led 1–0.

It was still 1–0 when the Cardinals batted in the last of the ninth. The dangerous Crespi, leading off, pulled away from a pitch, half swung at it and dribbled an easy ground ball to Camilli for the first out. The Dodgers mocked Crespi as he trotted past their bench on his way to the Cardinal dugout, and Crespi shouted back at them until he disappeared into the dugout. Marion popped up for the second out. Then a great hopeful cheer went up from the St.

Louis crowd when Slaughter, supposedly through for the season, came out of the dugout to pinch-hit for Cooper. He had been in the hospital that morning.

Even an injured Slaughter could be dangerous, and Durocher hurried out to talk to Wyatt. Leo returned to the dugout, and Wyatt commenced pitching to Slaughter. Ball one. Strike one, called. Slaughter swung at the next one and missed. Wyatt threw again; Slaughter swung and struck out. The game was over. Underdog Brooklyn had won, 1–0, and left St. Louis with a two-game lead.

ROBERT W. CREAMER

36

HOW TO BAT .400

A fter his glorious moment at the All Star game, Williams quietly moved offstage and left DiMaggio alone in the spotlight for the last week of his famous streak. It wasn't intentional; it was just that Ted went into a small slump and then got hurt. In the first game the Red Sox played after the All Star break the venerable Lefty Grove went after his 300th win. Grove was an extraordinary pitcher, the greatest in major league history according to Bill James in his *Historical Baseball Abstract.* He was held back in the minors in the early 1920s, pitching five successive years in the International League before he was able to break loose and make it to the bigs. He was twenty-five before he pitched his first major-league game, but he led the American League in strikeouts in his first seven seasons. He averaged almost twenty-five wins a year for seven straight years; he led in winning percentage five times and earned-run average nine times. In 1931 he won thirty-one games and lost only four.

His arm went bad after the 1933 season and he dropped from twenty-four wins to eight, but he worked his way back into shape and won twenty games again in 1935. In 1938 he had a 14–4 record in mid-July when his arm went dead in the middle of a game. He could not feel the ball; he was unable to grip it. It was a circulation problem. Doctors said that if he tried to pitch again he could irreparably damage his arm, maybe even risk amputation. His career seemed over.

Grove rested until the following spring and then started pitching again, although not as frequently. He won fifteen games and lost only four in 1939. In 1940 at the age of forty he struggled to win seven games, and going into 1941, with 293 career victories in hand, he was determined to win seven more. "I want my 300," he said. Only eleven men before him had won 300, and only five since 1900.

In 1941 Grove pitched sparingly, but he pitched well. On June 25 he worked a complete game to win 7–2 for his fifth victory of the year and the 298th of his career. Eight days later he won 5–2 for his 299th, and in his next start, going for his 300th after the All Star break, he pitched a complete game and gave up only six hits but lost 2–0.

In that game Williams went zero for four and his average dropped from .407 to .398, the first time he had been under .400 since he began his batting spree in May. The next day Williams went hitless again, sprained his ankle sliding and had to leave the game.

He didn't play for several days as DiMaggio's streak reached its crescendo. Then he pinch-hit a few times without hitting safely, and his average drooped all the way down to .393. Grove, meanwhile, tried again for his 300th, pitched ten innings this time and lost again. Old Mose, as he was called, was not a mild-mannered man, and it is reasonable to assume that he was getting a little mad along about this time.

Williams came to his rescue. Ted's ankle was better, and after

 ROBERT W. CREAMER

getting a pinch-hit home run he returned to the lineup. He had a hit one day, a couple more the next and a couple the day after that, and by July 25 his average had climbed to .398. That was the day Grove, now four months past his forty-first birthday, took the mound again. This time he didn't pitch well at all, but this time the Red Sox hit for him. The score was 6–6 when Williams hit a two-run homer to put the Sox ahead. Boston won 10–6, Grove finally had his 300th victory and Williams' batting average at the end of the game had climbed to precisely .400 (104 hits in 260 at-bats).

Grove never won another ballgame, although he started several more times. Something was gone. His arm hurt. Late in August he pulled a muscle in his side pitching to the leadoff man in the first inning and had to leave the game. That was pretty much the end. His last start was on the final day of the 1941 season. Grove gave up four hits in one inning of pitching and left the mound. After the season he retired.

But Teddy Ballgame, as Williams liked to call himself, had helped Old Mose win his treasured 300th.

Williams was hot again, amazingly strong at the plate. He was walked frequently—it was a rare day when he did not receive at least one base on balls—and frequently he had only one or two official at-bats. Yet he had a hit in practically every game. After his little slump he lifted his average twenty points in two weeks. Throughout August he stayed close to .410, sometimes rising a point or two above that, sometimes dipping a few points below. When he had a rare hitless day his average would drop several points, and then he would force it back up again. On August 18 he was down to .405, but in his next three games he had seven hits in twelve at-bats, including five home runs, to lift it to .412, and he was still hitting .410 half a dozen days into September.

Except in Boston, where even his teammates were rooting for him ("He's become positively popular with the other players this year," wrote one newspaperman with obvious surprise), his

.400-plus average had not generated a great deal of attention. Attendance in the American League dropped off sharply after the Yankees tore the pennant race apart and DiMaggio stopped hitting. Yankee home attendance in 1941 was actually down a little from 1940, and Boston's was almost precisely the same. Didn't Williams' .400 average excite people? Not that much—at least not until very late in the season. Sure, we all knew that .400 was something special, but it was not the utter rarity it would be today. People ten years older than I—people who were then in their late twenties—clearly remembered the spate of .400 averages in the early 1920s, seven of them in six seasons. Bill Terry of the Giants had hit .401 in 1930, only a decade earlier. In 1939 DiMaggio had carried a .400 average into September. Joe was batting .409 as late as September 9, only to fall twenty-eight points in the last three weeks of the season to finish at .381.

So Williams' .410 average in early September was splendid but not yet earthshaking. What was earthshaking—or fascinating, any-way—was the *way* he was hitting. He wasn't choking up on the bat and poking safe little singles. He was swinging hard, smashing out doubles, home runs, line drives, long fly balls. He had been well behind in the home-run race earlier in the year, but he hit so many late-season dingers that he moved past the Yankees' Charlie Keller into the league lead.

And he was getting few good pitches to hit. Everybody was walking him. He was given 145 bases on balls that year, almost seventy more than DiMaggio. Slowly the scope of his achieve-ment—refusing to swing at bad balls, waiting for the right pitch, whacking hell out of it when it was over the plate—began to be appreciated. Now fans in and out of Boston were applauding when-ever he came to bat, and they loudly cheered each hit. In New York a week into September he wowed a Yankee Stadium crowd by hitting two doubles and a single to lift his average to .413. The Yankee fans even jeered their old favorite, Lefty Gomez, when he walked Ted.

ROBERT W. CREAMER
≪≪≪≪≪≪≪≪≪≪≪≪≪≪≪≪≪≪≪≪

Williams held his average at .413 through September 11. There were only fifteen games left in the season, but maintaining the blistering pace was becoming increasingly difficult. For a man as sensitive to press coverage and fan comments as Williams was, the pressure must have been excruciating. There was the applause each time he batted, the pleas for a hit from the grandstand, the approving attention of his teammates and the concomitant need to come through. He was in the newspapers every day, and in Boston the press coverage was smothering: there were headlines about him, photographs, cartoons, news stories, features, columns, sidebars, special boxes of statistics on what he had done so far and what he had to do to hit .400.

He went hitless in two successive games (in only four official at-bats) and his average dropped four points to .409. It hovered there for a few more days before another hitless game dropped him to .405, with little more than a week to go. The Red Sox played their last home games of the season on Saturday and Sunday, September 20 and 21, and Williams had three hits in seven at-bats, including his thirty-sixth homer of the year. That splurge lifted his average only a point to .406.

The Red Sox had three games in Washington during the last week of the season and three in Philadelphia. Williams had one hit on the first day in Washington to keep his average at .405 (or precisely .4051, compared to the .4055 it had been the day before; people were beginning to use four decimal points when they discussed Williams' hitting). But the next day in a doubleheader against the Senators he stumbled badly, getting only one hit in seven at-bats—and that one an infield single that he barely beat out. One hit in seven at-bats, and his average plummeted all the way down to .401. He had batted only .270 since September 10, and his average had fallen twelve points.

The Red Sox had the next two days off before playing the final three games of the season in Philadelphia—a single game against the Athletics Saturday and a doubleheader Sunday. In Boston during the two days of waiting everyone became a statistics expert; everyone knew that two more outs would drop Ted's average below .400. A newspaper headline cried "WILLIAMS' BACK TO WALL IN BID FOR .400 AVERAGE."

People began to say that Williams ought to sit out the final three games and not play in Philly. That way he would end the season hitting .401. Joe Cronin, the Red Sox manager, toyed with the idea and mentioned it to Williams, but Williams insisted on playing. He wasn't talking much to the Boston writers, but Cronin passed the word along that Ted said he didn't want any mollycoddling to protect his .400 average. He'd hang in there. He'd play. The writers expressed approval. It seemed the right and proper thing to do.

Cronin wasn't so sure.

"You've got to admire the kid for being so courageous," he said, "but if he gets his hits I may yank him in the second game Sunday, and I'll tell you why. Shibe Park is the roughest ballpark in the world to hit in this time of year. The afternoon shadows from those high stands make it awfully tough on a batter in September. The pitcher is in the sun and the plate is in the shadows, and you can't see the ball. And Daylight Saving ends on Sunday. It could be pretty dark by the time the second game gets under way. I feel I have obligations and I may take him out of the second game, even if he doesn't like it."

In Philadelphia on Friday, an off day, Williams went to Shibe Park with a coach and a catcher and took some extra batting practice. He kept experimenting in the batter's box with the placement of his front foot, sometimes pointing the toe more toward second base, then again more toward third. A sportswriter watching said, "He's worried, though you can't get him to say so. He must be a little on the panic side."

If so, it didn't bother him much during that practice session. He lined ball after ball off the right-field wall and several over it. Afterward the writers asked him about Shibe Park.

ROBERT W. CREAMER
‹‹‹‹‹‹‹‹‹‹‹‹‹‹‹‹‹‹‹‹‹‹‹‹‹

"Hitting here this time of year is a headache," Williams said. "The shadows are bad. You don't get a good look at the ball.

"But I'm not alibiing," he said. "I want to hit over .400, but I'm going to play all three games here even if I don't hit a ball out of the infield. The record's no good unless it's made in all the games."

On Saturday Williams had only one hit in four at-bats and his average fell to .39955. Baseball's long-standing practice was—and is—to round off batting averages to the nearest three numbers. A .2994 average is rounded down to .299; a .2995 average is rounded up to .300. Technically, Williams' .39955 average would round off to an even .400 and would be so listed.

Again, there was talk about Cronin keeping Williams on the bench Sunday to preserve the .400 average. However, the hard fact remained that he was not hitting .400 but .39955. I remember a New York newspaper that Sunday morning saying "WILLIAMS DROPS BELOW .400." A Boston headline that same day referred to Williams' "controversial .39955." If Ted hadn't played on Sunday his batting average might have been listed in the record books as .400, but no matter how you rounded it off the .39955 figure would have echoed and reechoed through baseball history.

Cronin was besieged by newspapermen asking if he was going to keep Williams out of the Sunday doubleheader. The manager said he suggested it to Williams, but that Ted refused. Cronin said afterward that he was worried to death Sunday morning that his young slugger wouldn't make his .400 average that afternoon, and he wondered whether he shouldn't bench him anyway. Perhaps Cronin felt remorse for not having kept the youngster on the bench the day before, when his average was definitely above .400.

Williams didn't appear confident before the doubleheader on the last day of the season. About all he would say was "I hope I can hit .400," before turning the conversation to a postseason barnstorming trip he and Jimmie Foxx were going on.

Then the first game started. Williams, who was batting fourth, came up for the first time in the second inning. Batting against Dick Fowler, a six-foot-four-and-one-half-inch rookie righthander from Canada, he took ball one and ball two and then rammed a ground single through the right side of the infield. That lifted his average back over .400 to .401.

He came to bat for the second time in the fifth inning. Fowler missed with his first pitch but came in with the second, and Williams hit it 440 feet over the right-field fence for a long home run. His average was now .402.

The game had become a free-hitting affair, and he batted again the next inning. With the count two balls and no strikes, batting now against a lefthander named Porter Vaughan, he hit another grounder through the hole into right field for his third straight hit.

That raised his average to .404 and practically guaranteed he would finish over .400. He'd have had to go hitless in his next five times at bat for his average to fall below that mark. Everyone seemed aware of that and the Red Sox players in the dugout were cheering as vigorously as the crowd was. "His teammates don't consider him a necessary evil anymore," wrote a Boston sportswriter.

Williams came up again in the seventh inning. This time he cracked a line-drive single over the first baseman's head for his fourth straight hit. In the ninth he sent another grounder to the right side, but this one was bobbled by the second baseman for an error. He'd gone four for five. The Red Sox, losing 11–10 in the ninth, won the game 12–11 when their pitcher, Broadway Charlie Wagner, hit a single to drive in the tying and winning runs.

For all the hitting (the Red Sox had sixteen hits, the Athletics fifteen) the game was over in two hours and two minutes. The second game, called after the eighth inning because of the darkness in "the crater that was Shibe Park," as someone described the Philadelphia ballpark, took only an hour and thirty-one minutes to play. Williams batted three times. He hit yet another ground-ball single to right in his first at-bat, but in his second time

ROBERT W. CREAMER

Along with batting over .400, Williams achieved the single most gratifying moment of his long career in 1941. That came in the last half of the ninth inning of the All Star game when, with two out and two on, Ted hit a three-run homer to win the game for the American League. A youthful fan who had run toward home plate watched Joe DiMaggio (5) and Dominic DiMaggio (30) greet Williams as the grinning slugger crossed home plate. Joe Gordon of the Yankees, who scored on the home run, smiled at the happy scene, and a gleeful Cecil Travis of the Washington Senators (holding bats) ran toward the plate to add his congratulations.

DiMaggio's hitting streak preoccupied baseball in June and July as the Yankee hero batted safely in game after game, relentlessly passing one old record after another until he stood alone. In Cleveland on July 16 (above), he calmly watched a single fall safely in the first inning of a game with the Indians to extend his record to 56 straight games. The next night the Indians stopped him, and the great hitting streak was over.

The Yankees savored the hitting streak as much as DiMaggio did, cheering when he batted safely and sharing the joy. When DiMaggio smiled broadly after breaking George Sisler's modern record of 41 straight, even the unemotional manager, Joe McCarthy, cracked a smile as he shook hands with Joe. Infielder Gerry Priddy (left) and coach Art Fletcher were more restrained.

Tommy Henrich, the Yankees' reliable right fielder, took advantage of the three days he had off during the All Star break to marry pretty Eileen O'Reilly, a nurse he had met a year earlier when he was hospitalized with a leg injury.

At 41, Lefty Grove of the Boston Red Sox, called by some the greatest pitcher of all time, won his 300th game with the help of a Ted Williams' home run. It was Grove's last victory. His arm went bad and after the season he retired.

Under the astute direction of Manager Billy Southworth (right) the St. Louis Cardinals mounted a season-long challenge to the Dodgers in 1941, relying mainly on the speed, fielding prowess and batting skill of such brilliant players as the youthful Enos Slaughter (below, when he still had a full head of hair). Late in the season the Cardinals added one more glittering star to their roster when they brought up a hard-hitting rookie outfielder named Stan Musial (below, right), who hit .426 in September.

The Dodgers, led by the disputatious Durocher (2), were always arguing with and hassling umpires. In Wrigley Field Brooklyn first baseman Dolph Camilli (left) watched while Durocher poked a finger at little umpire Bill Stewart. Big umpire George Magerkurth (right) tried to make a point, but the argument ended with the Dodger manager tossed out of the game, which was nothing new.

Of all the umpires the Dodgers tangled with, Magerkurth, sometimes called "Meathead", was Brooklyn's most obvious antagonist. In a crucial game in September 1941 he called a balk on a Dodger pitcher that sent home the tying run, initiated a furious argument and led to fines for Durocher and several of his players.

Durocher relied heavily on 40-year-old Freddie Fitzsimmons in clutch games, and the burly veteran responded with key victories.

In the 1941 World Series, Joe Gordon of
the Yankees got on base his first eight
times at bat, hit safely in every game,
batted .500 against Brooklyn's pitching
and led all infielders with 19 assists.
He was the star of the show.

Brooklyn always lived on the edge of
doom. Before the fourth game of the
Series apprehensive Dodger fans
hung a sign from the upper deck in
Ebbets Field that said, WE WAITED
21 YEARS DON'T FAIL US NOW. But
fail them the Dodgers did. In the
ninth inning of that game, catcher
Mickey Owen could not hold on to
a third strike that would have ended
the game and tied the Series with
the Yankees at two games apiece.

The precise moment of doom for the Dodgers came after Henrich swung and missed, apparently striking out to end the fourth game of the Series, with the Yankees and Dodgers tied at two victories apiece. But the pitch, a low fast-breaking curve ball, eluded catcher Owen's glove (above). As it ricocheted away (below) Henrich sprinted toward first base and made it safely. The game was not over. The Yankees, given a life, exploded with a single, a double, a walk and another double to score four runs. They won 7-4 to take a three-one lead in games. The Dodgers were dead. The next day the Yankees won the Series.

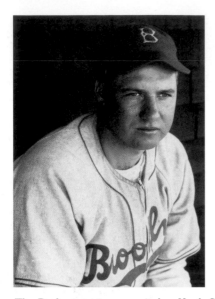

The Dodger goats were pitcher Hugh Casey and catcher Mickey Owen. Owen missed the pitch he should have caught, but Casey, who had pitched splendidly in relief for four innings, lost his poise after the incident and gave up three hits and two walks before the fateful inning was over.

Two months after the World Series ended the Japanese bombed Pearl Harbor and the United States was at war, as soldiers at the Presidio in San Francisco learned from radio and newspaper reports. Military service had called only two first-line major leaguers (Hugh Mulcahy and Hank Greenberg) during the 1941 season, but now hundreds more were to follow.

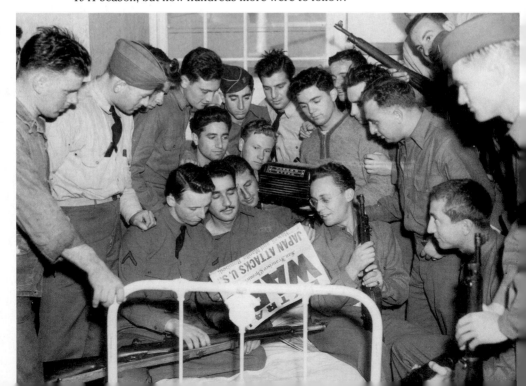

up, facing a rookie righthander named Fred Caligiuri, he hit a tremendous shot on a line to right center field that hit the loudspeaker horns of the public-address system under the 460-foot sign. One writer said it was the hardest Williams had hit a ball in his three seasons with the Red Sox. The ball punched a clean hole in one of the speaker horns, fell back onto the playing field, and Williams was held to a double.

It was the seventh straight time he'd been on base in the doubleheader. He had one more at-bat and for the first time all day he made out, hitting a fly ball to left field. He had had six hits in his eight at-bats and lifted his average six points on the last day of the season to .406 (or, to be precise, .4057).

"Can you imagine that kid?" a beaming Joe Cronin said after the game. "Four singles, a double and a homer when the chips were down!"

He kept talking about Williams.

"I tell you, I never came closer to crying on a ballfield than I did when Ted got that third hit. I really filled up. I was so happy the kid had done it. And without asking any favors or being given any."

Someone mentioned the Most Valuable Player award to Williams, and the youngster's face grew serious.

"Do you think there's a chance I could win it?" he asked.

Then, as though dismissing the idea (DiMaggio eventually won it), he smiled again and said, "Even if I don't, I'll be satisfied with this. What a thrill! I wasn't saying much about it before the game, but I never wanted anything harder in my life."

Later, some writers suggested that the Philadelphia pitchers had grooved pitches to Williams, but Bill McGowan, who umpired behind the plate in the first game, dismissed that idea.

"Don't let anyone tell you that," he said. "Those Philadelphia pitchers were bearing down. They threw some great curve balls."

But what the Philadelphia pitchers did to help Williams was to pitch to him. He did not receive one base on balls in the doubleheader. The five official at-bats he had in the first game were the most Williams had had in a game since September 1.

"If ever a player deserved to hit .400, it's Ted," said Cronin. "He never sat down against tough pitchers. He never bunted. He didn't have the advantage of the sacrifice-fly rule like those .400 hitters before him."

Under the sacrifice-fly rule a batter is not charged with a time at bat if a fly ball he hits drives in a run. For some reason the rule was not in effect for a number of years in the middle decades of the century, and 1941 was one of those years.

Cronin was asked, "How many sacrifice flies would you say Williams hit this year?"

"I'd say about fourteen," Cronin replied.

I have not been able to determine exactly how many sacrifice flies Williams did hit in 1941, but Cronin's estimate of about two a month seems reasonable. If those fourteen at-bats were deducted from the 456 official at-bats Williams was charged with, his final average in 1941 would have been .419 rather than .406, and we never would have had the drama of his final day.

ROBERT W. CREAMER

37

GENERAL LEAR
DEFENDS MEMPHIS

During the dramatic baseball summer momentous events were taking place throughout the world. The Germans kept pushing into Russia. American freighters and oilers were going down, most notably one called the *Robin Moor,* which was stopped by German raiders 750 miles off the west coast of Africa and sunk after the eight passengers and thirty-four members of the crew were put into four lifeboats. Roosevelt angrily protested that the ship was far from any war zone, and an attempt was made to turn the *Robin Moor* affair into a cause célèbre like the *Lusitania* in World War I or the *Maine* ("Remember the Maine!") at the time of the Spanish-American War. But Americans at the time were more interested in the *Robin Moor* as a saga of adventure; the lifeboats floated on the Atlantic for eighteen days before the people in them were rescued. Alfred Hitchcock's war movie *Lifeboat* was inspired by the ordeal.

Roosevelt and Churchill both mysteriously "disappeared" for a few days in August, and when they resurfaced in Washington and London it turned out that they had met secretly on board a U.S. cruiser off the coast of Newfoundland. Although America was not at war and Britain was, the two came to a basic agreement about what had to be done. Nazi Germany had to be defeated, and the postwar world should be a free world led by America and Britain. It didn't quite work out that way, but in August 1941 no one knew that the Soviet Union would not only survive the German invasion but would come out of the war a far more powerful nation than Great Britain.

Roosevelt and Churchill proclaimed their common purpose in what came to be called the Atlantic Charter, and photographs of the two sitting side by side surrounded by military aides provided a strong symbol of the unified aims of the two countries. A week or so later Churchill made a speech about the meeting that was carried on American radio. I remember being annoyed because Red Barber's play-by-play broadcast was interrupted in mid-game so that WOR could air Churchill's speech. However, I don't remember the speech. I must have turned the radio off.

What most people my age do remember about that meeting was that during it Roosevelt proclaimed the "Four Freedoms" that he said all mankind was entitled to. They were Freedom of Speech, Freedom of Worship, Freedom from Want, Freedom from Fear. Those words impressed a world battered by the Depression, totalitarianism and war. Norman Rockwell, the laureate of American illustrators, whose homey, idealized *Saturday Evening Post* covers of American life were enormously popular, did four paintings to illustrate the Four Freedoms, and I doubt you could find anyone of my generation who doesn't remember them.

Yet it was all part of our slide into war. I suppose, or I assume, that war was inevitable and that Roosevelt realized it was and was getting us ready for it. I don't recall paying much attention to events in the Far East before December, but I know now that the United States and Japan had been at economic war for at least two years and that the militarists and expansionists in Japan didn't seem to care that their country was on a collision course with America. But the moderate Japanese prime minister, Prince Konoye, was concerned, and after Churchill and Roosevelt met he suggested that he and Roosevelt meet, possibly aboard a battleship, to discuss ways of solving the problems between the two countries. Nothing came of it, and in October the militarists forced Konoye out of office and their head honcho, General Hideki Tojo, became prime minister. From that point on, though I didn't know it, war was imminent. It came seven weeks after Tojo took office.

The country was still pretty lighthearted on the surface, as interested in batting streaks and pennant races as it was in war and the threat of war. The military action that got the most attention in mid-summer was the conflict between a general and some soldiers who yelled "Yoo-hoo!" I still laugh, thinking back on the enormous fuss it raised in the summer of 1941. Most Americans, except for the relatively small number who were already in uniform, were not yet familiar with the term "chickenshit," but Paul Fussell has an entire chapter on it in his book *Wartime*. Chickenshit was pointless, unnecessary attention to military detail, and Lieutenant General Ben Lear, one of the highest-ranking officers in the U.S. Army in 1941, was a master at it.

Lear was playing golf on a course just outside Memphis on a hot Sunday late in July when a military convoy passed by on an adjacent road. The eighty-vehicle convoy was carrying troops and equipment of the 110th Quartermaster Regiment, which had just finished a month on maneuvers with the Second Army in central Tennessee. They were on their way to Camp Joseph T. Robinson in Arkansas, about 150 miles to the west of Memphis on the other side of the Mississippi River.

It was very hot, and most of the soldiers had unbuttoned their shirts and taken off the ties that were part of their everyday uniform. Many had also taken off their hats. The convoy was moving slowly as it passed the golf course, and the soldiers were waving and shouting what were later reported as "boisterous pleasantries" at civilians. The convoy passed some girls wearing shorts, and the soldiers whooped and hollered at them. There were wolf whistles. "Hey, babe!" the soldiers yelled. "Hi, sweetheart! Yoo-hoo!"

General Lear was at the first hole, getting ready to tee off, when he became aware of the whistling and shouting from the convoy. He was not in uniform, of course, and one of the passing soldiers called out to him, "Hey, buddy, you need a caddy?"

Lear's face froze. He was the commander of the Second Army and had directed the maneuvers that the troops were coming from. Furious, he walked off the tee toward the convoy. He was sixty-three, but he had been an old army first sergeant before becoming an officer, and he was tough. He vaulted over a low fence bordering the course and walked swiftly to the lead vehicle in the slowly moving column. The convoy stopped. Lear angrily dressed down the officers in charge before ordering them to go on to Camp Robinson, where they would hear more from him.

When the convoy reached the camp that night it was given orders to turn around and go back to Memphis. The slow-moving vehicles reached the city long after midnight. The troops were told to pitch tents in a grassy section of the Memphis airport and camp there.

Lear appeared the next day and chewed them out, calling them a disgrace to the army and criticizing what he called their loose conduct, their rowdyism, their breach of discipline. The convoy was ordered to return to Camp Robinson, but this time every man in the convoy except the drivers had to do fifteen miles of the distance on foot. It was ninety-seven degrees, the hottest day in Memphis in two years. All morning and afternoon the trucks leap-frogged each other, dropping troops, moving fifteen miles ahead, waiting there to pick them up again. Despite the heat, most of the soldiers handled the hiking without difficulty, and in the trucks where outsiders could not hear them they started singing a parody that began "Oh, General Lear he missed his putt, parlez-vous."

ROBERT W. CREAMER
‹‹‹‹‹‹‹‹‹‹‹‹‹‹‹‹‹‹‹‹‹‹‹‹‹

That should have been it, except that soldiers write home, and parents get upset and call congressmen and complain. Newspapers got hold of the story, and suddenly it was front-page news. The troops were called "the yoo-hoo soldiers" and Lear "the yoo-hoo general." One congressman called for an investigation. Lear defended himself, saying, "I am responsible for training of all elements in this army. Rowdyism cannot be tolerated."

Not good enough, said the congressman. "He's apparently engaged all the time in playing golf," charged another. The Senate got into it, one senator calling Lear "a superannuated old goat who ought to be retired."

The controversy spread. An army "mothers' club" in Arkansas demanded Lear's removal. A Tennessee newspaper printed a letter that said, "Maybe General Lear got his rulebook mixed and used the one for Russia." A soldier at Fort Lewis, Washington, tossed a note from a truck to a girl with the usual "Please write to this lonely soldier" message, but added, facetiously, "Please don't tell General Lear."

Westbrook Pegler, a right-wing columnist, defended Lear, but the fuss was so great that high army brass had to step in to calm things down. In one of those on-the-one-hand and on-the-other-hand statements the army said that Lear's methods might have been severe but his motives were good. They felt the affair ought to be quietly forgotten, and after a while it was.

I don't know what happened to General Lear. The controversy quieted down and he disappeared from the headlines, but everybody was aware of "the yoo-hoo general" that summer, and I don't recall him being much in evidence later on during the war. I assume he was unobtrusively moved into a less conspicuous post.

38

WINNING THE PENNANT

T here were only fourteen games to go when the Dodgers left St. Louis, but it still wasn't over. Brooklyn scrambled to a win over Cincinnati the next day, but the Cardinals beat the Giants twice, both times by one run, to again narrow the gap to one and a half games. Terry Moore appeared as a pinch hitter in the doubleheader. The Brooklyn-Cincinnati game was routinely exciting, the Dodgers taking the lead, losing it, taking it again and losing it again before finally winning 7–5.

The Cardinals didn't play the next day, but the Dodgers did, again against Cincinnati, and it was one of the oddest games ever played, a classic that turned into a farce. It began with an argument before the first pitch when Walker, leading off for Brooklyn, berated plate umpire Larry Goetz about something that had happened the day before. Goetz was a strong, capable, no-nonsense umpire who should be in the Hall of Fame, and he told Walker to stop yammering and to get in the batter's box and hit. Walker continued to jaw at him and Goetz motioned to the Cincinnati pitcher, Paul Derringer, to throw the ball, even though Walker was not in the batter's box. Derringer did and Goetz called it a strike. Walker yelled and Durocher charged from the dugout. Goetz motioned to Derringer to pitch again, but Durocher stood on home plate so that Derringer couldn't throw. When Leo, arguing with Goetz, moved away from the plate Derringer pitched again, but Goetz, busy with Durocher, didn't call that one.

The game got under way, went seventeen innings and was scoreless for the first sixteen. That must have seemed routine for Derringer, who had gone sixteen innings against the Dodgers in June before losing 2–1. This time he gave up fourteen hits and four walks in his sixteen scoreless innings, but the hits were all singles, and the Dodgers couldn't push a run across. They left seventeen men on base.

Johnny Allen pitched for the Dodgers, and he pitched well, too, better than Derringer, as a matter of fact, despite getting into a blustering argument with McKechnie, the Reds' manager, whose calm, scholarly demeanor had earned him the nickname Deacon Bill. Coaching at third for his team, Deacon Bill kept complaining loudly that Allen was throwing spitters. The Dodger pitcher kept his volatile temper under control until the fifth inning when he walked off the mound and went for the fifty-five-year-old Mc-Kechnie, waving an angry forefinger at him as though to say "I've had enough out of you!" The two were kept apart, but then Allen got into a shouting match with Jewel Ens, the Reds' first-base coach, who had been carping at Allen from the other side of the infield.

Thus beleaguered, Allen pitched the game of his life. He gave up just one hit in the first nine innings and only six all told, three of them scratch singles to the infield. After fifteen innings Allen was exhausted, and when he reached base in the top of the six-teenth Durocher lifted him for a pinch runner.

Hugh Casey pitched the last of the sixteenth and retired the

Reds without difficulty, and the game went to the top of the seventeenth, still 0–0. The umpires conferred. It was very dark, and ordinarily the game would have been called at that point. But the Cincinnati fans were yelling at them to let it continue, and because of the importance of the game in the pennant race the umpires decided to let it go one more inning.

As though on cue Reiser led off the top of the seventeenth by hitting a home run over the right-field fence to give the Dodgers a 1–0 lead. Disgusted, Derringer gave up singles to the next two hitters, and McKechnie replaced him with his best relief pitcher, Joe Beggs. By the time McKechnie had gone to the mound to console Derringer, and take him out, and bring Beggs in, and watch Beggs throw his warmup pitches, it was getting very dark indeed. Now the fans wanted the umpires to call the game; if the seventeenth inning could not be completed, the score would revert to the sixteenth and the game would end in a 0–0 tie instead of in a Brooklyn victory. Cincinnati fans hated to lose to Brooklyn. When the plate umpire motioned for the game to go on, they began setting newspapers on fire and waving them at the umpires.

The Reds began a delaying action on the field, prolonging the game in the hope that it would get so dark that it would have to be called. Beggs fielded a tap back to the mound and threw the ball past first base and another run scored. The catcher struggled with a tapped ball in front of the plate and found he couldn't pick it up until the batter was safe at first. A single through the suddenly immobile infield drove in two more runs to make it 4–0 Brooklyn, still with no one out.

At this point McKechnie decided to change pitchers again. He strolled slowly out to the mound, conferred with Beggs and then waved in another relief pitcher. A flagrant delay could result in the umpires forfeiting the game to the Dodgers, but a pitching change was a legitimate move and McKechnie took advantage of it. The Dodgers chafed as Jim Turner walked slowly in from the bullpen and warmed up. When the game resumed Casey hit into

ROBERT W. CREAMER
≪≪≪≪≪≪≪≪≪≪≪≪≪≪≪≪≪≪≪≪≪≪≪≪

a ground out the Reds could not avoid making and Walker hit an easy pop fly between third and short. No one bothered to catch the pop-up, but under the infield-fly rule it was an automatic out. Owen trotted from second to third after the ball hit the ground, but no one tried to stop him. Turner threw a wild pitch and Owen jogged slowly home with the fifth run.

Turner continued to throw pitches very wide of the plate, but the batter, Herman, swung at them anyway and struck out to end the inning. McKechnie, in an admirable display of chutzpah, protested to the umpires that Herman hadn't been trying. He then argued more validly that it was too dark to play any longer; lights being turned on in homes and offices were visible beyond the outfield fence.

The umpires waved McKechnie away and said finish the game. The Dodgers sprinted out to their positions for the last half of the seventeenth, but Casey, with a 5–0 lead, had trouble getting the ball over the plate. He walked one man, gave up a hit to another and walked a third to load the bases with one out. Durocher was going crazy. "Come on, Hugh, God damn it!" he cried. Casey got the second out on a force play as a run scored, and finally threw out Joost for the last out, amid mocking cheers from the fans.

THE Dodgers lost half a game in the standings when they lost to the Reds the next day while the Cardinals were tied by the Giants in a game that had to be called after ten innings. Brooklyn moved on to Pittsburgh, where they rallied to score five runs in the ninth to win 6–4, the key hit a 430-foot triple by Reiser. But in St. Louis the Cardinals won a doubleheader, to gain another half game. Now they were only one game behind, and they were raving about a rookie outfielder who had made his debut with St. Louis in the second game of the doubleheader. He was called Stanley Musial in the newspapers, and he doubled in two runs in the Cardinals' 3–2 victory.

Musial hit well the next day—he batted a memorable .426 in

the twelve games he played to the end of the season—but the Cardinals lost and so did the Dodgers, in Pittsburgh. The Cardinal defeat was just a common, garden-variety 4–1 loss; the Dodger defeat was a major event.

I remember that day because several distinctive things happened. Wartime gasoline rationing was not yet in effect, but a forerunner of it was imposed; gasoline stations along the east coast were closed from 7:00 P.M. to 7:00 A.M., part of an effort to reduce oil consumption. I had a date that night and had forgotten about the gas stations. I had borrowed my father's car, which was low on gas, and I was taken aback when I pulled into a station on my way to the girl's house and found it closed. It altered my plans. Instead of driving a few miles to the movie we wanted to see we had to stay close to home, and we ended up eating hamburgers at a local eatery called Annabelle's Diner. Annabelle's was at the top of a hill and as we walked to it from the car we noticed strange lights in the sky. At first we thought they were powerful searchlights, the kind that were used to attract attention to a small carnival or a church bazaar or the opening of a new store. But these lights were strangely erratic and seemed to come from widely different points. I had never seen anything like it. The beams seemed to shimmer across the sky in long twisted strands. We watched for about ten minutes before going into the diner and as soon as we sat down the lady taking our order said, "D'ja see the northern lights?" They were the aurora borealis, the northern lights of the Arctic, something seldom seen as far south as the latitude of New York City. I recall seeing them only once again in my life, one summer at Truro on Cape Cod twenty years later. It was an eerie, magical, unreal feeling.

That same night in the diner they were playing "Joe, Joe, DiMaggio, We want you on our side," on the jukebox. They played it over and over, and people were singing along with it. The song had been out for a few weeks and I am sure I had heard it before, but the repetition and the singing aloud and the juxtaposition of

ROBERT W. CREAMER
‹‹‹‹‹‹‹‹‹‹‹‹‹‹‹‹‹‹‹‹‹‹‹‹‹‹

closed gas station, date, diner and northern lights fixed the song in my mind that night.

I was surprised to discover in writing this book that the strange game the Dodgers played in Pittsburgh took place the same day, because I remember the game well, too. Fitzsimmons made his first start since his brave performance against the Cardinals but lasted only four innings. I liked Fitzsimmons a lot. He pitched in the first major league game I ever saw, back in 1931, and hit a home run into the upper-left-field stands. The fleshy Fitzsimmons was called Fat Freddie, but he was an athlete. He could pitch, he could hit and he could field, and I liked the way he spun around when he threw the ball. He was the sort of player everybody roots for, and I felt bad when the Pirates belted him around that day. And, of course, as a quondam Dodger fan I wasn't happy that Brooklyn was losing 4–0.

In the eighth inning the Dodgers struck back, as they had done so often that year. They rattled off six straight hits, scored five runs and went ahead 5–4. Casey took the mound. If he could hold the Pirates in the eighth and the ninth Brooklyn would have a two-game lead with little more than a week to go.

Vince DiMaggio, Joe's brother, led off the eighth with a double, went to third base on a fly ball and stayed there when the next batter grounded out. Two out now, man on third, Al Lopez batting.

DiMaggio waited quietly at third base until Casey began his pitching motion and then suddenly darted down the base path toward home before abruptly stopping and returning to third. That's a common-enough ploy today, but it was not as common then, and Casey, who had previously exhibited a tendency to lose his poise under sudden pressure, involuntarily reacted to it. Before he could complete his delivery Lopez leaped out of the batter's box, shouting "Balk!" George Magerkurth, the big umpire whose fate seemed inextricably bound with the Dodgers, agreed. He called the balk and waved DiMaggio across home plate with the tying run.

Casey ran toward the plate screaming at Magerkurth. Durocher was out of the dugout like a shot. He was on edge anyway from the tension of the road trip, and he hadn't been eating and had lost nearly ten pounds. He stuck his gaunt face up into Magerkurth's beefy one, yelled at him and refused to move away. Other Dodgers pressed around, joining in the argument before things quieted down and Durocher returned reluctantly to the Dodger dugout.

Consumed with anger, Casey resumed pitching and buzzed two fast strikes past Lopez. Then, chagrined by the balk call—and with no one on base and the count two strikes and no balls on the Pittsburgh batter—he took advantage of the opportunity to throw an irritated fast ball behind Lopez's head. He followed that message pitch with another in the same place, and then another. Umpires didn't eject pitchers for throwing at hitters in those days, but after the third one Magerkurth came out from behind the plate and yelled at Casey. Durocher ran from the dugout and got between the pitcher and the umpire. His comments this time were sulphurous, and Magerkurth threw him out of the game, although there were several minutes of loud, specific words before Durocher could be persuaded to leave the field. The papers the next day reported that on his way to the clubhouse Leo smashed every lightbulb in the runway.

The game resumed. Casey was still pitching, and he threw a fourth straight pitch behind Lopez's head. A reporter wrote, "Casey threw the ball right where he wanted to four times in a row. He should have control that good all the time."

At this point the game was tied, Lopez was on first base, there were two men out and the batter was Alf Anderson, the slender rookie shortstop who was trying without too much success to make Pittsburgh fans forget Arky Vaughan. Anderson was batting .215 and had had only two extra base hits all year. But Casey grooved one and Anderson hit a triple to right field that scored Lopez with the run that put the Pirates ahead. They won 6–5, and in the Dodger clubhouse after the game, hearing who had driven in the winning run for Pittsburgh, Durocher cried, "Alf Anderson? For Christ's sake, Alf Anderson? Who the fuck is *Alf Anderson*?"

Several Dodgers accosted Magerkurth under the stands after the game. No one hit him or even touched him, but their verbal abuse was impressive, and Magerkurth reported it to the league office.

MacPhail listened to the game over the radio in his office in Brooklyn while a tickertape relayed reports of how the Cardinals were doing in St. Louis. MacPhail was standing with papers in one hand talking about World Series ticket arrangements when some one shouted, "Casey balked! The score's tied!" MacPhail cried, "A balk? What the hell goes on out there?" He turned the radio up louder. "That's a fine time to pull a balk, for God's sake!"

When the game ended John McDonald, traveling with the club, phoned MacPhail long distance from Pittsburgh. His voice could be heard clearly by others in the office. He said to MacPhail, "I just want to tell you that that Magerkurth is a big meathead."

"I know he's a meathead!" MacPhail shouted. "Everyone knows he's a meathead. What's the idea of wasting money telephoning me from Pittsburgh to tell me Magerkurth is a meathead?"

McDonald had called MacPhail to tell him that Magerkurth was filing a report to the league office and to fill him in on the details of the altercation. The Dodgers, still a game ahead, moved across Pennsylvania to Philadelphia, where they had a day off on Friday but doubleheaders with the Phils on Saturday and Sunday and a single game on Monday. Frick, his chief umpire, Bill Klem, and MacPhail traveled from New York to Philadelphia; the league officials made the trip to interrogate Dodger players about the harassment of Magerkurth, while MacPhail went in order to discuss matters with Durocher and defend the Dodgers as best he could.

He was on the phone repeatedly with Durocher during the day and told Frick that the umpire had greeted Owen, the Dodger catcher, with an epithet at the start of the game. Frick eventually fined five Dodgers—Medwick, Camilli, Coscarart, Wyatt and

Franks—twenty-five dollars each for verbally abusing Magerkurth under the stands, and Durocher $150 for his behavior on the field.

By the end of that long Friday Durocher, tense and haggard, had a bigger problem on his hands. Outside the Warwick Hotel, where the Dodgers were staying, he was approached by an Associated Press reporter named Ted Meier. There are slightly differing versions of what was said between the two, but presumably the Philadelphia-based Meier, looking for a provocative local angle and knowing that seven of the Dodgers' nine remaining games were with the last-place Phils, asked Durocher, "Do you figure you'll beat the Phils all seven games?"

"I'm playing one game at a time," Durocher said curtly.

"It would make a good story if I could write that you said you'd beat them all seven."

"Don't quote me on things I haven't said," Durocher replied, his voice rising. He punctuated his remark with what a newspaper called "an uncomplimentary phrase."

Meier, who weighed more than 200 pounds, reacted angrily.

"Watch your mouth," he said. "You're not talking to Magerkurth, you know."

"You'd better get out of here," Durocher said, "before there's trouble."

Meier didn't get out of there, and there was trouble. The two moved a few steps away from the hotel into an alley and had a fight. Durocher knocked the reporter down twice with right hands.

Here is where those days differ from these days. Today the reporter would retain a lawyer and file a multi-million-dollar damage suit. The manager would issue a statement denying the whole thing. The lawsuit would be pending for a year or two and then would be settled out of court, with the reporter and the manager saying publicly it was just a misunderstanding, after the reporter received a quiet check for enough money to buy a new suit and a midsize car.

ROBERT W. CREAMER
‹‹‹‹‹‹‹‹‹‹‹‹‹‹‹‹‹‹‹‹‹‹‹‹‹‹‹

In those days, even though the president of the National League was in town investigating Dodger misbehavior the day before in Pittsburgh, Meier and Durocher returned to the Warwick lobby, where a short time later they shook hands. Hell, it was only a fight.

That evening Durocher also learned that the Cardinals had beaten the Cubs—young Musial went three for three—and were only half a game behind. But Mize was hurt again, this time with torn ligaments in his right arm, and would not play anymore that season.

Second-guessing a manager fifty years after the fact shows that I'm still a baseball fan at heart. Southworth was an exceptionally good manager, but I think he made a grievous blunder the next day against the Cubs. He benched Musial because the rookie batted lefthanded and the Cubs were starting a pitcher named Johnny Schmitz who threw lefthanded. In Musial's place he used another Cardinal rookie, Erv Dusak, who batted righthanded. Dusak later was given the memorable nickname Four Sack Dusak, although except for the euphony it's hard to see why. In a big league career scattered over nine seasons Four Sack Dusak hit only twenty-four home runs. His lifetime batting average was only .243.

Dusak went zero for four against Schmitz. Of course, there was no guarantee that Musial would have done better but, second guessing, in a crucial game in a close pennant race a week before the end of the season wouldn't you rather have had Stan Musial in there than Erv Dusak?

Still, it wasn't just the Dusak-for-Musial move that cost Southworth the game but also Crabtree-for-Triplett. The righthanded-hitting Triplett had doubled and singled off Schmitz as the Cardinals built a 2–0 lead, but in the eighth inning, when the Cubs shifted to a righthander, Southworth had the lefthanded-hitting Crabtree bat for Triplett (he had already used Musial as a pinch hitter). Estel hit a single, which was fine—the Cards scored another run—but if the manager had handled things differently perhaps the twenty-one-year-old Musial would have been in the outfield in the ninth inning instead of the thirty-eight-year-old Crabtree to help protect the 3–1 lead.

With a Cub runner on first base and no one out, Crabtree tried to make a shoestring catch of a little bloop hit and missed it. It went for a double and the Cubs had the tying runs on second and third with no one out. One assumes that Musial would have caught the ball. An intentional walk to fill the bases, an infield out and a single brought in the tying runs. Southworth called in his best relief pitcher, Howard Krist. Another intentional walk filled the bases again, and Bob Scheffing, a rookie backup catcher with the Cubs, hit the first pitch Krist threw to him for a grand-slam home run, the first homer of his big league career. The Cubs won 7–3. They scored *six* runs in the ninth after the Cardinals went into the inning leading 3–1.

That same afternoon in Philadelphia Wyatt and Higbe swept a doubleheader from the Phillies, and Brooklyn's half-game lead in the morning was two by nightfall. The undaunted Cardinals beat the Cubs twice the next day, Sunday, as Musial went six for ten in the doubleheader. (In the first game he scored the winning run in the last of the ninth by racing home from second base on a topped ground ball to the infield.) Because the Dodgers split two with the Phillies the up-and-down lead was down to one again. But Brooklyn beat the Phils on Monday when the Cardinals had the day off, and the lead was back to one and a half.

On Tuesday the Dodgers were idle, but it was a big day for Brooklyn. The Cardinals had a doubleheader with Pittsburgh; if they swept both games they would be only half a game behind, breathing down the Dodgers' necks going into the last four games of the season. But St. Louis lost the opener of the doubleheader, and that defeat eased the pressure on Brooklyn tremendously. It pushed the Cardinals two games back and gave the Dodgers the breathing room they needed. In White Plains, New York, near where I lived, Judge Lee Parsons Davis of the New York State Supreme Court interrupted proceedings in his court to announce from the bench that Pittsburgh had beaten St. Louis in the first game of the doubleheader. There were cheers in the courtroom, and then the case was resumed. Durocher listened to the game with members of the press, and a reporter said you could see the tension leave Leo's face and body when the Pirates won.

THE Dodgers went to Boston for the last two games of their marathon road trip. Thousands—literally thousands—of Brooklyn rooters followed them and boosted attendance at Braves Field for the next two days. On Wednesday the Cardinals defeated Pittsburgh—Musial batted in three runs—but the Dodgers maintained their one-and-a-half-game lead by coming from behind in the seventh inning to beat the Braves 3–2 with Dixie Walker hitting a bases-loaded double to drive in all three Dodger runs.

It came down to Thursday, September 25, three days before the official end of the season. The Dodgers scored a run against the Braves in the first, a run in the second, a run in the third and three more later on to win 6–0. Wyatt pitched a five-hitter. Just as he went to the mound to begin the ninth inning, the scoreboard posted the final of the Cardinals' game in Pittsburgh. The Pirates had beaten St. Louis. A Dodger victory would put them two and a half games ahead and clinch the pennant.

With the championship half an inning away, Wyatt threw nine pitches. He retired the first batter on a ground ball, the second one on a fly to left. He gave up a single to Paul Waner, but the next batter hit a grounder to third base and the great adventure was complete. Brooklyn had won the pennant.

"WE'RE IN!" screamed tabloid headlines in New York, and a gleeful celebration began in Brooklyn. In Boston the thirty-four-year-old Wyatt, a twenty-two-game winner in his twelfth big league season after winning more than nine games in a season only once, said,

"After all the things that have happened to me and being right on the verge of quitting the game, I just can't believe what has happened."

Durocher was uncharacteristically subdued. "We finally made it," he said quietly. "Give all the credit to the players. They're the ones who did it. I haven't done anything but sweat a little on the bench."

In Pittsburgh, where Musial scored the only run in the Cardinals' defeat, Southworth did not use his club's injuries as an excuse.

"We gave it all we had," he said. "I guess it just wasn't our year. My congratulations go to the Dodgers, who have just won the greatest pennant race in history."

39

THE WORLD SERIES: SPLITTING OPENERS

Dodger fans from all over New York went to Grand Central Terminal to welcome their heroes back from Boston. The train was due at 11:30 P.M., but by nine o'clock several hundred had already gathered, many carrying posters saying things like "THE BUMS DONE IT" and "MOIDER DUH YANKS" and "ARE THE GIANTS STILL IN THE LEAGUE?"

By eleven o'clock there were ten thousand people jammed into the station. "I've never seen anything like this," said a policeman, one of the dozens hurriedly assigned to keep the crowd under control. There were two impromptu bands tootling away, balloons rising toward the lofty ceiling, a constant happy noise rising from the crowd that burst into cheers when the first Dodgers walked from the train into the station. When Leo Durocher appeared, a dozen or so fans popped through the police lines and surrounded him; they stayed clustered around him as he made his way slowly, grinning all the time, to a waiting taxi.

In ten minutes all the Dodgers had run the cheerful gauntlet and were gone, and the big crowd melted away. There had been no speeches, no microphones, no carefully orchestrated plan, just a great, spontaneous welcome.

Larry MacPhail had not been in Boston with the team. He had listened to the game in Brooklyn and afterward celebrated with people from the Dodger front office. Branch Rickey was in New York and he came to Larry's suite at the Hotel New Yorker to congratulate him. Buzzy Bavasi was at the party, but as the celebration wound down he started to leave to drive to his home in Scarsdale, New York, north of the city.

"Wait a minute," MacPhail said. He had arranged with John McDonald to have the Dodgers' train stop at New York's 125th Street station, some four miles above Grand Central. Larry wanted to board the train there and ride triumphantly into Grand Central with the team.

"You can give us a lift, can't you?" he said to Bavasi. "It's on your way, isn't it?" MacPhail, Rickey and one or two others got in Bavasi's car and rode to upper Manhattan. A policeman let Bavasi park outside the station and he went up the stairs to the train platform with the others so that he could see the train come in and watch MacPhail and his party get on board.

However, on the ride down from Boston Durocher heard a couple of the players talking about getting off at 125th Street to avoid the crowd that would be in Grand Central. Afraid that most of his team would desert, and not knowing that MacPhail was waiting at 125th Street, Leo ordered the conductor not to stop but to go right on into Grand Central. So, with MacPhail and his entourage waiting expectantly on the platform, the train zipped through 125th Street and left them standing there.

Absolutely furious, MacPhail said, "Take me back!" Bavasi had no choice but to drive them all the way back downtown to the hotel. MacPhail was in the lobby waiting for an elevator when Durocher and Medwick and McDonald arrived. Glowering, Mac-

ROBERT W. CREAMER

Phail pointed to Durocher and McDonald and said, "I want to see you two. Come with me!"

They went up to MacPhail's suite, where Larry demanded an explanation of why the train hadn't stopped for him. Durocher said he had told the conductor not to stop.

"How dare you tell him not to stop?" roared MacPhail.

Leo tried to explain, but MacPhail wouldn't listen.

"You're not satisfied being manager of this team," he yelled. "Now you want to be the president. You're fired!"

When they met the next day, according to Durocher, MacPhail winked and said, "Got a little drunk out last night, didn't it?"

Leo was still the manager. The season ended two days later, with Brooklyn winning 100 games for the first time in club history, and the day after that there was a parade for the team in Brooklyn. That was extraordinary, too. At least a million people lined the streets along the route of march from Grand Army Plaza off Prospect Park to the reviewing stand at Borough Hall in downtown Brooklyn. Along with the hundreds of thousands on the streets and sidewalks there were people watching from practically every window in every building along the way. Others stood on roofs or sat on fire escapes. Trolley cars unable to move because of the parade were used as viewing stands. So were automobiles and trucks.

There were half a dozen organized bands marching in the parade along with horn blowers, bell ringers, dishpan whackers and wild-card drummers. Police and fire sirens wailed. The ragtag group of musicians who played in the aisles at Ebbets Field was there. Later the ballpark band became known as "The Dodger Sym-Phoney," but in 1941 they called themselves "The Dodger Discords" and "Our Bums' Symphony." It was still pretty spontaneous in those days.

A snowstorm of torn-up paper floated down on the Dodger players as they rode by in open convertibles, grinning and waving. There was an effigy of a New York Yankee that the crowd threw things at. People repeatedly broke through the police lines to run alongside the cars to say something to the players or to shake their hands. Some grabbed the players' arms. Some tried to kiss them. Some just patted their backs and yelled approval.

Hundreds of people dressed up in costume for the parade, any old costume they could find. There were clowns and pirates and cowboys and Uncle Sams and comic policemen and—a popular theme—tramps or bums. Many women wore dresses from the 1890s. There were hundreds of posters, as well as a banner strung across Fulton Street that said fervently, "We Are Proud Of You, Brooklyn Dodgers."

After the parade was over Meyer Berger of *The New York Times* interviewed a street cleaner who was helping to sweep up the mess left by the parade. "It's late," said the man, "and I'll miss my supper. But for the Bums, it's an honor. I'll tell my kids I swept up for the Bums."

THEN the Series began. Commissioner Landis held a meeting with the two managers before the first game and laid down some new rules for Series play. There would be no more big meetings at the mound, he said, no half dozen players gathering around as the manager talked to the pitcher. Only two players, other than the manager and the pitcher, could come to the mound. Also, he said, the manager could come out to the mound to talk to the pitcher only once during an inning, instead of the several trips Durocher was used to making in crisis innings. Finally, Landis said, there would be no protracted arguments. He said he expected the players and the managers to conduct themselves throughout the Series "in a proper manner." Since Joe McCarthy almost never lost his temper and seldom came off the bench, there was little doubt who was being cautioned by Landis' little speech.

Durocher shrugged it off and sat down to do some deep thinking about the Series, which was unfortunate for the Dodgers. Durocher,

ROBERT W. CREAMER
‹‹‹‹‹‹‹‹‹‹‹‹‹‹‹‹‹‹‹‹‹‹‹‹‹‹‹

who was a great tactician, decided to approach the Series strategically. Whit Wyatt and Kirby Higbe, his twenty-two-game winners, were well-rested, but Leo picked thirty-eight-year-old Curt Davis to pitch the first game. Twelve years earlier, in the 1929 World Series, Connie Mack had stolen a march on the Cubs, then managed by the same Joe McCarthy, by pitching a retread veteran named Howard Ehmke in the first game. Ehmke won and Mack came back with his ace, Lefty Grove, in the second game. The A's won both and went on to win the Series easily. Durocher apparently decided to try the same approach. Emulating Mack, he did not name Davis as his starter until just before game time. He even had Wyatt and Higbe warm up along with Davis. When reporters approached McCarthy with this exciting intelligence, the Yankee manager said irritably, "What the hell difference does it make which one pitches?"

Davis pitched reasonably well, but not well enough to win. Joe Gordon hit a towering home run into the left-field seats in the second inning, and Bill Dickey doubled home another run in the fourth. After Gordon's homer someone shot off a blank pistol three times in the left-field stands, and a Yankee fan from the Bronx who was sitting in the bleachers stood up and shouted, "T'ree Dodger fans has just blew their brains out."

The conservative McCarthy went with his ace, Red Ruffing, who unlike Davis pitched just well enough to win. Ruffing stifled the Dodgers' best hitters but gave up a run on a triple by Mickey Owen. The Yankees got that back when Gordon singled in a run, the sixth hit and the third run off Davis in five and a third innings.

Even so, the Dodgers might have won. In the seventh Cookie Lavagetto was safe on an error and Pee Wee Reese hit safely. Lew Riggs pinch-hit for Owen and singled to drive in Lavagetto. The Yankees still led 3–2, but the Dodgers had two men on and no one out, and Ruffing seemed to be laboring.

The pitcher was up and Durocher wanted a pinch hitter. He

grabbed Jimmy Wasdell off the bench and said, "Get in there and hit." Wasdell took him literally. After the first pitch he was given the bunt sign, but he took a full swing instead and lifted a foul near the dugout on the third-base side. Red Rolfe came over from third to make a nice catch of it, but Reese dashed from second base toward third after the catch. Phil Rizzuto sprinted from his shortstop position to third base just ahead of Reese, took Rolfe's throw and tagged Pee Wee out. It was a rally-killing double play. The Dodgers expected to have men on second and third with one out after Wasdell's projected sacrifice. Instead they had a man on first with two outs, and the abortive inning ended a moment later when Dixie Walker grounded to second.

The Dodgers made another gesture in the ninth when Medwick and Reese singled with one out to put the tying and winning runs on base. But the next batter was the weak-hitting Herman Franks, who had replaced Owen after Riggs pinch-hit for him. With Babe Phelps long gone, the Dodgers did not have a third catcher to replace Franks behind the plate if the Dodgers tied the score or went ahead. So Franks had to bat for himself, and hit into a double play to end the game.

"I didn't see any bunt sign," Wasdell said afterward, "but there must have been one because Durocher bawled hell out of me in the dugout. I can't blame him. It was my fault."

Durocher had cooled down by the time he showered and dressed.

"We blew our chance in that inning," he said. "That's when we should have come through, but we didn't. What the hell, it's just one of those things. It was a tough time to miss a bunt sign, but that's baseball. I'll take the responsibility. Don't blame Wasdell."

The Dodgers had obtained Wasdell from the Washington Senators, and the Washington manager, Bucky Harris, who was at the game, questioned what Durocher said. "I managed Wasdell for three years," Harris said. "Jimmy wasn't a smart ballplayer, but he never missed a signal. I doubt if Durocher gave him one."

ROBERT W. CREAMER
‹‹‹‹‹‹‹‹‹‹‹‹‹‹‹‹‹‹‹‹‹‹‹‹‹‹‹‹

There was also criticism of Durocher's decision to bypass his two pitching stars. As Murray Waldenberg, a Dodger fan, said, "We shoulda pitched Wyatt."

WYATT pitched the second game and beat the Yankees 3–2, ending their streak of World Series victories at ten straight. He got Joe DiMaggio to hit into a double play in the first inning to end a Yankee threat, but he was shaky through the first part of the game and gave up single runs in the second and third.

"I didn't feel good the first three or four innings," Wyatt said. "I told Leo I had nothing. Then all of a sudden, when I went out to the box for the fifth inning, my arm felt great. I had my stuff again. It's funny, I don't know why that is. I got faster as I went along, and I was mixing things up good, trying not to give those guys two of the same in a row to swing at."

Wyatt settled down after Spud Chandler, the Yankee pitcher, who reached base in the fourth inning, tried to go from first to third on a short single to Pete Reiser in center. Reiser threw a bullet to Lavagetto and Chandler was out. "I needed a perfect peg to tag out Chandler," Lavagetto said, "and Petey gave it to me."

After that, Wyatt gave up only two singles, while the Dodgers got to Chandler, who might have tired himself with that dash for third. They tied the game in the fifth inning, and in the sixth they moved ahead. Walker was safe on an error and Billy Herman singled, and McCarthy took Chandler out and brought in Johnny Murphy, the great relief pitcher, to face young Reiser. Murphy, who was never flustered (they called him "Grandma" for his rocking-chair pitching motion) struck out Reiser on four pitches, but Dolph Camilli singled on a three-and-two pitch to score Walker and put Brooklyn ahead.

Murphy allowed only one hit after that. With two out in the sixth the Yankees put two men on base, but McCarthy let Murphy bat for himself and the pitcher struck out. McCarthy was second-guessed after the game for not using a pinch hitter, but he defended his decision.

"I didn't put in a pinch hitter for Murphy because you just don't do things like that," he said. "You don't sacrifice your good pitcher for hitting that early in the game when your club is only one run behind. You'd run out of good pitchers all the time if you did. You want your good pitcher in there when he's going well to hold them, and Murphy was going well. He did his job, he held them. The hitters didn't go to hitting, that's all."

Rancor began to develop between the two teams. Reese slid hard into Rizzuto in the opening game, Johnny Sturm slid hard into Herman and Johnny Allen plunked Sturm with a pitched ball. In the second game Tommy Henrich threw a rolling block at Herman, and Gordon did much the same to Reese. Herman said nothing, and Reese did no more than glare at Gordon. Then, with the hard-bitten Owen on first base in the fifth inning, Wyatt grounded into a double play, Gordon to Rizzuto to Sturm. Owen was clearly out, but he came into Rizzuto spikes-high and spilled him as the shortstop made his relay to first to complete the double play. Rizzuto got up angrily and turned on Owen, but the Dodger catcher didn't seem to notice him and trotted off the field. Henrich, coming in from right field, eased Rizzuto toward the Yankee dugout.

"Well, you'd get sore, too," Rizzuto said after the game, "if he banged into you the way he banged into me. He tried to spike me, and he had no reason. The play was over."

"Owen threw a football block at Phil," DiMaggio said. "He must have gone ten feet out of his way to smack him down."

"They're gonna get some of that rough stuff, too," Gordon said, "and you can put that in the paper."

During the game, after Owen slid into Rizzuto, the Yankees began to get on the Dodger catcher from the bench.

"They called Mickey some nice choice names," said Charlie Dressen, whose position in the third-base coach's box was in front

ROBERT W. CREAMER

of the Yankee dugout. "We were told by Judge Landis we couldn't holler at each other, so I asked the umpires, what about it?"

Owen didn't seem too upset.

"Sure, I gave him the business," he said, "but nobody's sweet and gentle with me either. They give me the works all the time at home plate. That's baseball."

When he learned that Rizzuto said his slide was too high, Owen snorted.

"That's too bad," he said sarcastically. "I feel so sorry for him, so, so sorry.

"Hell, I wasn't trying to spike him. I was trying to break up the double play. They don't ask permission to come into me at home plate. I catch plenty of hell back there. They come in hard. And why shouldn't they?"

Owen was told that the Yankees had threatened to retaliate. He shrugged.

"I ain't going nowhere," he said.

"They want to play rough?" Durocher said. "Well, that suits us. That's when we play our best ball."

40

FREDDIE FITZSIMMONS' KNEE

The Series was scheduled to be played in seven days, one after the other, with no travel days, no rest days, no time off at all. But it rained, and the game scheduled for Ebbets Field on Friday, the third game of the Series, had to be postponed to Saturday. So everyone got a day off anyway.

I was at the beginning of my second year of college, going now to Fordham as a day-hop, repeating my freshman year, working at odd jobs now and then to pick up spending money. School and weekend jobs kept me from even thinking about going to any of the Series games, but Arnold Benson and his kid brother Warren went to the second game. They took a bus from Mount Vernon to the subway terminal in the Bronx and for a nickel each rode down to Yankee Stadium. They got on line for tickets at about nine in the morning, waited patiently until the windows opened, shuffled along with the other fans and for $3.30 each bought a ticket for a decent seat in the upper stands in left field. It was that easy to get World Series seats in those days, and it made for a livelier, more knowledgeable crowd, at least after the first game, which was something of a social event for very important people.

I wasn't even able to listen to the third game on the radio. I went to the Polo Grounds that day to see Fordham play football. But the blessed people who worked in the Polo Grounds scoreboard set up a line score, the way they did at regular-season baseball games, and we could follow the Series game inning by inning. It was quite a game, with the zeros parading slowly along from the first inning through the seventh, neither team scoring.

Durocher picked the reliable Fred Fitzsimmons to pitch. McCarthy countered with Marius Russo, who was from the same section of Queens that Rizzuto came from. Russo had been the best Yankee pitcher after Ruffing for a couple of seasons and would have started the second game except that he came down with a bug, and McCarthy held him out. Gomez, who had made a great comeback in 1941 with a 15–5 record, was having arm trouble again and did not appear at all in the Series.

The zeros on the Polo Grounds scoreboard reflected the superb pitching that Russo and Fitzsimmons were doing. Russo walked Herman in the first inning, but Reiser hit a comebacker to the pitcher and Joe Medwick flied out to end that threat. DiMaggio singled off Fitzsimmons in the second, Joe's first hit in the Series, but with two men out Gordon flied to Walker, the first time in three games that Gordon failed to reach base safely.

Henrich got on base on a force-out in the fourth but was picked off by Owen, who snapped a throw to Camilli. Henrich irritably kicked at Camilli's glove and tried to slap the ball out of it and Camilli shoved him. Before the two could do anything more than that, Larry Goetz, umpiring at first, stepped between them and quieted them down.

One other thing happened in that inning that was hardly noticed at the moment it occurred but which meant that Brooklyn was in trouble. On the force-out, Henrich had hit to Reese, who began to toss the ball toward second to Herman for the beginning of what might have been a double play. Herman was very slow coming toward the bag, and Reese had to run over himself to tag it for the out. It developed that the second baseman had pulled a muscle in his rib cage during batting practice and was in great pain. He tried to play and got away with it for a few innings. He didn't have to swing the bat in the first inning when he drew his base on balls, and he had only one easy chance in the field. But he couldn't move freely and he was unable to swing the bat properly, as he discovered in the bottom of the fourth when all he could do was tap a soft ground ball toward Gordon. Durocher had to take him out of the game and use Pete Coscarart at second for the rest of the Series.

Gordon just missed hitting a homer in the fifth when he whacked Fitzsimmons for a triple off the left–center field wall. Fitzsimmons then walked Rizzuto intentionally, ignored Phil when the youngster stole second and struck out Russo, a good hitting pitcher, to end the inning.

The Yankees were pressuring Fitz every inning, but the old-timer kept holding them off. In the sixth Sturm singled and stole second and Henrich walked, but with two on base, one out and DiMaggio and Charlie Keller coming up, Fitzsimmons settled in. He got DiMaggio on an easy pop fly to right and Keller on a weak grounder to first base. Relieved cheers went up from the Brooklyn crowd and Fitzsimmons received an ovation as he walked to the bench. Meanwhile, the Dodgers were doing nothing with Russo. In six innings he gave up only one infield hit, a topped roller along the third-base line that barely stayed fair.

In the top of the seventh Fitzsimmons walked Gordon, who was on second base with two out when Russo batted again. Russo was an excellent athlete, one of the best college basketball players in the country before he turned to baseball, and he knew how to handle himself as a hitter. His career batting average was .213,

ROBERT W. CREAMER

which is very good for a pitcher, and that year he hit .231, which was 102 points higher than Coscarart hit.

Against Fitzsimmons, Russo had flied out before striking out in the fifth, but now he leveled in on one of the Dodger pitcher's deliveries and hit a vicious line drive directly back at him. The ball hit Fitzsimmons on the left leg and the pitcher fell down, obviously badly hurt. The ball ricocheted toward Reese, who caught it and threw to first base, but Russo beat the throw as Gordon moved from second to third.

Time was called and everybody gathered around Fitzsimmons. The ballplayers thought his kneecap was broken. Lavagetto and Dressen helped the pitcher to stand on his good leg and, with his arms around their shoulders, helped him off the field and into the Dodger dugout. Fitzsimmons' wife and daughter were sitting near the dugout, and they had their hands to their faces in distress as they watched him being carried off.

He was taken to a hospital and X-rayed. It was not a fracture but a very bad bruise. The ball had hit just above the knee and had broken the skin, but it was a painful rather than a serious injury. Fitzsimmons, limping badly, was at the ballpark in uniform the next day. He pitched no more in the Series and appeared in only one game the next season, but in 1943, at the age of forty-two, he relieved a wartime pitching shortage for the Dodgers by starting seven games and winning three before retiring for good.

Back on the field there was consternation and confusion. The Yankees assumed that Russo had reached first safely, that the inning was alive and that they had runners on first and third with the top of their batting order coming up. But the umpires realized what the Yankees—and Reese, for that matter—hadn't. Russo's line drive hadn't touched the ground, either before or after it hit Fitzsimmons, and when Reese caught the ball after it ricocheted off Freddy's leg it was the third out of the inning.

Somewhat stunned, the Yankees took the field and, somewhat

stunned, the Dodgers came to bat. The score was still 0–0, but there was an unreal quality to the game now. Reiser brought it back to shouting reality when he led off the bottom of the seventh with a tremendous double against the screen beyond the scoreboard in right center. It didn't miss being a home run by much. It was the first hit of the Series for Reiser, the first real hit off Russo, and the first time a Dodger base runner had gone beyond first base.

Calmly, the lefthanded Russo struck out the righthanded Medwick. The third strike bounced away from the catcher and Medwick had to be thrown out at first base, but Reiser had to remain at second. Lavagetto hit a bounding ball through the middle that looked like a base hit, but Gordon, ranging far to his right, made another fine fielding play behind second base and threw Lavagetto out, with Reiser moving to third.

Camilli was up. Russo threw him a ball, then a called strike, then another called strike. Camilli swung on the next pitch and fouled it off, fouled off another. Then Russo threw an off-speed curve and Camilli was caught flat-footed, watching it break across the plate for a called third strike.

Now it was the eighth inning, still 0–0, but soon in the Polo Grounds we saw a "2" go up on the scoreboard for the Yankees. Hugh Casey had been in the Dodger bullpen during much of the game, throwing easily whenever it appeared that Fitzsimmons might be getting into trouble. After Russo's liner knocked the old pitcher out of the game Casey continued to throw slowly, but when he came into the game it was glaringly apparent that for all his warming up Casey was not ready. Sturm, leading off, flied to center, but Casey then gave up four straight hits and made a serious mistake in the field. Rolfe began the trouble with a solid line drive to right center, and only deft fielding by Walker held him to a single. On a hit-and-run Henrich hit a ground ball to the right side just beyond Camilli's reach. Coscarart, moving to his left, fielded the ball and would have thrown Henrich out at first

ROBERT W. CREAMER
⋘⋘⋘⋘⋘⋘⋘⋘⋘⋘⋘⋘

base except that Casey failed to come off the mound in time to cover the bag. That should have been the second out. Instead the Yankees had two men on with only one out, and DiMaggio was up. As Casey pitched, Coscarart moved toward second as though for a pick-off play on Rolfe, and DiMaggio hit a single through where the second baseman had been. Rolfe scored, and the Yankees led 1–0.

Casey went to two balls and a strike on Keller, and Durocher trotted out to the mound. He talked earnestly to Casey and returned to the bench just in time to see Keller hit a single to left to drive in Henrich. Durocher made the trip to the mound again, this time to take Casey out. Larry French came in and got Dickey to hit into a double play to end the inning, but Fitzsimmons' lovely shutout was gone, and the Yankees led 2 0.

Then we saw a "1" for the Dodgers in the bottom half of the inning. Walker doubled to open the eighth, the second straight inning in which the leadoff batter doubled off Russo, but the pitcher made a nice play on Owen's tap to the mound, holding Dixie at second while he threw Owen out at first. He struck out Augie Galan, batting for French, but Reese sliced a single to right to score Walker and close the score to 2–1. Herman would have been the next hitter, but Billy was on the bench, and Coscarart popped up to end the rally.

Allen pitched the ninth for Brooklyn and retired the Yankees 1–2–3 on hard-hit balls to the outfield. Now it was the last chance for the Dodgers. They had roughed up Russo a little in the seventh and had scored on him in the eighth. The meat of their batting order was up—the third, fourth and fifth hitters. But Reiser struck out, Medwick popped up and Lavagetto grounded out, and it was over. The Yankees had won, and the Dodgers had suffered a bitter defeat.

"You can't win if you don't hit," Durocher said philosophically. "We had our righthanded hitters up there in the seventh and the ninth, and they couldn't hit the ball out of the infield. That's a hell of a note when your best righthanded hitters can't hit a lefthander."

Asked if Casey should have covered first base in the eighth inning, Durocher said coldly, "I have no comment on that." But it was obvious that he had already commented on it to Casey, who looked woebegone sitting in the clubhouse after the game. One reporter said he had that "glazed look in his eyes that you see in Joe Louis' victims." Casey was the last Dodger to leave the clubhouse that day.

The pragmatic McCarthy said, "They got a bad break when the ball hit Fitzsimmons, but we got a bum break on that, too. If the ball hadn't hit him it would have gone into center field and Gordon would have scored from second."

MacPhail was ranting in the press room, blaming Durocher for the defeat, saying he never should have brought Casey into the game. "He hadn't warmed up in the bullpen," MacPhail argued. "He was just lobbing the ball, and he didn't bear down at all. He shouldn't have brought him in. He had another pitcher warmed up and ready to go. He had French. A lefthander. And the first three Yankee hitters in the eighth were lefty!"

Durocher was used to that sort of stuff, and MacPhail almost always calmed down after popping off, but it certainly reminds you of George Steinbrenner, doesn't it?

ROBERT W. CREAMER

41

MICKEY OWEN'S BOO-BOO

Thus the fourth game of the 1941 World Series became a must game for the Dodgers. They had to win it. They had no choice. They simply could not afford to lose and fall behind three games to one to a team as powerful as the Yankees. In Ebbets Field, fans sensing this hung a banner from the upper stands that pleaded, "WE'VE WAITED 21 YEARS. DON'T FAIL US NOW."

McCarthy started Atley Donald, the young fireballer who had won only nine games that season but who had beaten Feller a couple of times. Durocher started Higbe, at long last. Higbe did poorly, had trouble putting the ball where he wanted and gave up six hits and three runs in the three and two-thirds innings he worked.

Worse, that was all the pitching the twenty-two-game winner did for Brooklyn in the Series. Durocher had outmaneuvered himself with his rash decision to use Davis in the opening game. During the season he depended tremendously on Wyatt and Higbe

("Those boys are going to start every fourth day for me," he had said in Philadelphia in May), but in the World Series, where dominant pitchers are so important, he put himself in a position where even in a seven-game Series he would have been able to use Higbe only once in the normal course of things. His decision kept Higbe, who thrived on work (he was second in the league in innings pitched in 1941), idle for an inordinate length of time since his last regular-season start. It was not surprising that he wasn't sharp against the Yankees. "I'd have licked them easy if I'd have had my control," he said afterward.

Higbe should have been a much more important factor in the Series, but in the fourth game he was struggling from the start. With two outs and a man on first in the first inning he yielded a walk and a base hit to give the Yankees their first run. He got through the second inning and scraped through the third, when Sturm lined hard to right, Rolfe singled to center, and Henrich hit a long fly on which Walker made a fine catch.

In the fourth he gave up a double to Keller, a walk to Dickey and a single to Gordon to load the bases with no one out. He got Rizzuto to hit into a force at home plate and struck out Donald, but with two away Sturm hit him for a single that drove in two runs, and the Yankees led 3–0. The gloom in Flatbush was profound.

Durocher took Higbe out and replaced him with French, who got out of the inning without retiring a batter. French threw a pitch in the dirt that bounced off Owen, and Sturm broke for second. But the catcher, who had blocked the ball with his body, picked it up and threw behind Sturm to Camilli. Rizzuto, on second base, had seen Owen block the ball and knew he had no chance to get to third, but with Sturm headed for second Rizzuto took off. Camilli threw to Riggs, who threw to Reese, and Rizzuto was out in a rundown to end the inning.

Down 3–0, the Dodgers struck back. With two out and nobody on Donald walked Owen and then he walked Coscarart, which

ROBERT W. CREAMER
≪≪≪≪≪≪≪≪≪≪≪≪≪≪≪≪≪≪≪≪≪≪≪

must have given McCarthy pause. Wasdell batted for French and roused the crowd by hitting one high over the screen in right, but just foul. He then hit one down the left-field line that was fair by a foot. He got a double, two runs scored to make it 3–2, and the Dodgers were back in the ballgame.

Allen came in to pitch for Brooklyn and was terrible, quickly loading the bases with Gordon coming to bat. At that point Gordon had been to the plate seventeen times in the Series and had been on base eleven times. Durocher went out to the mound and waved Casey in.

"Yesterday's goat," somebody muttered, but Casey got Brooklyn out of the inning when Gordon hit a fly to left field for the third out.

Escaping trouble that way pepped up the Dodgers. Walker led off the fifth by doubling to left, and Reiser rammed Donald's first pitch to him over the scoreboard for a homer. It was Brooklyn's only home run of the Series, but it put the Dodgers ahead 4–3.

Casey protected that slender lead beautifully. He was his old tough self again. Sturm got a two-out single in the ninth, and DiMaggio beat out an infield hit in the seventh, but otherwise Casey was perfect. Rizzuto popped up, Rolfe popped up, Henrich popped up, Keller popped up. The Dodgers did very little themselves with the Yankee relief pitchers, but it didn't seem to matter. They were in front, and Casey was mowing the Yankees down.

In the eighth he got the side out in order.

In the ninth Casey got Sturm on a ground ball to second and Rolfe on a little tap back to the mound. One more out and the Dodgers would win, and the Series would be tied at two games each.

Henrich was the batter. Casey's first pitch to him was a ball, the next two were called strikes. Casey was still overpowering, and Henrich seemed outmatched. One more strike, and the game would be over.

Henrich got his bat on the next pitch and fouled it away. Casey wasted one outside and then came back with a beauty just off the plate. It could have been called a strike, but Goetz, who was umpiring behind the plate, said it was ball three. Casey wound up and threw the next pitch, and Henrich swung and missed for strike three.

"I was fooled," Henrich said. "Casey threw me a heck of a pitch. It was a great curve. He didn't usually have a good curve, but this one exploded. It looked like a fast ball but when it broke it broke down so sharply that it was out of the strike zone. I committed myself too quickly. I tried to hold up but I wasn't able to."

Goetz's right arm shot up in the umpires' signal for a strike. Fans ran on the field. Henrich had fanned! The game was over! The Dodgers had evened the Series!

But the pitch got away from Owen, glancing off the edge of his mitt and angling away toward the box seats near the Dodger dugout. Many people have decided since that it was a spitball that Casey threw, and that was why the unsuspecting Owen was unable to catch it.

"It wasn't a spitter," Owen told Don Honig. "It was a curve ball, as good a curve ball as Casey ever threw, and missing it was my own fault. Casey had two curve balls, a big curve and a short quick one. He'd been throwing the short quick one for five innings. We had only one sign for the curve ball. I gave him the sign and he threw the big curve. I should have had it, but it got away from me."

Henrich said, "I knew it was going to be strike three, but even as I was trying to hold up on my swing I was thinking the ball had broken so fast that Owen might have trouble with it. That went through my mind. I was looking back, and I saw it bouncing. It rolled all the way to the fence."

Henrich ran and made it to first base safely. He had struck out, but the game was not yet over. And DiMaggio was at bat.

As he had in other tense moments, Casey lost his poise. DiMaggio

ROBERT W. CREAMER

hit a hard single to left field, so hard that even with two out Henrich had to stop at second lest he be thrown out at third. Keller was up. He swung at Casey's first pitch and missed. He swung at the second and missed. Once again the Dodgers were one strike away from victory.

"That's where I pulled a rock," Durocher said. "I told the writers that if they really wanted to get the reason why we lost the game they should blame me. Casey gets two quick strikes on Keller and we're only one strike away from winning. My mistake was that for the first time in my life I was shell-shocked. I should have got off the bench and gone out to the mound to talk to my pitcher in a spot like that. Especially after what had happened. I *got* to go out there and talk to him, slow him down. I got to say to him, Look, you got this guy where you want him. Take your time. Waste a couple of pitches. Maybe he'll go after a bad one.

"Instead, I sat on my ass and didn't do anything. And Casey comes right back in with a pitch and Keller hits it off the wall for a double."

The double off the screen scored Gordon easily from second with the tying run, but DiMaggio, starting from first base, had to power his way around the base paths to score the run that put the Yankees ahead. With all his myriad talents, the one thing DiMaggio had that is often overlooked was his extraordinary speed, his talent as a base runner. He came around third like an express train as Walker retrieved the ball and threw it home, and he just did slide under Owen's tag to score.

Durocher continued to sit, shell-shocked, as Casey walked Dickey and gave up another double to Gordon, a long drive off the left-field wall that Wasdell just missed catching. Two more runs were in, and the victory that had turned into defeat changed into debacle. Still on the mound, Casey walked Rizzuto before Murphy ended one of the most memorable half innings in baseball history by grounding out to the shortstop.

In their half of the ninth the Dodgers went down meekly. Reese fouled out. Walker grounded to short. Reiser, the last faint hope, hit an easy grounder to first.

The game was over. And so was the Series, although the two teams had to go through the formality of playing again the next day.

THE Yankees were exultant in their clubhouse after the game, their traditional cool abandoned. The day before they had expressed sadness and sympathy for Fitzsimmons and praised his ability and courage, but today they were triumphant and contemptuous in their derision of Owen.

"The right guy got it," said Atley Donald. "He tried to cut Phil down. He played dirty ball. He's only getting what he deserves."

Even DiMaggio said, "As long as there has to be a goat, I'm glad it was him. We're not a bit sorry for him."

After the last out, as Owen trudged to the Dodger clubhouse along a high wire-mesh fence that separated the players from the spectators, he took a lot of abuse. "Hey, Owen, you bum you!" cried one man. "Hey, Owen, you're lousy, you know that?" shouted another. A kid yelled, "Whose side you playing on?"

In the clubhouse he sat on a bench, red-eyed and exhausted, talking with reporters.

"Sure it was my fault," he said. "It hit the edge of my mitt and bounced off. I should have had it."

He stood up and slowly undressed. "I don't mind being the goat," he said. "I'm just sorry for what I cost the other guys." Then he limped off to the shower.

The next day, the last game of the Series, Henrich batted in the first inning and received a base on balls. The crowd gasped when the fourth ball got away from Owen and bounced all the way into the Yankee dugout. In the second inning the same thing happened when Keller walked, a pitch squirting away from the plate. Yet when Owen came to bat for the first time in the bottom of the second inning, the Brooklyn crowd stood and applauded him, the ovation lasting nearly thirty seconds before it finally quieted down.

But it was like a wake. The Yankees scored twice in the second inning, the fifth straight game in which they took a two-run lead before Brooklyn could score, and they added another in the fifth. The Dodgers picked up a lone run in the third. And that's the way it ended, 3–1 Yankees.

Wyatt pitched bravely, giving the Yankees only one hit after the second inning (a home run by Henrich), and he struck out DiMaggio the first two times Joe batted. That was the only time all season that DiMaggio struck out twice in the same game.

But Wyatt was frustrated and angry, as were all the Dodgers ("Those lucky Yankees," they kept muttering.) He took it out on DiMaggio. Back in the summer when Johnny Babich of Philadelphia said DiMaggio wouldn't get a hit off him because he would keep the ball away from him, Wyatt mocked that approach and suggested pitching in tight instead. "If DiMaggio was playing in the National League," he said, "he'd have to swing while he's flat on his ass."

Wyatt attempted to put that theory into practice, throwing very close to DiMaggio before striking him out the first two times he batted. When DiMaggio came to bat a third time, right after Henrich hit his home run, Wyatt threw at him again. This time DiMaggio hit a long hard fly to Reiser in deep center. After the ball was caught he turned and trotted across the infield toward the Yankee dugout, and as he went past the mound he said something unpleasant to Wyatt. Wyatt said something unpleasant back and DiMaggio, nearly to the foul line, turned and went for the pitcher, who stepped off the mound to meet him. The alert Goetz, umpiring this day at third base, quickly got between them and there was no fight, although players from both teams raced to the scene, the Dodgers rallying behind Wyatt, the Yankees behind DiMaggio. "There was considerable milling and mouthing," said a newspaper, but nothing more.

The Brooklyn fans in center field threw things at DiMaggio as he went to his position the next inning, but the game ended quietly. The Dodgers got only one hit in the last five innings off the Yankees' Ernie Bonham, the fifth different starting pitcher McCarthy used in the Series, and they seemed almost in a hurry to get the thing over with. Bonham threw only four pitches in the sixth inning to retire the side in order, and only three pitches the next inning. DiMaggio singled off Wyatt in the seventh, the last hit of the year for the Yankees, and in the last half of the ninth the final play of the game, the final play of the 1941 baseball season, was a long fly ball that DiMaggio caught near the exit gate in center field.

It was a fitting climax to a remarkable season. At the other end of the spectrum the ebullient Yankee coach, Arthur Fletcher, kept shouting in the Yankee clubhouse, "We moidered duh bums. We moidered duh bums."

I felt some sadness for the Dodgers, but mostly I gloated over the Yankee victory as a Yankee fan had a right to do, and I couldn't resist rubbing it into friends of mine who were Brooklyn rooters all the way.

They looked at me resentfully and said, "Wait till next year."

42

AND EVER AFTER

Two months and one day after the fly ball settled into DiMaggio's glove the Japanese bombed Pearl Harbor, and everything changed. In 1942 I registered for the draft. In 1943 I was in the army. In 1944 I went overseas. In 1945 there was the atom bomb. In 1946 the war was over and I went to work. In 1947 I got married. In 1948, in the middle of June, I became a father.

Seven years earlier in the middle of June the most important thing in the world to me was DiMaggio's hitting streak, more important at the time than Hitler and Japan and President Roosevelt. In 1948 the most important thing was my family—my wife, my son. They meant more than the Cold War and Harry Truman, and they meant more than the Yankees and the Dodgers and Jackie Robinson and "Spahn and Sain and Pray for Rain."

Things had changed. Hank Greenberg was discharged from the army two days before Pearl Harbor because of a rule releasing draftees over the age of twenty-eight; two days after Pearl Harbor he reenlisted and was gone "for the duration." When he returned after the war he was an old man as ballplayers go and though he won another home-run championship and helped the Tigers win a pennant, he played only two and a half seasons before ending his abbreviated career.

DiMaggio played one season after Pearl Harbor and had a bad year, for him. He hit only .305 and then went into the army. Williams also played another season and won the batting title again before becoming a navy flier. Joe and Ted came back and flourished after the war, but neither of them ever reached the heights they attained in 1941.

Reiser played one more year before going into the navy and in mid-season of 1942 was hitting .350. He seemed on his way to a second straight batting championship when on July 19, desperately chasing a fly ball, he rammed his head into the concrete outfield wall in Sportsmans Park in St. Louis. Amazingly, he was out of the hospital and back in the Dodger lineup four games later and actually improved his batting average to .356 before dizzy spells began to harass him. He had to sit out many games and his average plummeted nearly fifty points by the end of the season. Brooklyn, nine and a half games ahead of St. Louis when Reiser was hurt, was unable to hold off the Cardinals this time and lost the pennant. Reiser never played really well again. He came back after the war, was repeatedly injured and soon faded into a shadow of the great star he had been. By 1948 he was a part-time player. By the time he was thirty-three he was all washed up.

MacPhail resigned from the Dodgers after the 1942 season to accept a commission in the army, and Branch Rickey, of all people, replaced him. At the end of the war the Yankees were sold by the Ruppert estate to a partnership that included, of all people, MacPhail. Baseball had changed. Players who had been there in 1941 were still around after the war—Feller, Musial, Slaughter,

Mize, Keltner, Henrich, Marion, Rizzuto, Reese, Gordon, Hopp, Pollet . . . but they had changed, too.

I still loved the game and continued to follow it, and do to this day. I've been writing about it for decades. I treasure my memories of baseball after World War II and in all the decades since. I can't imagine that I'll ever grow so decrepit that I'll forget the excitement of Jackie Robinson, the fun of Stengel, Bobby Thomson's home run, Willie, Henry Aaron, Brooks Robinson, George Brett, Rickey Henderson. I have forty-five seasons of postwar baseball tucked away in my memory bank to go along with those I remember from the 1930s.

But none of them measures up to 1941.

Acknowledgments

I talked to or heard from a great many people about 1941, and here I try to thank them all: Bud Livingston, Bud Schelz, Henry DeMayo, Red Barber, Mel Allen, Mike Seidel, Pete Williams, David Halberstam, Fred Opper, Arnold Benson, Charles Einstein, Harold Rosenthal, Sterling Lord, Phil Rizzuto, Buddy Hassett, Bill Mazer, Martha Creamer, Jane Daych, Elizabeth Hains, Marius Russo, Marvin Breuer, Lee MacPhail, Buzzy Bavasi, Branch Rickey III, Tuga Clements, Mary Rickey, Tommy Henrich, Pee Wee Reese, Fred Golomb, Tom Rizzo, Tom O'Connor, Jim Russell, Dave Oppenheim, Jack Tobin, Andy Crichton, Jerry Tax, Les Woodcock, Jerry Astor, Dick Schulz, Ray Robinson, Milton Epstein, Pete Coutros, Gene Ferrara, Jack Rosenstein, Tony D'Addario, Chuck Painter and Mary Ellen Hill. I hope those I have failed to mention will forgive my absentmindedness.

Anyone interested in baseball in 1941, and particularly in Joe DiMaggio's hitting streak, should read Al Silverman's *Joe DiMaggio: The Golden Year, 1941* and Michael Seidel's *Streak: Joe DiMaggio and the Summer of 1941*. I also found much material of interest in Leo Durocher and Ed Lynn's *Nice Guys Finish Last;* Ted Williams and John Underwood's

My Turn at Bat; Arthur Mann's *Branch Rickey: American in Action;* Donald Honig's *Baseball Between the Lines;* Paul Fussell's *Wartime;* J. G. Taylor Spink's *Judge Landis and Twenty-five Years of Baseball;* William B. Mead's *Even the Browns;* Robert Obojski's *Bush League;* SABR's *Minor League Baseball Stars, Volume II;* Charles Einstein's *The Fireside Book of Baseball* in its various editions; Dominic DiMaggio and Bill Gilbert's *Real Grass, Real People;* Ray Robinson's *Iron Horse;* Art Hill's *I Don't Care If I Never Come Back;* Peter Williams' *The Joe Williams Baseball Reader;* Hank Greenberg and Ira Berkow's *The Story of My Life;* Red Barber's *Rhubarb in the Catbird Seat;* Bill James's *Historical Baseball Abstract;* Frank Graham's *The New York Yankees;* Joe Reichler's *The World Series;* and Fresco Thompson's *Every Diamond Doesn't Sparkle.* I also made continual reference to *The Baseball Encyclopedia;* to *The World Series,* by Richard Cole, David S. Neft, Robert T. Johnson and Jordan Deutsch; to *Daguerrotypes of Great Stars of Baseball,* by Paul MacFarlane; to *Total Baseball,* by John Thorn and Pete Palmer; and to *Sports Illustrated.*

Al Silverman, my editor and friend, suggested the book and was a warm support while I was writing it. I thank him for that and for his perceptive editing of my copy.

I owe great thanks to my son—Bob Creamer, for his help in editing and preparing the manuscript; to Jim Creamer, for his editorial comments and for research efforts that went beyond the call of filial duty; and to John Creamer, for reading the final draft and making helpful suggestions.

My thanks go, too, to the Tuckahoe Public Library, the Eastchester Public Library, the White Plains Public Library and the New York Public Library.

Finally, I thank my loving and patient wife, Margaret, for not shooting me after I reneged on my promise never to write another book under deadline.

Index

INDEX

⋘⋘⋘⋘⋘⋘⋘⋘⋘⋘⋘⋘